The Horned
Moses
in Medieval Art
and Thought

CALIFORNIA STUDIES IN THE HISTORY OF ART

Walter Horn, General Editor

Advisory Board: H. W. Janson, Donald Posner, Wolfgang Stechow, John R. Martin

The Horned Moses
in Medieval Art
and Thought

by RUTH MELLINKOFF

Wipf and Stock Publishers
EUGENE, OREGON

The Horned Moses in Medieval Art and Thought
is a volume in the California Studies in the History of Art sponsored in part by the Samuel H. Kress Foundation

Wipf and Stock Publishers
199 West 8th Avenue, Suite 3
Eugene, Oregon 97401

The Horned Moses in Medieval Art and Thought
By Mellinkoff, Ruth
Copyright© January, 1970 by Mellinkoff, Ruth
ISBN: 1-57910-088-0
Publication date: September, 1997
Previously published by U of California, January, 1970

TO
WALTER HORN

Preface

As ITS title suggests, this book is an interdisciplinary study touching not only upon medieval art, but also upon such disciplines as medieval history, history of the Church, Latin and vernacular literature, both religious and secular, medieval drama, mythology, and folklore. To provide an iconographical interpretation of horned Moses in as deep a sense as possible has been my goal. The many diverse elements from different areas of medieval thought associated with the horns of Moses were compelling reasons for my using methods of approach and study suggested by the late Erwin Panofsky: "The art-historian will have to check what he thinks is the *intrinsic meaning* of the work, or group of works, to which he devotes his attention, against what he thinks is the *intrinsic meaning* of as many other documents of civilization historically related to that work or group of works, as he can master."

A project such as this involving so many humanistic disciplines would have been impossible without the assistance of others. In acknowledging with gratitude the interest and counsel of a number of individuals, I must first express my thanks to Professor Walter Horn who has given generously and continuously of his time and scholarly guidance throughout the preparation of this book, always providing lucid and objective criticism.

The completion of this book was assisted by many and I am grateful to all who have helped. Special thanks are due to Professors Jaan Puhvel, Herbert Morris, Philip Levine, LeRoy Davidson, and the late Ralph Altman, for their suggestions and criticisms. The final revision of my manuscript was immeasurably aided by the erudite criticism of Professor Meyer Schapiro, to whom I express my grateful thanks. While I am indebted to all for help, the responsibility for errors and imperfections is exclusively mine.

I would also like to express my appreciation to Ingrid Frank for her assistance with the Latin translations, to the many librarians who helped me countless times in my search for obscure references, and to all those individuals associated with the University of California Press who contributed to the preparation of this book.

Contents

CONTENTS

List of Illustrations

Introduction

To MOST present-day observers the visual image of a Moses with horns is striking and strange, as any guide to the famous statue by Michelangelo in the church of San Pietro in Vincoli in Rome can report (fig. 84). Twentieth-century connotations of a man with horns on his head are mostly negative; one thinks of horns as symbols of dishonor. They conjure up pagan deities, the Devil, the cuckold. A horned Moses seems somehow absurd, insulting, and ridiculous. And because a horned Moses seems so strange, men of the twentieth century have been led to ask why Michelangelo, whose artistic representations of Old Testament prophets rank among the most powerful and magnificent of all time, should have chosen horns for this Judaic-Christian prophet.

These horns of Moses, represented by Michelangelo and other artists, medieval and later, have traditionally been explained as the offspring of a translator's mistake. It is said that they derive from an error made by Jerome in his translation of the Old Testament, namely, a mistranslation[1] of the Hebrew word, *qeren*, in Exodus 34:29:

וַיְהִי בְּרֶדֶת מֹשֶׁה מֵהַר סִינַי וּשְׁנֵי לֻחֹת הָעֵדֻת בְּיַד־מֹשֶׁה בְּרִדְתּוֹ מִן־הָהָר
וּמֹשֶׁה לֹא־יָדַע כִּי קָרַן עוֹר פָּנָיו בְּדַבְּרוֹ אִתּוֹ:[2]

where *qeren* (קרן) can mean "horns" or "rays of light."[3] It is here, in Exodus 34:29, that Jerome translated the Hebrew, *qeren*, as Latin *cornuta*, "horned":

> Cumque descenderet Moyses de monte Sinai,
> tenebat duas tabulas testimonii, et
> ignorabat quod cornuta esset facies sua
> ex consortio sermonis Domini.[4]

1

[And when Moses came down from mount Sinai,
he held two tables of the testimony, and
he knew not that his face was horned from
the conversation of the Lord.][5]

This translation problem does not arise in the rendering of the account of Moses receiving the Law for the first time. In the third month after the Exodus, Moses received the first two tablets of stone, written either "by the finger of God" (Exod. 31:18, and see further description of the tablets at Exod. 32:15, 16), or by Moses (see the Ten Commandments at Exod. 20:2–17). After forty days of communion with the Lord, Moses descended from the Mount and found the people worshiping the Golden Calf. Enraged by this idolatry, Moses shattered these first tablets (Exod. 32:19). It is later in Exodus that Moses is directed by the Lord to renew the tablets (Exod. 34:1–27). Moses again remains on Sinai for forty days and nights, and finally descends with a second set of Law tablets (Exod. 34:29). Now Moses is marked in a special way after his communion with God. It is at this point in the narrative that Jerome describes the change as *cornuta*.

Jerome's translation, later known as the Vulgate, was made between 382 and 404.[6] By the eighth or ninth century it became the generally accepted version,[7] yet no visual representation of a horned Moses appeared until the eleventh century. Why this gap? This time gap between the appearance of *cornuta* in the Vulgate and the later appearance of the horns on Moses in art, as well as its significance, seems thus far to have been overlooked by scholars. Thus it is the alleged mistranslation, and the late appearance of the Moses horn-motif in art, which lead into the main problems of this study: When, where, and why did the horns of Moses first appear in art? And, when the horns of Moses finally did become visual, what did they mean to medieval man? Before the major problems just outlined are considered, however, it would seem helpful and appropriate to indicate some of the ancient background for the motif of horns on heads. The usefulness of a brief survey of this kind will become increasingly apparent in subsequent chapters of this book.

The continuity of horns as an important symbol for mankind (on many different levels and with both positive and negative connotations) will be seen as indeed relevant to a study of horned Moses.

While most of us today might view with alarm the horns on Moses, seeing in them symbols of dishonor, horns were not always so understood. The history of religions could almost be written as the history of horned gods and goddesses. From ancient civilizations into modern times, the horned head or headdress symbolized divinity, honor, power. This universally utilized motif has been as much at home among American Indians as in ancient Mesopotamia or Egypt.[8] Among the Egyptians, Mesopotamians, Hittites, Greeks, Etruscans, Gauls, Celts, Buddhists, Scandinavians, and others, many of their major deities were represented with horns or a horned headdress, or they were represented by the horned animal itself (e.g., a ram, bull, or goat),[9] which was sacred to the particular god. Myths and cults, and their artistic renderings, reserved some aspect of the god as particularly representative. The frequent choice of horns as eminently appropriate for this purpose is not difficult to understand. Man's observation of their destructive use by the animals themselves, their use as tools and weapons by man, and the incorruptibility of the substance of the horns, all emphasized their power. This power seemed innate, and thus by ready inference it followed quite naturally that horns could function independently.

Horns could transfer divinity and power to those things on which they were placed. Such transference was ubiquitous in the ancient world. A horned headdress for kings and priests was common and appropriate. In Egypt the king as the incarnation of deity wore a headdress with horns.[10] The ram's horns of Alexander were representative of his legendary descent from Ammon[11] and they appeared in art (fig. 1). The Mesopotamian gods consistently wore a horned cap in distinct contrast to the headdress of men,[12] a distinction reinforced by a notable exception. When the priest-king played the role of the god in the ritual of the sacred marriage, he also was given the prerogative of wearing the horned cap.[13] The Mesopotamian king, Naramsin, is represented with a horned headdress on a stele where the headdress serves as a symbol of victory and deification (fig. 2).[14]

Horns used for their apotropaic, magical qualities are of great antiquity and are still so used in twentieth-century Italy.[15] Horns served as amulets;[16] they were placed on houses[17] and on graves.[18] But nowhere is the apotropaic and protective usage of horns more evident than when they were placed on helmets.[19]

One can quickly conclude, therefore, that horns on men in the milieu of the ancient world had primarily a positive connotation, symbols of honor rather than dishonor. They represented the gods and occasionally they denoted kingship (probably divine kingship). The contained innate power and strength and were symbolic of victory. As powerful representatives of the gods, they were wonder-working as protective devices.

If horns were one of the most common attributes of the gods in the ancient world, others were also popular. "Rays of light" were often used to represent deities in their celestial aspects, that is, as sun, moon, or stars. An ancient god often had several symbolic attributes, horns representing him in his animal aspect, a sun disk in his celestial aspect, and so on. Not unusual was the simultaneous representation of different attributes of the god, for example: Isis with horns and solar disk, Ra sometimes with the disk and ram's horns. This combination of motifs is splendidly illustrated with the ancient Mesopotamian sun god, Shamash: horns and rays of light are both represented on an Akkadian seal of the period (ca. 2340–2180 B.C.),[20] and again, later,[21] on the Hammurabi stele. In each instance Shamash wears the horned cap of divinity, while rays of light issue from his shoulders (figs. 3 and 4). A late Hellenistic syncretistic example of the combination of symbolic motifs can be seen on an abraxas gem where Jupiter is simultaneously represented with the rays of Phoebus, the basket of Serapis, and the horns of Ammon (fig. 5).

The metaphorical meaning of horns or horned in the Bible continued the ancient meaning of horns as symbols of honor, divinity, strength, kingship, and power.[22] In Jerome's time, therefore, his translation of Exodus 34:29 as described above, may not have seemed strange. That a man of Jerome's scholarship should have chosen *cornuta*, however, indicates that at the very least he did not find such language either offensive or nonsensical. Jerome's understanding of this is discussed more fully in Part II which is concerned specifically with interpretation of the horns.[23] What is of essential importance to us here is that Jerome's version became *the* Bible of the Latin Church in the Middle Ages. It formed the ultimate source for Moses' horns.

The Jerome translation, while giving us the biblical basis for the horns of Moses, does not explain why approximately six hundred years pass before they appear in art. Why this gap between their first occurrence in the Bible and their first visual representation? Perhaps the long delay cannot be fully explained, but several observations regarding the earlier iconography of Moses may give some perspective. These observations are presented here only briefly and in outline form, for the early iconography of Moses is a vast subject in itself.

First of all, it should be noted that in the earliest period of Christian art, especially in the catacombs, it is not Moses receiving the Law, but Moses striking the rock miraculously producing water for the Israelites, which is by far the most popular Moses episode.

Second, once the reception of the Law did become an integral part of the repertoire of early Christian art, the renewal of the Law (Exod. 34:29) as distinguished from the initial reception of the Law (Exod. 31:18) was not stressed.[24] The iconography that developed was limited to a more generalized image of the reception of the Law and established a pattern that was generally adhered to. There were some variations, as will be pointed out, but significant innovations and changes do not seem to occur until the eleventh century. At least as early as the sixth century A.D., there are very clear examples of an established iconography for Moses receiving the Law. Generally he is youthful, unbearded, nimbed, his hands covered (or draped), and he is shown standing receiving the tablets of the Law usually in the form of a scroll from the Hand of God, which is issuing from the arc of heaven.[25] Usually his shoes are removed or he wears only the barest of thong-sandals. Moses is so represented in a mosaic in San Vitale in Ravenna (fig. 6). Moses, as described above and as represented in the mosaic at San Vitale, may possibly have had a prototype as early as the somewhat damaged male figure in a painting from the Dura-Europos synagogue (mid-third century A.D.).[26] In any case, the iconographic type as represented at San Vitale was, at least in its general outlines, maintained through the Middle Ages in the miniatures and mosaics of the Eastern Church. The Eastern Church retained the Septuagint version of the Bible, which as mentioned earlier, "glorified" Moses, but did not give him "horns." Byzantine versions varied only slightly;[27] the basic pictorial type remained constant[28] and without horns. For example, in the Cosmas Indicopleustes (Vat. Gr. 699) several scenes from the life of Moses are combined: the Calling of Moses, Moses and the Burning Bush, and the Reception of the Law.[29] And in the tenth-century Bible of Leo the Patrician (Vat. Reg. Svev. Gr. 1) Moses is shown removing his shoes and then is shown receiving the Law, this time in the form of a tablet rather than a scroll.[30]

In the Byzantine Octateuchs (manuscripts containing the first eight books of the Bible) of the eleventh and twelfth centuries, there is an interesting addition[31] to the Moses iconography, namely, a scene that represents his "shining" or "glorified" face after the renewal of the tablets. Four of the five[32] extant Octateuchs contain this scene: folio 118^v in Vat. Gr. 747, the earliest of the group, dating in the eleventh century; folio 258^v in Constantinople Seraglio 8, dated 1081–1118; folio 110^v in the now destroyed Symrna Cod. A, dated twelfth century;[33] and folio 254^v in Vat. Gr. 746, dated twelfth century.[34] Figure 7 is an example of this type.

The West too retained much of the same early Christian iconography through the Carolingian period with some minor variations. Changes do occur with regard to Moses' beard, nimbus, and the draping of his hands. On a folio of the Grandval Bible (Br. Mus. Add. 10546),[35] 834–843, Moses is shown with a beard, he lacks a nimbus and his hands are not covered (fig. 8); however, he does receive the Law from the Hand of God from heaven's arc. On a folio of the Vivian Bible (Bibl. Nat. Lat. 1),[36] 844–851, Moses retains his nimbus, but again he is bearded and his hands are not covered (fig. 9). In the lower half of this same folio, Moses is reading the Law to the people, this time in the form of a giant codex, and here we see that his left hand holding the codex is draped. The reception of the Law is similarly represented on a folio from the Bible of San Paolo fuori le mura in Rome, variously ascribed to Charles the Bald (840–877) and Charles the Fat (876–887).[37] In this case Moses' hands are covered, he has a nimbus, but once again he is bearded (fig. 10). These examples represent relatively minor changes; basically the ancient tradition is continued.

Bolder changes and innovations do not appear until later. One of the most fascinating new pictorialized concepts of Moses receiving the Law is found in the early eleventh-century Farfa Bible (Vat. Lat. 5729).[38] It is on folio 6ᵛ that one of the artists has not only represented Moses as he receives the Law (the renewal), but also his appearance after he has "veiled" his face (Exod. 34:33;[39] see fig. 11). This is indeed a departure from the early Christian archetype. Here Moses is seen kneeling (instead of standing), hands draped, receiving the tablets (or codex) from the Lord who is no longer represented by his hand but is shown as a full figure in a mandorla. Neuss has pointed out that all elements of the subject matter of this folio (as well as some others) are not always entirely clear,[40] that it is very difficult to explain why the animals of Exodus 13:13 are found here, and that it is not known why Moses, together with one of the Israelites, holds a stylus.[41] (Note that the arm of Moses which holds the stylus is bare, that is, it appears uncovered or white. I would suggest that a possible explanation for this unusual representation is to be found in Exod. 4:6 where the hand of Moses was made "leprous as snow" by the Lord as one of the signs to be used by Moses before the people. The Lord restores the hand to normal flesh in Exod. 4:7.[42])

Neither Neuss nor anyone else thus far to our knowledge, however, has pointed out that the extraordinary veiling device used for Moses after he has received the Law (Exod. 34:33) is a mask. This is made clear by the artist's technique of picturing Moses in the manner of Picasso, that is, part of his real face shown in a three-quarter front view and simultaneously part of his mask shown in profile (fig. 11).[43] How does this come about? A linguistic controversy surrounds the interpretation of the Hebrew describing Moses' "shining face" (Exod. 29–35). Some scholars have argued that the appropriate Hebrew should be translated and interpreted as a "sacred mask"; others say that such an approach and interpretation is unsubstantiated.[44] One can only speculate as to whether or not the artist who painted folio 6v had access to an interpretation of the text which indicated a mask for Moses.

In the frescoes of Saint-Savin-sur-Gartempe of the end of the eleventh or early in the twelfth century, another significant variation in the representation of the scene of Moses receiving the Law (fig. 12)[45] can be noted. In this painting, as in the Farfa Bible just discussed, the Lord is no longer represented only by his Hand issuing from the arc of heaven. Here too the Lord is totally present. He stands inside a mandorla wearing a cross-nimbus and hands two tablets with letters inscribed on them to Moses. Moses kneels, presumably on Mt. Sinai, as he receives the Law. He is without a nimbus and his hands are not covered. And an interesting addition to the scene is found on either side of Moses and the Lord where angels are depicted blowing trumpets announcing the Covenant. This fresco then represents another example of change in the representation of this scene.

The amazing miniature of the Farfa Bible, and the fresco at Saint-

Savin serve as only two examples of the new medieval iconography that was sprouting in the West. While they do not give us a horned Moses, they do represent dramatic breaks with tradition. We must look to England for the first example of a horned Moses in art.

PART I Where, When, and
Why Did the Horns
First Appear
on Moses in Art

I Eleventh-Century England, the Place Where Moses First Is Represented with Horns

THE EARLIEST artistic representation thus far found of horns on Moses is in eleventh-century England, in the Aelfric Paraphrase of the Pentateuch and Joshua, British Museum Cotton Claudius B. IV.[1] Neither Émile Mâle nor Louis Réau was aware of this eleventh-century horned Moses. They both have noted the first appearance of this horn–motif as occuring in the twelfth century. Mâle believed that the horns appeared for the first time as one of the iconographic innovations produced by the liturgical drama.[2] Réau argued that they could as easily have occurred first in manuscript illumination.[3] He explained their appearance in art by means of the "Jerome mistranslation" mentioned earlier.[4]

Arthur Watson, criticizing Mâle's hypothesis that the horn-motif of Moses was introduced by the liturgical drama, was the first to direct attention to the fact that this English eleventh-century horned Moses in the Aelfric Paraphrase of the Pentateuch and Joshua (hereafter referred to as the Aelfric Paraphrase) was earlier than the twelfth-century examples.[5] Neither Watson nor others, however, noted the highly important detail that in the Aelfric Paraphrase Moses has a hat with horns, rather than horns growing from the head. (Several hypotheses evolve from this observation, as will appear later in this study.[6])

This very important Anglo-Saxon manuscript is profusely illustrated with more than four hundred pictures,[7] depicting events from the Pentateuch and the book of Joshua. Among them are a multitude of pictures of a horned Moses. (For a few examples, see figs. 13, 14, 15, 16, 17, 18, 19, 20, 21, 22, 23, 24.) One may still wonder—were these the first? While it seems there are no extant examples of a horned Moses in art earlier than those in the Aelfric Paraphrase, this does not prove that there were none. There is considerable opinion that the Aelfric Paraphrase had a much earlier model lying behind its miniatures. Francis Wormald has stated that the prototype must have been an important early Christian manuscript, though probably the artist had no more than a good tenth-century copy before him.[8] M. R. James held a similar opinion, comparing the many scenes of births, deaths, burials, and family groups of patriarchs in the Aelfric Paraphrase with an early Christian manuscript such as the Greek Cotton Genesis.[9] He argued that Canterbury might have owned an ancient picture Bible, one that could have served as the older model.[10]

Hanns Swarzenski, on the other hand, has stated that the Aelfric Paraphrase shared a common prototype with the Bible of San Paolo fuori le mura, namely a conjectured Rheims model.[11] He compares the double scene of "Moses Blessing the Tribes" and the "Death of Moses" in the Bible of San Paolo fuori le mura (fig. 25), with the comparable folio (139ᵛ) in the Aelfric Paraphrase (fig. 24). These folios do have certain characteristics in common: the design layout of the pages is similar, and the episodes from the life of Moses are the same. There the similarities end. They differ far more than they are alike. Not only are the styles different, but the iconographic details differ in almost every way. Compare, for example, the ultrarealistic treatment of the "Death of Moses" in the Aelfric Paraphrase, with that in the Bible of San Paolo fuori le mura. In the former (fig. 24), his death is visibly mourned by the Israelites by means of hand gestures, his shroud and burial box are shown—the burial box represented as actually being lifted up—and finally, we see Moses being led into heaven. By contrast, the same scene in the Bible of San Paolo fuori le mura (fig. 25), is represented in a more abstract, symbolic fashion: In the upper left of the page an angel lifts a "sleeping" Moses into the clouds, thus simultaneously representing his death, burial, and reception into heaven;

while in the upper right of this folio Moses is shown again communicating with the Lord, possibly being told of his imminent death. Thus, the comparison of these two scenes seems to provide little justification for asserting a common Carolingian prototype for the two manuscripts. Their similarities could as easily be due to a common dependence on an early Christian manuscript of a kind suggested by M. R. James and Francis Wormald.

The opinion that the Aelfric Paraphrase might have been based on an ancient model is supported by evidence of the arrival of early Christian manuscripts in England not long after the conversion to Christianity. Otto Pächt believes that the Aelfric Paraphrase does reflect an older model, and he states that the late seventh century, the period of the mission of Abbot Hadrian and the Archbishop Theodore of Tarsus, was the most likely time when such picture cycles could have come to England. He has suggested that the iconography points to Eastern, pre-iconoclast cycles of Bible illustration.[12] During this same period England began to collect books at a rapid pace. Benedict Biscop acquired and brought to England many books from his several trips to Rome and a stay of two years at Lerins.[13] And before A.D. 700, books were already being copied by English monks in their own scriptoria.[14]

All of these opinions as to earlier models for the Aelfric Paraphrase are based on suppositions. While interesting and relevant, they cannot serve as evidence for arguing that the iconography remained constant. Even if it could be demonstrated that an earlier model definitely existed and was used, this does not imply that the model included representations of the horned Moses. The Aelfric Paraphrase, at the present time, appears to be the first tangible evidence[15] of the appearance of the horns of Moses in art.

The Aelfric Paraphrase has been assigned to Canterbury[16] and is dated about A.D. 1050,[17] plus or minus a few years, but definitely before the Conquest. The artists (several hands worked on the manuscript)[18] are more distinguished by an apparent creative imagination than by any technical facility. The drawing and painting are clumsy—not up to the quality of the earlier English manuscripts. This aspect of the illuminations has often been alluded to. E. M. Thompson, Francis Wormald, and David Rice agree on this score and refer to the style of these representations as "rough,"[19] "incompetent,"[20] and "not of outstanding artistic importance."[21] The pictures in the Aelfric Paraphrase are there to teach and explain, rather than to beautify. They reflect an attempt to translate literally —into pictures—the narrative, textual content. Many of the illustrations are unfinished, particularly those toward the end of the manuscript. The work on the pictures appears to have been done in stages: first, patches of color were brushed in without any preliminary drawing; next, the general outlines were added; and last, specific features were drawn in. The colors used were nonnaturalistic, in keeping with other English manuscript illuminations of the period.[22] The beautiful fluttering linear work of the Anglo-Saxon artists of the late tenth and early eleventh centuries, as for example in the Benedictional of St. Aethelwold, is almost totally lacking. When it does exist, it is superficial, and almost certainly a later addition.

The Aelfric Paraphrase, which seems to be outside the mainstream of English illumination does, however, evidence an apparent kinship with certain works dating from shortly before the Conquest. These manuscripts have a distinctive character.[23] The Caedmon manuscript, Junius 11 of the Bodleian,[24] ca. A.D. 1000, belongs with this group, as does the Prudentius's treatise on the Virtues and Vices (the "Psychomachia" illustrated in outline at Malmesbury about 1040–1050),[25] and so does British Museum Tiberius C. VI,[26] dated about 1050.[27] These manuscripts were all characterized by a new freshness and a freedom from convention. This is combined with a diminution of the linear agitation of the drawing of earlier manuscripts of the so-called "Winchester school." But perhaps even more significant are the iconographic innovations that are found in these manuscripts. The Aelfric Paraphrase shares all the characteristics of this group of manuscripts, and, not least, their iconographic inventiveness.

While the Aelfric Paraphrase has been settled upon as the earliest attestable occurrence of the horns on Moses in art, there is some question as to exactly where, in the manuscript itself, the artist first so represented him. Moses has horns as early as folios 78^v, 79^r, and 79^v, but these particular horns give every indication of being much later superimpositions. Even a casual look at the illuminations shows up some heavy inking-over of earlier drawings. Folio 128^r (fig. 20), and folio 113^v (fig. 16), demonstrate this same inking-over process in the drapery of some of the clothing. (E. M. Thompson has noted this peculiarity at various points in the manuscript.[28]) The probability that the horns on Moses on the three folios (78^v, 79^r, and 79^v), were later additions finds internal support in the manuscript itself. There is no textual basis for the introduction of the horns at this point in the manuscript, nor is there any continuity of the horns on subsequent drawings of Moses. Not until the significant point in the biblical text is reached where Moses renews the tablets of the Law (Exod. 34:29), do the horns occur again. And it is at this point in the text—folio 105^v—that we find the first horned Moses that is of prime concern to us (fig. 13).[29]

Folio 105^v is divided into upper and lower portions. In the upper part we see Moses in the process of renewing the Law; here he has no horns. Moses, having descended from Mt. Sinai, is holding the tablets of the Law and he is now adorned with two tremendous horns on a hat or headdress which he keeps throughout the rest of the manuscript—even in his final scene where he enters heaven (fig. 24). The design of the horns on the subsequent folios[30] varies somewhat. But although more than one hand can be distinguished, all represented the horns as horns on a hat or headdress, not as organic growths. This horned headgear for Moses appears to be unique; later representations of a horned Moses do not show the horns as part of a headdress.[31] But before leaving the Aelfric Paraphrase, it now seems in order to introduce several possible explanations (none mutually exclusive) for the horn-motif appearing first in England.

II Eleventh-Century England:
A Place of Originality

IN THE preceding pages the illustrations in the Aelfric Paraphrase were established as the earliest attestable examples of a horned Moses in art. In what follows, I propose to demonstrate that the Aelfric Paraphrase belongs to a cultural milieu likely to produce artistic innovations, an England bursting with novelties. It has already been noted that the Aelfric Paraphrase is part of a group of manuscripts not only having style affinities, but filled with examples of iconographic changes and inventions. The innovations of this period in England, that is, shortly before the Conquest, have been stressed again and again. Meyer Schapiro refers to this school as:

> one of the most original and precocious in creating new conceptions of the traditional themes.[1]

Arthur Haseloff has summed it up in this way:

> La peinture anglaise des xe et xie siècles offre le contraste le plus nettement tranché avec la peinture allemande du même temps. Si l'on est tout à fait en droit de voir dans l'art allemand une sorte de Renaissance d'art primitif chrétien ou la continuation de traditions carolingiennes et byzantines, en revanche, ce que créa l'art anglo-saxon de la même période fut absolument neuf et original.[2]

And Adolph Goldschmidt expressed himself in similar terms.[3]

There is little doubt that eleventh-century England represented a time and a place when the earlier conventions were no longer always adhered to. New versions of old themes appeared. For example, the "labors of the months," traditionally represented by single figures, were transformed into landscape friezes of a kind that did

18

not reappear until a much later period, in the art of the fourteenth-century.[4]

It is the English, about this very time, who develop and create the fierce demons in art we have come to associate with their later portrayals in medieval painting and sculpture. British Museum Harley 603, a copy of the Utrecht Psalter, is full of zoomorphic hybrids,[5] monster types, demonstrating a decided taste for these weird monsters, demons, and unreal animals—a taste only comparably met with in the later medieval art of men like Schongauer and Bosch.[6]

This preoccupation with monsters and devilish beings perhaps contributed to another English artistic creation, a grotesque gaping monster's mouth as the entrance to hell. This is new iconography, and it is credited to England. This hell-mouth is dramatically and startlingly represented in several manuscripts. One is struck by the daring realism of these folios. For example, in the scene of the "Harrowing of Hell," of British Museum Cotton Tiberius C. VI (ca. 1050), folio 14[r], we find a Christ triumphant who tramples down a dragon plus a handcuffed Satan, and who also pulls the "saved" ones from the monster hell-mouth.[7] A similar mouth-entrance can be seen in the "Last Judgment" scene in a folio in the Register of Newminster (ca. 1016–1020), British Museum Stowe 944 (fig. 26).[8] Here we see St. Peter, key in hand, in the upper part of the picture, welcoming the "elect" at the gate to heaven; while in the lower portion of the same folio a winged angel (St. Michael?) locks a door leading into an arena where a giantlike man shoves the "damned" into the hell-mouth. And note the scene in the middle portion of this same folio where the struggle for the possession of the "souls" is taking place, with Peter and Michael on one side and Satan on the other. Little is left to wonder about. The whole story is told to those who look at the page. This literal, superrealistic presentation is typical of these manuscripts and of the Aelfric Paraphrase. (We will have more to say about this aspect of the art a little later.) A similar hell-mouth is portrayed in two of the folios in the Junius 11

Caedmon manuscript in which the Fall of the Archangel and his cohorts is represented.[9]

There is more evidence of English originality. The practice of drawing in different colored inks and with tinted colored outlines has been traced to the Anglo-Saxons, and English embroidery art has been cited as its stimulus.[10] So too the earliest series of full-page pictures preceding the psalter is found in England,[11] an idea widely adopted in other countries during the following centuries.[12] British Museum Tiberius C. VI, described earlier, with its folio of the "Harrowing of Hell," is an example of one of these full-page psalter pictures. This very same psalter is responsible for more "firsts," introducing new scenes not found in earlier English art, scenes from the life of David and the life of Christ.[13]

Recently it has been argued that folio 8ᵛ of the Aelfric Paraphrase contains the earliest pictorial record of Cain using a jawbone as his murder weapon.[14] There is no murder weapon mentioned in the biblical account; nevertheless, the jawbone as Cain's weapon became one of the most unusual English medieval iconographical motifs, later serving in illustrations on the Continent, and ultimately ending up in the Ghent Altar.[15]

Meyer Schapiro has shown that the new dramatic representation of the Ascension of Christ was an Anglo-Saxon creation.[16] In the earlier Ascensions, Christ either stands or sits in the sky, above the Apostles; or, he is shown ascending toward the Hand of the Father. Around the year 1000 there is a new and radical variation introduced: Christ is represented with only his legs showing, while the rest of his body remains hidden by clouds.

An eleventh-century Anglo-Saxon crosier-head, with scenes from the Nativity (now in the Victoria and Albert Museum) also demonstrates originality in the realm of sculpture. H. P. Mitchell's description of this object stresses this:

> The highly unconventional composition of the subjects, the freedom of poses of the figures, and the fanciful representation of the whole, in places bursting from the surface of the ivory,

all is daringly original and unorthodox. So too, is the choice of subjects from the opening and close of our Lord's life. . . . The representation of the dead Christ with the eyes of a living man offers a sort of parallel to the crucified Christ of the 13th century. It seems probable that only in Anglo-Saxon art could such a work have been produced at this date, for there only did the necessary artistic power exist sufficiently freed from the trammels of both classical and Byzantine tradition.[17]

Thus it is suggested that the originality of this period of English art offered favorable conditions for the introduction of a novelty such as the horned Moses. It should be stressed, however, that while English innovations of this period were both abundant and influential, they were part of a general pattern of a changing medieval world. It was mentioned earlier that the Catalonian Farfa Bible and the frescoes of Saint-Savin-sur-Gartempe represented important departures from the older traditional iconography.[18] Breaks with tradition can be found throughout the West,[19] and so while England of the eleventh-century is a place of great originality, this cannot serve as a sufficient explanation for the first appearance of horns on Moses in art. It is in the life of early eleventh-century England that we look for additional explanations for this new motif.

III The Stimulus from Vernacular Texts

It MAY not be mere accident that the horns on Moses appear for the first time in the illustration of a vernacular text. There is a possibility that the vernacular Old English may have acted as a stimulus in changing traditional iconography as well as in helping to create new artistic images.

From the seventh century on, the Anglo-Saxons evolved a vernacular literature, beginning with poetry, epic and lyrical, containing both pagan and Christian elements.[1] The eleventh-century illustrated Caedmon Junius 11 manuscript of the Bodleian Library, referred to earlier, contains two Old English poems probably composed around 871, the time of Alfred. The poetry in the Caedmon manuscript demonstrates the Anglo-Saxon taste for apocryphal biblical literature and for the violent battle scenes of the Old Testament. For example, the one poem known as Genesis B deals with the Fall of Satan and the Rebel Angels; and the other known as Genesis A, is primarily an enthusiastic account of the battles in Exodus. Certainly the daring innovations in the illustrations of the Junius 11 manuscript are in no small measure due to the extraordinary vernacular text.[2]

The aim of Christian vernacular poetry was, as R. H. Hodgkin put it:

> to present Christian teaching in such a mode that it might appeal to the ordinary man, the man on the mead-bench.[3]

The poets only strayed from the original biblical narrative to make the story more vivid:

> Thus in Genesis God appears as "a chief of thegns." Satan also has his "strong retainers," and he can boast that they will not fail him in the fight.[4]

22

No doubt the authors of the poems formerly ascribed to Caedmon emphasized the biblical battle scenes as a means of stimulating the interest of their fellow countrymen:

> Here then we see the form in which popular Christianity was conveyed to the ordinary Englishman. His attention was turned to the Old Testament rather than the New. He was fed on the spirit of the Old Testament as well as its stories. The new religion was coloured as a new form of warfare, to attract a pugnacious people.[5]

The earliest version in a vulgar tongue of the *Physiologus*, was written in Old English verse, probably in the second half of the eighth century.[6] It derived ultimately from a Greek version that was translated into Latin before A.D. 431;[7] it came into the Middle Ages as the standard work on animals. The *Physiologus* and the Caedmon Junius 11 texts are only two examples of English vernacular poetry. There were of course many others including the famous *Beowulf*.[8]

While Old English poetry goes back to the seventh or eighth centuries, the development of vernacular prose came later. It began with King Alfred (849–899) and his translations of popular Latin works of his time,[9] among them the "Dialogues" and "Pastoral Rule" of Gregory the Great, the "Consolations" of Boethius, the "History" of Orosius, and the "Soliloquies" of St. Augustine. This tradition of vernacular prose translation was continued by others. Byrhtferth, a monk of Ramsey, wrote a *Manual* or *Enchiridion*, a handbook to the elementary science of the day.[10] Wulfstan, bishop of London, and later of Worcester, wrote powerful sermons denouncing the evils of his age.[11] This Old English literature that had no vernacular counterpart in any other country of this period had a tremendous appeal, amply demonstrated by the many manuscripts that still survive.

Aelfric (born ca. 955, died ca. 1020) has been called the father of vernacular English literature.[12] His writings are distinctive in their quality and quantity.[13] He was educated in his early years by a secular priest, one whose ignorance Aelfric despised.[14] It was only later that Aelfric became a pupil of Bishop Aethelwold at Winchester.[15] Perhaps the experience with the ignorant secular priest helped to develop Aelfric's educational zeal, a zeal that impelled him to translate Latin works into Old English. His Catholic Homilies, two series of sermons, dating probably to 991 and 992, were also written in English.[16] His *Lives of the Saints* (in Old English) was issued a few years later.[17]

Aelfric's was a concern for the whole Church and not just for the monastic community. His patrons were important members of the lay nobility as well as churchmen. The Aelfric Paraphrase itself is prefaced by a dedication to Aethelweard, a nobleman who held office as an ealdorman in the western part of Wessex.[18] Aethelweard had asked Aelfric to translate the Old Testament into English.[19] Sometime after Aelfric completed the Bible translations, he wrote a treatise on the Old and New Testaments, a kind of layman's guide or introduction to the Bible. It too is prefaced by a letter to a nobleman, Sigwerd.[20] In this preface Aelfric says:

> Thou hast oft entreated me for English Scripture, and I gaue it thee not so soone, but *thou* first *with* deeds hast importuned me therto; at what time thou didst so earnestly pray me for Gods loue to preach vnto thee at thine owne house: and when I was *with* thee, great mone thou madest that thou coudst get none of my writings. Now will I that thou haue at least this little, sith knowledge is so acceptable vnto thee, and thou wilt haue it rather than be altogether without my bookes.[21]

There is no doubt that Aelfric's translations were intended for the instruction of village priests and for those of the noble laity who could not read Latin. Aelfric, however, "would have regarded a clerical training based exclusively on the vernacular as disastrous for religion."[22] He wrote Aethelwold's biography in Latin, and his abridgment of the *Regularis Concordia* for the Eynsham monks was also done in Latin. Aelfric considered his English translations concessions to the needs of the time. In his preface letter to the

Genesis translation he tells Aethelweard that he will not translate anything more:

> I pray thee, dear ealdorman, that thou bid it me no more, lest I be disobedient to you or a liar if I do it.[23]

Aelfric's vernacular works, however, had the greatest appeal. Their popularity is emphasized by the fact that they were copied steadily, both before and after the Conquest, along with the texts of other Old English writers.[24] That seven copies of the Aelfric Paraphrase still exist, argues for the supposition that many more were originally made.[25]

The biblical translation itself was probably done shortly before 1000. It is referred to in the literature varyingly as the Old English Heptateuch, or as the Aelfric Paraphrase of the Pentateuch and Joshua. Aelfric used Jerome's Vulgate as the basis for his translation,[26] and it seems probable that Aelfric had read the Old Testament only in Latin, for it is doubtful that he knew either Greek or Hebrew.[27] His version is not a strict translation but, as its name correctly suggests, is a paraphrase.

Aelfric's Paraphrase, a simplification of the biblical text, may have aided in focusing attention on the more picturesque details. No doubt with an eye toward his audience, Aelfric eliminated such things as catalogs of names, abstruse passages, and details that were not pertinent in carrying forward the biblical history.[28] "He wishes to furnish," as Caroline White pointed out, "a practical, easily-understood rendering of the parts which are most important for the laity to know. All else he passes over."[29] This principle of omission was a part of Aelfric's general approach. This is expressed in one of his own homilies where he says:

> This day's gospel is also difficult for laymen to understand; it is chiefly occupied with names of holy men, and they require a very long exposition according to the ghostly sense; therefore we leave it unsaid.[30]

Aelfric's writings give attention to those things that are concrete, specific, literal, and uncomplicated by abstract speculation or allegory. Vernacular prose of this kind may readily have influenced the artists who in the only extant illustrated copy of the Paraphrase, British Museum Claudius B. IV, depicted the stories, the words and phrases directly—that is, literally. For now, in the case of the horned Moses, the Latin of Jerome's translation of Exodus 34:29 is translated into Anglo-Saxon so that:

> Cumque descenderet Moyses de monte Sinai, tenebat duas tabulas testimonii, et ignorabat quod cornuta esset facies sua ex consortio sermonis Domini.[31]

became in Aelfric's Old English:

> Ða Moyses nyðer eode of Sinai dune, he haefde þa tabulan on handa, 7 nuste þaet he waes gehyrned, for ðam þe he wið God spraec.[32]

The Latin *cornuta* is thus changed into plain English so that all who know English can now read: Moses had become *gehyrned* from speaking with God.

It appears reasonable to conjecture that this vernacular text had a special influence on the artists who illustrated it, on artists probably unaware of the symbolical and metaphorical aspects of biblical language. Thus they translated *gehyrned* into a literal image, a horned Moses. It is Beryl Smalley who has pointed out that "the Anglo-Saxon on the eve of the Conquest may have been a good artist and poet; he was not intellectual."[33]

The very development of vernacular prose stressed the concrete as against the vague, the literal as against the metaphorical. This outlook in itself assisted in the breakdown of old traditions and conventions, and in the creation of new ones. Meyer Schapiro states that it was just such a focus that contributed to the new Ascension of Christ around the year 1000:

> We may even speak of the image of the disappearing Christ, in a broad sense, as a vernacular achievement in art, not only

because of its relation to the Blickling homily, but because of its essentially empirical attitude to the supernatural religious objects.[34]

This is a time when the English inclined toward the conversion of a generalized concept or mystery into a concrete pictorial image. Otto Pächt alluded to some of the iconographical innovations of this type in the twelfth-century St. Albans Psalter. For example, it is in this psalter that the words of Pilate, "His blood be on us," are made visible through an illustration of Pilate's gesture, that is, a literal translation of the metaphor.[35] And in another place in this psalter, a lasting iconographic change is achieved when the artists create a concrete image of the "cup of bitterness," in the "Agony of the Garden," by representing it as a chalice standing on a rock in front of Jesus.[36]

These are examples of a technique of word-illustration which the Middle Ages developed at an early time, and had special appeal for the English.[37] Was it this attitude of mind which led to the literal representation of *gehyrned*? Was it the concrete image of a horned Moses that the artist of the Claudius B. IV. manuscript tried to represent? That they did not read the language in its metaphorical sense to mean abstract power or abstract symbolism of any kind, is clear from a glance at the illustrations. What may now appear to us as ridiculous, did not seem so to the eleventh-century English artist. If one considers the total context of the period, a country and a time in which change is rampant, then the sudden appearance of a horned Moses does not seem quite so astonishing; Moses with horns fitted the spirit of the period. It was the appropriate moment. For hundreds of years those who could read Latin read *cornuta* in the Vulgate, but never before had anyone dreamed of literally representing it. Now in the eleventh century, clergy not learned in Latin, as well as the Old English reading laity, could read it in their own language as *gehyrned*, and as everyone knew, that meant very simply—horned.

IV The Possible Influence of
Liturgical Drama on the New
Iconography for Moses

THE EMPHASIS on the literal, the concrete, the active was essentially an emphasis on the popular. And this was nowhere more apparent than in the development of the liturgical drama. In searching out all the factors that may have influenced the change in Moses' iconography, Émile Mâle's hypothesis—that the original impulse for giving Moses horns came from the liturgical drama[1]—should also be considered.

Mâle's theory has been praised and criticized. Arthur Watson took a very dim view of Mâle's hypothesis,[2] pointing out that the only evidence to support it is a fourteenth-century *Drama of the Prophets* from Rouen in which Moses is costumed with horns—very late evidence, indeed, to justify an innovation of a much earlier date. The stage directions in the Rouen manuscript give Moses horns, saying:

> Tunc Moyses, tenens tabulas legis apertas,
> indutus alba et cappa, et cornuta facie,
> barbatus, tenens uirgam in manu, dicat:[3]

Watson argued that this costuming of Moses with horns in the stage directions of a fourteenth-century text cannot be used to prove that liturgical drama influenced the change in iconography. He further points out that this stage direction, or costuming instruction, does not occur in any other of the extant prophet-dramas.[4] It should be remembered, however, that very few documents remain; and even absent written evidence of a direct stimulus for the creation of this iconography, some aspects of the historical development of religious drama do make us consider the possibility, though

28

unclear, that it may have influenced the introduction of the horns of Moses in art.

The drama of the Middle Ages grew out of the Church liturgy. From probably the ninth century onward, the liturgical texts were enhanced with dramatic interpolations known as "tropes," consisting at first of just a few words. The earliest example of this on record is the *Quem quaeritis in sepulchro, o Christicolae?* of a manuscript from St.-Gall, dating from the end of the ninth, or the beginning of the tenth century, and chanted on Easter Day.[5] By about A.D. 975 this simple "trope" had already grown into an elaborate ceremony. Evidence of this appears in the well-known *Regularis Concordia* compiled by the English Benedictine, St. Aethelwold. Aethelwold states that he modeled this practice of adding the dramatic interlude after Fleury on the Loire. The scene that was acted out was the visit of the three Marys to the tomb of Jesus for the purpose of anointing his body. There they are met by the angel who greets them with the verses attributed to the ninth-century monk, Tutilo of St.-Gall:

> *Quem quaeritis in Sepulchro, o Christicolae?* (Whom do you search for in the sepulchre, O servants of Christ?) *Jesum Nazarenus, crucifixum, o coelicolae!* (Jesus of Nazareth, crucified, O servants of Heaven!)[6]

The text of the *Regularis Concordia* describing this dramatic "trope" is particularly important, for it furnishes the earliest documentation for a complete dramatization in the Church. It demonstrates that as early as the last quarter of the tenth century elaborate costuming and settings were already a part of these plays. And it further demonstrates that the liturgical drama reached out to the same kind of audience for whom the vernacular prose texts were written, namely, the unlearned majority—clergy as well as laity. We read of this in the text of the *Regularis Concordia* itself, in the directions of what should be done with reference to the burial of the Cross on Good Friday (a preliminary to the performance of the *Quem quaeritis* which followed the Resurrection):

Now since on that day we solemnize the burial of the Body of our Saviour, if anyone should care or think fit to follow in a becoming manner certain religious men in a practice worthy to be imitated for the strengthening of the faith of unlearned common persons and neophytes, we have decreed this only: on that part of the altar where there is space for it there shall be a representation as it were of a sepulchre, hung about with a curtain, in which the holy Cross, when it has been venerated, shall be placed in the following manner: the deacons who carried the Cross before shall come forward and, having wrapped the Cross in a napkin there where it was venerated, they shall bear it thence, singing the antiphons *In pace in idipsum, Habitabit* and *Caro mea requiescet in spe,* to the place of the sepulchre. When they have laid the cross therein, an imitation as it were of the burial of the Body of our Lord Jesus Christ, they shall sing. . . . In that same place the Holy Cross shall be guarded with all reverence until the night of the Lord's Resurrection.[7]

While Aethelwold's *Regularis* demonstrates a desire for informing the ignorant by means of the drama, other churchmen of the Middle Ages were not always in accord with this more popular method of education. Liturgical buffoonery of the clerics such as the Feast of the Fools, and the Feast of the Boy Bishop, were widely condemned, as were various *ludi* of the people. It is not always certain how the more serious plays dramatizing sacred events were regarded by responsible Church authorities.[8] Karl Young, in this context, draws attention to Gerhoh of Reichersberg (1093–1169), a firm supporter of the papacy, who condemned all who interested themselves in dramatics, holding the conviction that all such activities only provided incentives for conviviality.[9] Even Herrad of Landsberg, an abbess of the monastery of Hohenburg (1167–1195), who believed that the Church plays were designed to strengthen the belief of the faithful, after observing that the performances had become occasions for buffoonery and disorder, proclaimed that those in authority should prohibit the plays.[10]

The vivid, down-to-earth dramas had tremendous popular appeal. The stage settings, fairly elaborate structures in later plays, replete with such devices as the ass of Balaam in the *Ordo Prophetarum*, and the furnace of Nebuchadnezzar, were probably thoroughly enjoyed by the less learned clergy, as well as by the laymen.

Even as early as the tenth-century *Regularis Concordia*, there is mention of a curtain and a costume for the angel. This is extremely important evidence for establishing an early date for costuming instructions and for stage sets. Because it is so important, part of a translation of this drama that is included in the *Regularis Concordia* is quoted here. It has already been mentioned that the sepulchre for the performance is arranged in a vacant part of the altar and is provided with a curtain around it,[11] which we may assume can be drawn open and closed. The description of the impersonations are as follows:

> While the third lesson is being read, four of the brethren shall vest, one of whom, wearing an alb as though for some different purpose, shall enter and go stealthily to the place of the "sepulchre" and sit there quietly, holding a palm in his hand. Then, while the third respond is being sung, the other three brethren, vested in copes and holding thuribles in their hands, shall enter in their turn and go to the place of the "sepulchre," step by step, as though searching for something. Now all these things are done in imitation of the angel seated on the tomb and of the women coming with perfumes to anoint the body of Jesus.[12]

And ultimately "the other three brethren" show the clergy the grave linen, demonstrating that the Lord has risen and is no longer wrapped in it. The play is brought to a conclusion by beginning the *Te Deum*, thus signaling the sounding of the bells.

While this play within the tenth-century *Regularis Concordia* presents specific evidence of costuming and stage settings, curtain and all, of a very early period, it does not set a standard, or a pattern, for a subsequent continuous development. There seems to be no rhyme or reason for the particular inclusion, or the exclusion, of stage directions or costuming instruction in later plays. Both Karl Young,[13] and more recently, O. B. Hardison,[14] have shown that most of the liturgical plays were developed between the tenth and thirteenth centuries. Young has pointed out that the texts of the plays are not uniform in communicating information about costuming or other devices used for impersonation. He has stressed this aspect of these dramas, calling our attention to the fact that some plays that are relatively longer and more elaborate, display rubrics that are remarkably silent on details of impersonation.[15] Hardison also emphasizes this erratic, nonevolutionary development of Christian drama in the Middle Ages. He points out that simple drama forms occur at later dates, while not infrequently, an early form of a particular drama is more complex than a later one.[16] Furthermore, his investigation suggests that the vernacular tradition of the drama developed simultaneously, and perhaps separately, from the Latin dramas.[17]

Our particular interest in the liturgical drama centers on the *Drama of the Prophets* (also known as the *Procession of the Prophets*, or the *Ordo Prophetarum*), for "Moses" is part of the dramatis personae. This play was not based on a "trope," but rather on an apocryphal text, the pseudo-Augustinian *Contra Judaeos, Paganos, et Arianos Sermo de Symbolo*,[18] probably written in the sixth century but ascribed to Augustine throughout the Middle Ages. The portion of the Sermon used was addressed specifically to the Jews (eight chapters out of a total of twenty-two) attempting to convince them of their errors. The technique is that of using Old Testament prophets as witnesses, each summoned singly, giving his testimony. Moses is an important member of the group. This sermon was the basis of dramatization at least as early as the eleventh century as witnessed by the text of a play at St.-Martial of Limoges.[19] The fourteenth-century Rouen text (which may be based on a much earlier one), the one on which Mâle based his hypothesis,[20] contained the rubric costuming Moses with horns.

While all of the dramatizations are based on the *Sermo*, they are not carbon copies, either of the sermon itself or of one another. For example, there is a text from Laon which also has an impressive list of detailed costuming instructions like the Rouen play—yet, each play includes details of costuming not included in the other.[21] Thus far, the fourteenth-century Rouen text is the only one found which specifically includes a costume instruction for a horned Moses. Our knowledge of liturgical drama, however, is very dependent on the manuscripts that have survived. It is this chance survival of relatively few manuscripts, plus the erratic development of the drama that was mentioned earlier, which makes it almost impossible to establish with any degree of certainty whether or not Moses was costumed with horns at an earlier time. In other plays now lost, or in performances where costuming was not provided in a text, perhaps Moses was costumed with the horns. There is also the further possibility that the horns were so much de rigueur that they were not stressed in stage directions or other instructions. For, as already noted, liturgical dramas did not always include stage directions or costuming instructions, which, of course, did not mean that the performers were not costumed.

There is some internal evidence in the manuscript of the Aelfric Paraphrase itself which provides a hint of possible influence from liturgical drama. This evidence, not commented on in the literature, is not conclusive, yet it seems of sufficient interest to be included in this study. Let no stone go unturned.

First, and most important, as noted earlier, although the horns of Moses vary to some extent in their design throughout the manuscript, they are always represented as horns on a kind of hat or headdress and not as organic growths. What is suggested then is that from this treatment of the motif it is possible to infer that the artist based his pictorial representation on a costume worn by a person impersonating Moses. (See figs. 13–24). This hatlike headdress with the horns is seen whenever Moses is represented, after his renewal of the tablets of the Law. In the Aelfric Paraphrase men who do not wear hats of one kind or another are easily recognized. Their hatless state is made more apparent by the conventionalizations for hair. Here, for example, is one type often used in the Aelfric Paraphrase:

Note in particular the conventionalized part in the hair above the forehead.

Moses himself in folio 105ᵛ (fig. 13), in the upper portion of the picture, has this conventionalized hairdo. He has not as yet received the horns. After his renewal of the Law, in the lower portion, the conventionalized hairdo is gone, and he now wears the headdress (or hat) with the horns.[22]

The second piece of internal evidence in the Aelfric Paraphrase is the screen by which Moses veils himself (Exod. 34:33) after he has received the horns from God—after he has renewed the tablets of the Law and is reading it to the Israelites. This screen suggests a stage prop (fig. 13). There was a reference earlier to the unique representation of a mask for the veiling of Moses' face in the Catalan Farfa Bible (fig. 11). In the Aelfric Paraphrase, however, this veiling is represented by what appears to be a kind of portable curtain-screen. There is no biblical basis for this whatsoever. If the artist was not influenced by a dramatic enactment of this scene, then the very least he should be credited with is another iconographical invention, that is, a novel interpretation of what it meant for Moses to veil himself. For in this case the vernacular usage appears to be the same as the Latin. The Anglo-Saxon *hraegl* (like the Latin *uelamen*) means a garment, a covering, a cloth.[23] The idea of a curtain-screen, therefore, does not appear to derive from the text, either Latin or Anglo-Saxon.

Admittedly the evidence just discussed—headdress with horns, and portable curtain-screen—does not furnish a base sufficiently firm for concluding without any shadow of doubt that these attributes were the results of influence from the liturgical drama. Tenuous as it is, this argument should nevertheless not be wholly discarded.

It is Otto Pächt who has reopened the whole question of whether or not the liturgical drama was a major factor in influencing the pictorial arts.[24] More specifically, he has been concerned with whether or not it was a major factor in the twelfth-century revival of pictorial narrative. He presents convincing evidence for just that, namely, that liturgical drama influenced not only the iconography, but also the overall spirit of pictorial narrative of the twelfth century. For example, he shows that the influence of the Peregrinus play had an effect on the costuming of both Christ and the pilgrims in the St. Albans Psalter, and furthermore had an effect on the very pictorialization of spoken words.[25] In essence the mystery was brought down to earth. Pächt says with reference to the new Resurrection iconography that it is animated with the same aim as the new Emmaus iconography: "to express mystery in terms of dynamic physical action."[26] He then points out:

> But as soon as we see Christ rising bodily from the tomb, as soon as the mystery becomes, so to speak, tangible, pictorial representation begins to trespass the boundary separating the arcana from the realm of natural causality and with it shifts the whole ground on which Christian art had rested.[27]

This bringing-down-to-earth of the mystery was part of the spirit of the eleventh century, and of the twelfth century. It should be stressed that the same impulses at work in the realistic dramatization of religious mystery were at work in the vernacular texts with their iconographic novelties. Both emphasized the literal, the concrete, the immediate, the popular—in short, those aspects of things that could be readily understood.

While it is difficult to say whether or not there was an eleventh-century *Drama of the Prophets* that costumed Moses with horns and thus ultimately influenced the artists of the Aelfric Paraphrase, it can be said that if such a play had been performed, with Moses so costumed, it would have been in keeping with the spirit of the period. Further, it should be added, that once Moses appeared on stage, adorned with horns, this would invariably have helped to spread and popularize the motif.

V Ancient Use of Horns on Helmets Reflected in the Honed Headdress of Moses in the Aelfric Paraphrase

IN THE preceding chapter the possibility was discussed that the horned headgear of Moses in the Aelfric Paraphrase might have its origin in the liturgical drama of the period. A question that now arises (which to my knowledge has not previously been formulated) is whether the horned headdress of the Aelfric Paraphrase, and of its possible prototype in a liturgical play, might not have a common source in an even more ancient usage of horns on helmets.

The custom of wearing horned helmets may have derived from a more ancient tradition of wearing a headdress composed of the skin of the head of an animal with horns still attached,[1] as evidenced by its modern survival forms in primitive American Indian societies.[2] But at least as early as the ancient Mesopotamian and Egyptian civilizations, horned helmets were in use, as was mentioned at the beginning of this study.[3] Such helmets with horns were similarly worn in Greek, Etruscan, and Roman civilizations,[4] providing both physical and magical protection for the wearers. James Turnure, in his recent discussion of two pieces of Etruscan ritual armor (a shield and a bronze helmet), has pointed out that the ram's horns on either side of the head of the helmet were connected with battle helmets, that they were an indication of the strength, courage, and masculinity of the wearer, or else they served as a sort of charm to provide the wearer with those virtues.[5] They were used to ward off evil spirits and helped to frighten away the enemy.[6] When these horned helmets were made for funerary purposes, the symbolism connected with them continued into the grave, providing protection from demons of the underworld.[7] The horns of rams and bulls were worn as amulets by the Romans,[8] and the *corniculum*, a military mark of distinction in the form of a horn or horns on helmets, was conferred upon the Roman soldiers for proven bravery.[9]

But of special interest here is that similar traditions were associated with horns in Northern Europe. Archaeological finds—horned helmets and horned headdresses for gods or warriors or both—are available, dating as early as the Bronze Age. Horned persons appear in Scandinavian rock carvings, probably in the period of the Middle Bronze Age (1000–800 B.C.).[10] (See fig. 27.)[11] These rock carvings are evidence of Bronze Age cults.[12] Represented in these rock carvings are what E. O. G. Turville-Petre refers to as the oldest attributes of Thór:

> The goat, the hammer and the axe were, as it seems, the oldest attributes of Thór, and as symbols of divinity were perhaps older than Thór himself. Scandinavian rock-carvers of the Bronze Age depicted human figures, often ithyphallic, swinging an axe and sometimes a hammer, showing that the axe was a fertility symbol. At least one of these figures, grasping two hammers, has a head horned like that of a goat.[13]

It has also been suggested that the horned figures could represent men wearing horned helmets or that they might be representations of the more primitive headdresses of the skins of animals with their horns attached, worn as masks.[14]

Late Bronze Age horned helmets have been found at Viksø in Denmark, dating probably somewhere between 800 and 400 B.C. (fig. 28). Johannes Brøndsted marks this as the moment "when the isolation of the North had been broken and the gates to the South thrown open."[15] The Viksø helmets themselves seem to be imitations in metal of an animal mask; note that they are provided with eyes and a nose (fig. 28). The Viksø helmets had their counterpart in some small bronze statuettes, figures that Brøndsted said probably represented Danish twin gods.[16] These statuettes were part of a find made in the eighteenth century in South Zealand, but for years the find and knowledge of it were lost. Recently two con-temporary drawings[17] were discovered, the collections of the Na-tional Museum were then searched, and two of the original six fig-ures were found, including one of the two men with the horned helmets (fig. 29). While the Viksø helmets seem to have been made in northern Italy, the statuettes appear to be native to Denmark.[18]

The famous silver Gundestrup cauldron, a Celtic work of art of the early iron age (ca. 400 B.C. to end of first century B.C.), probably dating from the latter part of that epoch,[19] demonstrates the ancient tradition of helmets ornamented or mounted with various animal or bird motifs. On one of the inner plates of the cauldron (fig. 30), a human sacrificial scene is represented, while a procession is held in honor of this ritual-ceremony. These appear to be high-ranking warriors, and each wears a helmet adorned with a different motif—a crescent (or stag's horn), a goat's horns, a boar, and a bird. Every deity on this Gundestrup cauldron is represented as either a very large person or as a bust.[20] One of these gods who is represented as a bust in a wheel-turning scene is of particular interest, because a warrior who grasps the wheel is wearing a horned helmet. (fig. 31.) It has been suggested that the deity in this scene might be Taranis, the counterpart of Jupiter.[21] A magnificent example of an actual Celtic horned helmet (now in the British Museum), was dredged from the Thames, and dates around 25 B.C. (fig. 32).[22]

The evidence briefly reviewed here shows that before the Chris-tian era horns on helmets were well known in the northern lands as well as in the ancient Near East and among the Greeks, Romans, and Etruscans. It is significant, however, that the tradition of the horned helmet continued among the northern peoples long after it was no longer in use in the Roman world. For after the beginning of the Christian era examples of the horned headdress can still be found in use in the North. There is evidence of this in the unusual portrayal of the warriors on the Arch of Constantine in Rome. Here represented in relief are those who aided Constantine in the decisive Battle of the Milvian Bridge in 312. These fourth-century reliefs include, among others, a Teutonic regiment in the Roman army called the *cornuti*, the "horned ones." The *cornuti* are easily singled out by the horns on their helmets, for Roman helmets did not have horns in late imperial Roman times[23] (see fig. 33). This Teutonic contingent wore goat's horns,[24] and these horns probably represented the sacred origins of their tribe or their clan.[25] It should be added that in this case their ancestor might have been Thór, the god to whom the goat was sacred.

The goat-horned warriors of the Arch of Constantine were not the only ones among the northern tribes to wear an animal motif into battle. There is ancient literary evidence that documents the importance of the boar in this reference. Tacitus, in the first century A.D., speaks of the tribes of Aestii, whom he says resemble the Suevi in rites and fashions, but whose language is more like the British. These Aestii,[26] he says, wear the emblem of the boar for protective purpose:

> They worship the mother of the gods, and wear as a religious symbol the device [mask] of a wild boar. This serves as armour, and as a universal defence, rendering the votary [worshipper] of the goddess safe even amidst enemies.[27]

The written testimony is supported by later archaeological evidence from some warrior graves of the fourth-century A.D. in northern Gaul. One such grave and its contents have been described in detail by Joachim Werner.[28] Among the contents of this grave is an ornament fashioned out of two boar's tusks and mounted in a silver fastening. It was found in a large red clay bowl. Werner states that the manner in which the silver plate is fastened to the tusks argues for its use on a leather helmet, rather than as the top of a standard. This very same grave also contained a belt buckle deposited within a clay bowl. The leather belt and its companion, the leather helmet, had crumbled to dust with the passage of time, leaving behind the less corruptible buckle and boar's tusk ornament.

Werner also refers to additional evidence and examples of similar boar's tusk ornaments from a private collection in Brumath-Stefansfeld,[29] and points out that metal helmets were not in general use among the free Germanic tribes in the fourth century, in contrast to those who fought within the Roman army. He notes that metal helmets begin to make their appearance in the territory of the free Germanic tribes only in the fifth century.[30] And when ultimately they were formally adopted by these peoples, they were reserved for kings and nobles because of their costliness. Perhaps the ordinary soldier would do well if he managed a leather helmet with a boar's tusk ornament.

It seems fairly certain that these emblems of horns or tusks, placed on headgear or on standards, denoted the sacred origins of the clan or tribe of those who wore them or carried them. They may have represented the god whom the men worshiped, or perhaps the legendary ancestor of a tribe.[31] Certain animals were sacred to certain gods, and these gods could occasionally be represented by the animals themselves, or by some distinctive part of the animals such as their horns or their tusks. Thus, Thór was represented by the goat or goat's horns; Frey and Freya by the boar or boar's tusks.[32] Heimdall was associated with the ram, Odin with wolves, ravens, and a horse with eight legs.[33] It is interesting to learn that Thór was: "the god whom the invaders of England loved most,"[34] and had been known to the English pagans as Thunor. While Frey and Freya were gods of peace, Frey was also a warrior and defender.[35] And we are told that "Another name for Freyr is *Atriði*, probably implying, 'one who rides to battle.'"[36] What better to wear or take into battle than an emblem of the god worshiped, goat's horns or a boar's tusks? (See again the procession of warriors on the ancient Celtic cauldron, fig. 30, and the goat-horned warrior on the Arch of Constantine, fig. 33.)

Ornamenting of helmets with animals, or animal motifs, continued to be an important practice in the North. Although archaeological evidence is sparse, what there is when combined with literary evidence demonstrates that this was part of the northern tradition at least as late as the ninth century, and probably later. Both the archaeological evidence and evidence in literary sources reviewed in the following pages, demonstrate this point.[37]

The corselet and helmet are extremely rare in both Anglo-Saxon burials and in Teutonic burials elsewhere in Europe.[38] The same is true of the later Viking period. Yet the tradition of the Viking with his helmet adorned with horns is part of our twentieth-century concept of the Vikings—a common trademark used for identifying something as Scandinavian. (See fig. 34, a trademark for a baking pan.) Even present-day Danes have associated themselves with this same concept as part of their past tradition. A recent photograph of a Dane advertising a Copenhagen restaurant shows him wearing a leather helmet with horns (or tusks) attached to it (fig. 35).

While only a few helmets have been found, those few are of immense significance. They demonstrate the continuity of the ancient traditions. Ornamental helmets belonging to chiefs have been found in the graves of the latter migration period from Vendel, Uppland, Sweden, of about the seventh century A.D.[39] Bronze plates of the same time) were found in Torslunda, Öland, Sweden, which were most probably used as stamps for making the plates for decorating those or similar Vendel helmets (figs. 36 and 37). One of these plates contains a "dancing" warrior (probably a religious ritual war dance) who wears a horned headdress (fig. 36). Two men in their war gear, each wearing a helmet surmounted with a boar are represented on the other bronze plate (fig. 37).

The remains of another helmet, found at Benty-Grange, Derbyshire (fig. 38), dating perhaps in the sixth or seventh century A.D.,[40] still has a very recognizable boar figure on the top of one of the helmet's ribs where it served as the crest.[41]

The bronze Öland plates and the Benty-Grange iron helmet supply evidence of the continuity of the practice of decorating or mounting a helmet with an animal or animal motif. (Compare the Gundestrup cauldron of figs. 30 and 31 with the bronze plates from Sweden, figs. 36 and 37.) But this evidence is strengthened immeasurably by the seventh-century Sutton Hoo boat grave with its great treasures, including a magnificent helmet (figs. 39 and 40).[42] The motifs on the Sutton Hoo helmet bring it very close to the Swedish Vendel helmet motifs as seen on the bronze plates. Compare, for example, the horned figure of the Swedish plate (fig. 36), with the similar figure on the Sutton-Hoo helmet (fig. 39 and details on fig. 40).

The Sutton Hoo helmet from East Anglia, England, dramatizes the impact of archaeology on historical theory. Because of the Sutton Hoo type of burial (boat grave), and because of the affinities of the helmet and shield with the Swedish Vendel plates, it has now become easier to explain the Scandinavian elements in *Beowulf*, the eighth-century English epic poem. The Sutton Hoo discoveries show that pagan art and manner of burial did not completely wither away with the conversion of the English to Christianity.[43] (It is not material here whether this was or was not a Christian burial, for certain pagan elements are still present.) Charles Green in his book on Sutton Hoo has convincingly demonstrated that East Anglia was invaded and settled by Scandinavians probably between A.D. 520 and 531,[44] not long after the Angles, Saxons, and Jutes invaded England. This can only mean that Scandinavian influences were important in this part of England long before the first of the later ninth-century Viking raids.

Very recently another unusual find was excavated (1964 by Mrs. Sonia Hawkes) from the Anglo-Saxon cemetery at Finglesham, near Deal, in east Kent. This is a buckle from grave 95, dated in the seventh century,[45] which has as its main feature a man wearing a horned helmet (fig. 41). The buckle's horn-helmeted figure has iconographic affinities with Swedish Vendel helmet decoration, like the figure from Torslunda (fig. 36) as well as the Sutton Hoo helmet (fig. 40). It seems certain, however, that it was made in England; Mrs. Hawkes has pointed out that its general form and construction place it in the group of a well-known west Germanic type that was current in Kent during the first half of the seventh century.[46] Thus while we have been reconciled to the hypothesis of a direct connection between East Anglia (Sutton Hoo) and Sweden, a relationship between Kent and Sweden is something new. This find, unique thus far in Anglo-Saxon archaeology, can perhaps remind us of how little is still known about this period of history. (It has been suggested that the Finglesham man with his horned headgear point to an association with Odin or Wodan, the god of battle and of the dead.[47])

The helmet from Sutton Hoo (sixth or seventh century A.D.)[48] with its horned-warrior figures (there are two), is both interesting and important archaeological confirmation for the many helmets in the poem *Beowulf*.[49] This great English epic poem vividly demonstrates the ancient and honored traditions of the helmet with animal figures or animal motifs on it. *Beowulf*[50] tells a story of the ancient Scandinavian world, but it is addressed to an English audience of about the eighth century. The strange enigma of a Scandinavian story for an English audience is explained by the discovery of Sutton Hoo. It suggests then that the poet composed a Scandinavian theme for a Scandinavian dynasty, in an environment where both had become quite thoroughly English.[51]

Some observations are in order at this point concerning later evidence that may demonstrate the continuity and relevance of an animal headdress, animal mask, or helmet adorned with an animal motif, as late as the eleventh century. First of all, on one of Sweden's most remarkable rune stones from Sparlöse in Västergötland, there is a carving of a mounted warrior who wears a helmet with a horn-shaped or bird-beak motif (fig. 42). This stone has been dated in the beginning of the Viking period, around A.D. 800.[52] The pictures on the stone have been described but not interpreted.[53] Mårtin Stenberger notes that the rider wears a helmet, and he describes him as a "triumphant one";[54] however, he does not say anything about the unusual design of the helmet. Because this figure is represented in profile, it is difficult to say exactly what the motif may be.

It is in a tapestry reconstructed from fragments of the Oseberg boat grave of ca. A.D. 850 that we point out a horned, helmeted figure with two horns (fig. 43).[55] This is indeed remarkable evidence; it significantly demonstrates the continued usage and understanding of such symbolism in the North—into the Viking period. This unusual tapestry has been very carefully and accurately reconstructed. While the original drawing of the helmet appears somewhat indistinct,[56] assurance has been given that it does in fact represent a helmet with horns.[57] The importance of the Oseberg boat grave that was carefully excavated in 1904[58] can scarcely be overemphasized. To date, this is probably the greatest of the Viking age discoveries, both in its scope and in its many valuable treasures.[59] This grave is generally believed to have been the burial chamber of a highborn woman, possibly a queen.[60] This burial chamber was probably surrounded by tapestries that were long and narrow, perhaps hung as a frieze on the wall;[61] the reconstructed portion containing the horned, helmeted figure probably formed a part of such a frieze.

Unfortunately so much of our knowledge of northern history and mythology has been lost that only very well-known stories can be easily identified. Thus far, the portion of the Oseberg tapestries which includes the horn-helmeted figure has not been interpreted. Turville-Petre has referred to some of the motifs on this tapestry— for example, he speaks of the horses and chariots as "symbols of death and rebirth,"[62] and of the "swastikas and other mystic signs"[63]—but does not comment on this figure and its significant helmet. Perhaps one can at least speculate that this figure may have represented a god or demigod; his scale suggests no ordinary mortal. Note that he is by far the largest figure in the tapestry (fig. 43).

Evidence that a horn-helmeted figure was still of some importance during the Viking period is further demonstrated by a small metal figurine from Birka[64] which dates in the tenth century[65] (fig. 44). This figurine is at least one link with the Oseberg figure, and it is of no small interest to note that the horns on this helmet (meeting at the center with bird-beak or serpent-head endings) are related to those on the Sutton Hoo helmet (cf. fig. 40), the Finglesham buckle (cf. fig. 41), and the Torslunda figure (cf. fig. 36).

A late example of a boar's mask on the eleventh-century runic stone from Ramsundberget, Södermanland (fig. 45) should also be mentioned. The scenes on this stone represent events in the life of Sigurd. Attention is called in particular to the representation of Sigurd's head when he slays the dragon Fafner.[66] Here he seems to wear a boar's mask, or headdress, or perhaps even the head of a boar (lower right of fig. 45). Note the two tusks. Later he is represented with a normal head when he roasts the dragon's heart at the smithy. Here he tries the dragon's heart to see if it is properly cooked and has put his sore thumb, which he burned, into his mouth to ease the pain (left center of fig. 45). (It is from the dragon's blood he has just tasted that he learns the language of the birds who are represented in the tree on the stone.) Note also that Regin whom Sigurd slew lies beheaded (left of fig. 45). Regin, too, appears to have worn a boar's mask or boar's tusk.

A. T. Hatto has pointed out how ancient was the appreciation of the protective and defensive character of the boar, and the practice of wearing the tusks attached to helmets, or as masks.[67] We know from *Beowulf* that the helmets protected the face as well as the skull by means of visors (*grīm-helmas*).[68] It has been noted how much more terrifying the helmet looked with its visor than without, judging from the Sutton Hoo helmet.[69] The battle-*grīma* may have been as important for its disguise or mask as for its physical protection. It has been suggested that perhaps the primary purpose of the boar mask was that of defensive magic against the aggressive magic of the snake-sword.[70] Hatto contends that the boar helmets probably developed from the boar masks.[71] He notes that on the sides of the seventh-century Vendel helmets discussed earlier, there are warriors wearing helmets of a type he believes to be more archaic than the ones they decorate[72] (fig. 46). One of these warriors wears what seems to be a boar mask or a helmet and visor with a protruding tusk (see again fig. 46).[73] It seems at least very possible that the helmet adorned with an animal or animal motif, the animal mask, and perhaps even the wearing of the animal's head, all coexisted. Note, for example, that on one of the Vendel plates referred to earlier (fig. 36), both a helmeted figure with horns as well as a figure who wears an animal's head are represented. The eleventh-century representation of Sigurd wearing a boar's tusk headdress is late evidence of this practice.

The archeological evidence just reviewed is supported by literary evidence. The eighth-century English poem, *Beowulf*, mentioned earlier, underscores the relevance of the animal or animal motif on helmets with its numerous allusions to helmets and to the boar's images on them. The many references to helmets in *Beowulf* may be explained by the fact that the poem speaks of kings and nobles whose social status called for the helmet as ordinary equipment. Recall that the Sutton Hoo helmet has boars' heads at the ends of the eyebrows as can be seen in fig. 39; in *Beowulf* we read of similar boars over the cheek-guards:

> —Then shone the boars over the cheek-guard; chased
> with gold, keen and gleaming, guard it kept
> o'er the man of war,[74]

Beowulf's helmet itself is described as being protected by swine-forms:[75]

> And the helmet white that his head protected
> was destined to dare the deeps of the flood,
> through wave-whirl win: 'twas wound with chains,
> decked with gold, as in days of yore
> the weapon-smith worked it wondrously,
> with swine-forms set it, that swords nowise,
> brandished in battle, could bite that helm.[76]

The copious descriptions of helmets[77] and their boar decorations in the poem, emphasize the possibility that as late as the middle of the eighth century in England, such armor and its symbolic ornamentation was still well understood by the audience for whom the poem was written. It is also possible that this understanding continued to a much later date.

Beowulf is supposed to have been written by a contemporary of Bede (d. 735), but of this there is no direct evidence. The poem, however, must have been composed no earlier than the end of the seventh century, nor much later than the beginning of the ninth.[78] While the poem's composition is generally dated in the eighth century, we know it only from a single manuscript copy now in the British Museum made about 1000.[79] This can only mean that the English were still interested in this epic, at least to the extent that it was painstakingly copied. One can with some assurance argue that as of the period when it was copied, that is around 1000, it may have been understood—helmet, emblems, and all. And the possibility thus suggests itself that perhaps even as late as the eleventh century, the same century in which Aelfric's Paraphrase was illustrated in the Cotton Claudius B. IV. manuscript (ca. 1050), the tra- . dition of a symbolic headdress or helmet with an animal or animal motif was still part of the commonly understood heritage of the men of England.

This suggestion is given additional support by similar references elsewhere in the literature of the Old English period, allusions to this old tradition of horned helmets, or to helmets with a boar's decoration. The great poem, *Elene*, now generally attributed to Cynewulf of the late eighth century, alludes to helmets very much like those in *Beowulf*. This is a poem based on the legend of the recovery of the True Cross by Constantine's mother, Helena (Elene). In the poem we read that Constantine, about to go to battle, sleeps, dreams, and awakes with a boar helmet on his head, no doubt a protective device for him:

> he woke up from sleep
> covered with his boar-shaped helm.[80]

A little later in this same poem is a similar description of the helmets worn by Elene's warriors:

There was on the man
easy to be seen
the twisted mail-shirt
and the chosen bill,
the ready war-dress,
many a helmet,
beauteous boar-shaped ensign;[81]

Elene was discovered only in 1822. It is number CXVII of the library of the Cathedral of Vercelli in northern Italy. While the poem itself was probably composed in the late eighth century, we know it from the Codex Vercellensis (or Vercelli Book),[82] which belongs to the last decades of the tenth century,[83] or possibly the eleventh century.[84] Thus again, evidence of the animal-ornamented helmet appears in an earlier text that is still being copied in a later period close to if not in the very century of the Aelfric Paraphrase.

Another reference to helmets occurs in the Old English poem known as the *Finnsburg Fragment*, or the *Fight at Finnsburg*. Place and date are almost impossible to determine, but the poem is thought to be as early as *Beowulf*.[85] In it one reads:

Then in hall the sound of slaughter was heard;
the hollow shield in the hands of the bold,
the horned helmet, burst, the house-floor dinned,[86]

The "horned helmet" of this poem is a rendering of the Old English, *bānhelm*.[87] *Bān* means "bone" or "tusk";[88] thus the helmet may have been one adorned with horns[89] or, perhaps, with boar's tusks.

In Scandinavia the same tradition of a helmet with animal decoration is evidenced in the latter Eddas and Sagas, for example we read:

Thus the helmet which King Aðils took from the dead Ali was called variously Hildisvín, "Swine of battle," and Hildigoltr, "Boar of battle." The latter name was used by the skalds as a general term for "helmet," while Hildisvíni, according to one of the Edda poems, was the name of the boar owned by the goddess Freyja.[90]

One can conclude, therefore, that the English and other northern peoples, had an ancient tradition in common of helmets adorned with symbolic ornamentation of animals, or their horns or tusks. The fact that these are common traditions of all peoples of the North is not so strange. The diverse racial strains of the English have often been exaggerated for:

> Angles, Saxons, Frisians, Jutes, Danes and Norsemen were little more than tribal names of folk of closely-related stocks, of cognate speech and culture . . .[91] and as modern Dark Age studies progress, the mixed Anglo-Saxon and Scandinavian origin of a large proportion of the English nation becomes even clearer.[92]

The sixth-century Scandinavian migration to the east coast of England referred to earlier[93] helps explain the Sutton Hoo grave goods and their tie with the Scandinavian bronze plates from Öland, as well as their relationship with Scandinavian elements in *Beowulf*.[94] All these things suggest that Scandinavian influence in England began long before the ninth-century Viking raids.

This all becomes pertinent with regard to the Aelfric Paraphrase, for this manuscript has often been described as one of a group of manuscripts showing Viking taste in their illuminations:

> This episode of Viking taste in the second quarter of the eleventh century is a strange one, because it does not appear to be the result of imposition by the conquering Cnut, who seems to have had works of art executed in a purely English style.[95]

Whether or not so-called Viking taste was wholly the result of the ninth-century raids should now be questioned. Perhaps this "taste" was already part of the English tradition, only needing to be revived. This so-called Viking taste manifests itself in a style that has been described as "violently stylized and sometimes grotesque,"[96] as represented in texts such as the Aelfric Paraphrase and in the Caedmon Junius 11 of the Bodleian Library. Wormald says:

It is also indicated by an emaciation of the old acanthus or-nament into a kind of stringy interlace which in its most extreme form develops into the whole-hearted Scandinavian Ringerike ornament. There are also some animal forms, par-ticularly heads, which equally reflect this same taste.[97]

Various theories have arisen from this belief in a special kind of Scandinavian artistic influence in eleventh-century England. With reference to the Caedmon manuscript, T. D. Kendrick has stated that the artist may have tried to please two masters, Viking royalty and English ecclesiastic, a union that he thinks was made easier by the "existing barbaric tendencies in south England art."[98] Wilhelm Holmqvist has argued that the Scandinavian influences in the Caed-mon manuscript are really English,[99] and that the dragons with snout lappets in the Aelfric Paraphrase could just as easily come from the south of England as from Scandinavia.[100] Similar taste has been noted in the Bayeux Tapestry and parallels that of the Aelfric Para-phrase.[101] All these comparisons and analyses strengthen the hy-pothesis that Anglo-Saxons, Danes, and Normans had artistic ties that went back at least to their days together in a homeland on the Continent or in the North.

It seems at least within the realm of possibility that the horned hat or headdress which Moses wears in the Aelfric Paraphrase was wholly in keeping with the English-Scandinavian tradition of hel-mets adorned with animals or animal motifs. Let us recall that both archaeology and literature tell us that the ornamental helmet is a mark of the circle of leadership, worn exclusively by rank—the chief, the king, the nobility. It has even been suggested that the hel-mets from the Vendel period of the sixth and seventh centuries in Sweden were themselves an innovation in Scandinavian culture, giv-ing expression to a new ambition of chiefs striving after greater po-litical power.[102] Helmets were treasured and are among those things mentioned as part of the dragon's hoard.[103] Stjerna has observed that there is an association of ideas between the word, *helm*, a word re-curring in *Beowulf* to mean "king" or "lord" or "protector" (verses

371, 456, 1321, 2381, 2705), and to the helmet itself. He states that on account of their elevated position and luster these helmets were well fitted as symbols of chieftains.[104] Even the Lord is called "Heaven's Helmet":

> Almighty they knew not, Doomsman of Deeds
> and dreadful Lord, nor Heaven's-Helmet heeded they
> they ever, Wielder of Wonder.[105]

Thus in the context of an England where those ancient traditions were but slowly erased, one can the more readily appreciate how appropriate a helmet headdress would seem for Moses, who was also a chief, also a leader of his "chosen people."

A helmet for Moses probably would have been considered appropriate. Even a helmet (or headdress) adorned with horns would not be at all shocking to a nation in which the old heathenism was still active just below the surface of Christianity. The mission of Augustine was confronted with a heathenism rooted in the soil by the practice of generations.[106] While it is almost impossible to find out how extensive was the heathenism of the Anglo-Saxons after their conversion to Christianity, there is evidence that the Church tried to ease the transition from old pagan practices to Christian ones. Bede, for example, tells us in his *Ecclesiastical History*, that as of A.D. 601, Pope Gregory in a letter to Abbot Mellitus encouraged the adaptation of pagan sites and rites to Christianity to aid in true and lasting conversion:

> we wish you to inform him that . . . and have come to the conclusion that the temples of the idols in that country should on no account be destroyed. He is to destroy the idols, but the temples themselves are to be aspersed with holy water, . . . For if these temples are well built, they are to be purified from devil-worship, and dedicated to the service of the true God. In this way, we hope that the people, seeing that its temples are not destroyed, may abandon idolatry and resort to these places as before, and may come to know and adore the true

God. . . . They are no longer to sacrifice beasts to the Devil, but they may kill them for food to the praise of God, and give thanks. . . . If the people are allowed some worldly pleasures in this way, they will more readily come to desire the joys of the spirit.[107]

The Church retained such things as the charming (now the "blessing") of the plow, and bringing in the Boar's Head at Christmas. The most vivid application of this approach was their retention of the name of Eostre, a heathen goddess, for the most sacred of Christian holidays. Saints such as St. Michael and St. George were particularly popular and, perhaps, helped to take the place of such a god as Thunor (Thór). Welund (Wayland the Smith) turns up in an English version of the *De Consolatione Philosophiae*, as he does on the eighth-century Franks casket. On the casket we find Wayland the Smith represented without caption on the front panel, while in another scene, the presentation of the gifts of the Magi to Christ, it was found necessary to provide a title in runes: MFXI ['Magi'].[108] Perhaps the new Christians might not so easily recognize the scene of the Wise Men presenting gifts to the Christ Child; the story of Wayland the Smith would be recognized by one and all and needed no caption.[109]

The nature of Christianity in northwestern Europe was different from what it had been in the East. Conversion of the West to Christianity was more apparent than real.[110] Christianity in the Northwest was not a popular movement. It did not begin with the lower classes. It quite often began with the conversion of a king or chief who then became the bellwether for the conversion of his followers.

Even though the Church made every attempt to prevent a knowledge of heathen ways from being perpetuated in writings, it is certain that the people often relapsed into idolatry. We are informed by Bede of the revival of idolatry in Kent (ca. 616) after the death of Ethelbert (twenty-one years after the conversion of Kent),[111] and similarly the revival of idolatry of the East Saxons after the death of King Sabert, who left three pagan sons to inherit his realms.[112] The

East Saxons, later reconverted, once again in A.D. 665 relapsed into idolatry, hoping for protection from a devastating plague.[113] And Bede tells us of the conversion of King Eorpwald, the son of Redwald, King of the East Anglians saying:

> His father Redwald had in fact long before this received Christian Baptism in Kent, but to no good purpose; for on his return home, his wife and certain perverse advisers persuaded him to apostatize from the true Faith . . . and he had in the same temple an altar for the holy Sacrifice of Christ side by side with an altar on which victims were offered to devils.[114]

The old gods were difficult to dispose of. While some could be incorporated into Christianity, the Church more often than not, tried to remove them to another world, namely, the underworld. There they were transformed into devils. An Old Saxon Catechism in which the German converts of the English missionary St. Boniface were required to renounce heathenism is evidence of this. The intention of the Church is quite clear:

> Do you forsake the devil?
> *Resp.*: I do forsake the devil.
> And all the devil's bribes?
> *Resp.*: And I forsake
> all the devil's bribes.
> And all the devil's works?
> *Resp.*: And I forsake all
> the devil's works and words
> Thunor and Woden and
> Saxnote and all the unclean spirits who are
> their friends.[115]

Aelfric echoes these ideas in his life of St. Martin:

> With a thousand wily arts did the treacherous devil strive in some way to deceive the holy man, and he showed himself visible in divers phantasms to the saint, in the appearance of the gods of the heathen; sometimes in Jove's form, who is

called Thor, sometimes in Mercury's who is called Odin, sometimes in that of Venus, the foul goddess, whom men call Fricg.[116]

Christianity had a long and hard struggle against heathenism in England. Aelfric, at the end of the tenth century, was attempting to cope with this aspect of English life, for heathenism probably still existed in northern and eastern parts of England,[117] possibly enhanced by the Scandinavians who fostered anew the "old propensity of the Saxons and Angles to the customs of their forefathers."[118] (The Norse god Thór was well known in England in Viking times. Turville-Petre had suggested that the "Fishing Stone" of Gosforth indicates that the pagan myth of Thór, the giant Hymir, and the World Serpent had infiltrated the Christian legend of Leviathan.)[119] Aelfric, who thought that England was not facing a revival of heathendom, but rather an introduction of an alien religion, spoke out against some forms of magic which were practiced by the English.[120] Yet Aelfric, who in accordance with Church practice at that time rejects the curse, allowed that it had power.[121] And Aelfric says with reference to the cross (trying to help his audience to distinguish between pagan tree worship and Christian theology with reference to the cross) says: "The sign of the cross is our blessing, and we pray to the cross, yet not to the tree, but to the Almighty One who for us hung upon it."[122]

Aelfric, who tried to rid the English of certain "heathenisms," at the same time tried in every way to make both profane and biblical history more available to the laymen. He enlivened his writings with "local color," and he included as much of the familiar as was possible. He did this with special regard to the social stations of persons of high rank: Moses is thus called *heretoga*,[123] an Anglo-Saxon word that has been variously translated. Dr. Caroline White translated *heretoga* as "mighty duke,"[124] William d'Lisle's 1623 translation of Aelfric's treatise, "On the Old and New Testament," gives "great commander" for *heretoga*:

We nimaeð of ðam bocum ðas endeburdnesse, ðe Moyses wrat, þe maera heretoga, swa swa him God sylf dihte on heora sunderspaece, þa þa he mid Gode wunode on þam munte Synai.[125]

[We will follow the order of *Moses* the great commanders bookes, who wrote as God himselfe directed in their priuat conference while he abode with God vpon . . .]

Heretoga occurs in the Paraphrase itself at Numbers 13:1, where Aelfric, apparently wanting to make the story clearer, adds to the Latin text in his translation. He makes the figure of Moses more understandable, more dramatic, and more a figure of Aelfric's own time by expanding considerably on the Latin of the Vulgate which says only this:

Profectusque est populus de Haseroth, fixis tentoris in deserto Pharan.[126]

Aelfric's longer paraphrase of this Latin verse reads:

Aefter ðamðe Moyses, se maera heretoga, mid Israhela folce, swa swa him God bebead, ofter ða Readan Sae ferde, Farao adrenced waes, syððan se aelmihtiga God him ae geset haefde, ða ða seo fyrd com to Pharan ðam westene,[127]

And Aelfric in his homily, "Of the Prayer of Moses," again refers to Moses as the *maera heretoga,* so that it reads in translation:

After Moses the great leader [after ðam ðe Moyses
se maera heretoga]
had departed from the land of Egypt
with his people,
and they had journeyed on foot
over the Red Sea,
and come into the wilderness, there
warred mightily against them
Amalek the king, fighting with his people.[128]

It is clear that *heretoga* in the eleventh century means "commander," or "general," or "chieftain."[129] That being so, the fragments of surviving old traditions discussed on the preceding pages suggest that the historical and mythological association of the concept of leadership and power with the motif of a horned helmet was still sufficiently alive in eleventh-century England to be revived in the image of a great biblical leader who had guided his people from slavery into freedom. The victory of Moses over the Egyptians as a feat of military prowess could be readily understood by Englishmen engaged in their own numerous battles. Aelfric himself tried to infuse his fellow countrymen with patriotism by giving examples of victorious kings such as Alfred, Aethelstan, and Edgar, kings who as leaders of the people were conducted to greatness and power by God.

A visual analysis of the Moses representations in the Aelfric Paraphrase, as demonstrated earlier, shows clearly that the horns with which the great biblical leader is equipped are not organic growths but are part of a hat or headdress, possibly reflecting a costume for Moses as seen in a liturgical drama. Until such time as another, more compelling explanation of the appearance of this motif can be found, I should like to suggest the theory that the horned headgear of Moses in the Aelfric Paraphrase represents an eleventh-century revival of an ancient motif of a pagan nature—transposed to the Judaic-Christian-prophet-leader, Moses.

PART II The Meaning of
the Horns of Moses:
Their Interpretation
and Significance

VI The Spread of the Horned Moses Image

PART II of this book is concerned with delineating and speculating on what the horns of Moses meant to medieval men. As a prelude to interpretation it will be desirable to indicate at least the general outlines of the how, the when, and the where of the diffusion of the horned Moses image in western Christendom. Insofar as possible, the evidence will be presented chronologically and geographically.

The eleventh-century representations of horned Moses in the Old English Aelfric Paraphrase, discussed in Part I, stand apart in vivid isolation. They are the only examples thus far found which show a hat or headdress with horns for Moses, and are the only artistic evidence of a horned Moses in the eleventh century. There is a puzzling hiatus of approximately three-quarters of a century before another horned Moses can be found. This gap in the evidence may be due to the haphazard survival of documents. The pictorial tradition of a horned Moses may or may not have been continuous. The period in England after the Norman Conquest has been described as "one of the meagre periods for art, as to both quality and quantity,"[1] and this may possibly partially explain the gap in the evidence. These barren years ended around 1120 with an amazing revival of pictorial narrative, described as an "unparalleled outburst"[2] in the north and south of England. It is about at this point that horned Moses suddenly reappears. The absence of evidence of continuity of the image presents a formidable enough art historical problem; it is compounded by evidence of an almost simultaneous reappearance of horned Moses in England and Austria. For as we look to England for the first example of horned Moses after the Aelfric Paraphrase, and find him in the Bury Bible of ca. 1135[3] (Cambridge Corpus Christi College MS 2) and in the Shaftesbury Psalter (Br. Mus. Lansdowne 383) dated in the second quarter of the twelfth century,[4] we can at about the same time, ca. 1130, find horned Moses represented in one of the most important Salzburg productions—the Gebhardt Bible from Admont (Vienna National-bibliothek, Ser. nov. 2701).[5]

But while the reappearance of horned Moses seems to occur at about the same time in England and at Salzburg, a comparison of the examples indicates differences both in the design of the horns and their context. The Bury Bible folio 94r[6] (fig. 47), shows a horned Moses in both the upper and lower registers; in the former he is expounding the Law to the Israelites, and in the latter he expounds the Law of the unclean beasts. In each case Moses has horns, but in addition he is pictured with a halo. The Shaftesbury Psalter, related in style to the St. Albans Psalter,[7] provides a horned Moses in a depiction of the Tree of Jesse (fig. 48). Here Moses is portrayed at one side of the tree with gigantic horns, but unlike the Bury example, he does not have a halo; Abraham is represented on the other side of the tree with a halo. The Gebhardt Bible provides an excellent example of Moses before and after, i.e., the effect on Moses of his renewal of the tablets of the Law. On folio 68v (fig. 49) he is in the midst of receiving the Law and is not horned; on folio 69r (fig. 50) he has completed his task and now is horned, but like the example in the Shaftesbury Psalter he does not have a halo. This same before and after effect is seen in the Aelfric Paraphrase, but both before and after are represented on a single folio (fig. 13). The two twelfth-century English examples cannot be convincingly described as a prototype, either one for the other or for the Salzburg Moses; nor can the Salzburg example be described as a model for the English examples. The still somewhat tenuous dating of the manuscripts makes it difficult to determine which example is the earliest.

The Salzburg horned Moses seems to be an isolated occurrence in that part of Europe during this period. There does not seem to be additional evidence of the use of this iconography in this region until the thirteenth century. This is contrasted with England where we find two other very important manuscripts (soon to be discussed), where Moses is horned. All four of the English manuscripts are clustered together in the second quarter of the twelfth century. This suggests that horned Moses may indeed have been well known in England during the post-Conquest period although no concrete evidence remains today to prove it. If then, we were to assume not parallelism but rather English origin, we would have to ask how the horned Moses image reached Salzburg. If one postulates that there were liturgical dramas that costumed Moses with horns during this period, possibly he was seen there; or perhaps English clergymen traveled to Salzburg either with manuscripts containing this image, or with some knowledge about it. Both England and Salzburg were major centers where Bible manuscripts were produced in the twelfth century. The connections between England and Salzburg are hazy; however, there is some evidence indicating close contact between these two great centers. Otto Pächt has shown that there is another unusual iconographic parallel between a manuscript in England (the St. Albans Psalter) and one in Salzburg. In each case, the rare motif of a devil manikin seen entering Judas's mouth is depicted.[8] Perhaps other parallels exist. The image of horned Moses may have traveled via manuscripts that have not survived the ravages of time and misfortune.

As mentioned, horned Moses is found in two other twelfth-century English manuscripts.[9] In the Lambeth Palace Library MS 3, dated ca. 1150, within an initial to the book of Leviticus,[10] a very lively horned Moses is shown rushing forward to receive the Law (fig. 51); note that here he has a halo. The lower portion of the initial illustrates a burnt offering (Lev. 1:5). Moses can also be seen horned on folio 198[r] of this same manuscript in a depiction of the Tree of Jesse (fig. 52 in the upper right of the six central medallions); however, here he does not have a halo.

A fascinating horned Moses also occurs in the magnificent English psalter (Br. Mus. Cotton Nero C. IV) executed for Henry of Blois, Bishop of Winchester, between 1150 and 1160.[11] Here on folio

4^r (fig. 53) Moses is represented with his arms partly covering the lower part of his face while he receives the Law from the hand of the Lord. His horns (shown here without a halo) are very long and large in proportion to the rest of his body, and they give the distinct impression of organic growths.

If the evidence of artistic relationships between England and Salzburg seem uncertain, the opposite might be said of the situation as between England and France in the eleventh and twelfth centuries. Potent English influences were at work both in Normandy and in Burgundy.[12] The evidence, however, for twelfth-century French examples of the horned Moses is sparse; but there is some. Again we are faced with the possibility that time has destroyed artistic documents that might have contained this imagery. The reasonableness of this hypothesis is supported by convincing evidence that in the second half of the twelfth century a horned Moses stood among the portal sculptures of the Romanesque church of Saint-Bénigne at Dijon. This sculptured Moses no longer exists and were it not for the fact that it is preserved in a drawing by Dom Plancher in his *Histoire de Bourgogne*,[13] today's students would be oblivious of its ever having existed. It is certainly possible that the portal sculpture was stimulated by English influence. At the beginning of the twelfth century, two completely different art styles appeared in Burgundy. One of these styles definitely looked to England, affected perhaps by the fact that the English monk Stephen Harding became abbot of Citeaux in 1109 and ruled until 1133.[14] English influence is particularly noticeable in some of the manuscripts illuminated at Citeaux during this period.[15]

Northern France, where one would expect strong English influence,[16] does provide an example of a horned Moses in a manuscript of the end of the twelfth century coming from Corbie (Bibl. Nat. Lat. 11564).[17] On folio 2^r (fig. 54), Moses is pictured with horns and a halo opposite Aaron who wears a bishop's mitre and also has a halo. André, prior of Cluny, kneels before St. Peter in the lower part of the miniature.

There is an unusual representation of Moses, folio 41^r of the second Bible of Limoges (Bibl. Nat. Lat. 8), dated ca. 1100,[18] where at first glance Moses seems to be represented with either two horns or two rays of light. A haloed Moses stands before the Lord in this scene. Two light areas within Moses' halo, giving the appearance of horns or rays, are not clearly delineated and contrast with the very definite marking of the cross inside the nimbus of the Lord. A black-and-white photograph does not adequately demonstrate this. A close analysis of the color indicates that the green paint may have been scratched off at some time, or may have accidentally flaked off, thereby coincidentally giving the appearance of two rays or horns. While it might be tempting to include the Limoges example among the examples of horned Moses, the evidence seems too equivocal.

English influence in France was so great in the late twelfth and early thirteenth centuries, that it is often difficult to categorically assign a manuscript to either side of the Channel.[19] For example, the late twelfth-century Manerius Bible (Bibl. Sainte-Geneviève MSS 8–10),[20] containing examples of horned Moses, was executed in France, yet it was probably illuminated there by an Englishman, Manerius of Canterbury. (See for example folio 69^v, fig. 55.)

It is of some additional interest to note that the flourishing Mosan art of this period does not reflect an iconography of horns for Moses.[21] And it will be shown later in this chapter that a no-horns-for-Moses tradition runs parallel with a horns-for-Moses concept, throughout the Middle ages and during the Renaissance.

As we move into the thirteenth century, we are met with a proliferation of examples of horned Moses in England and France. There are also extremely interesting, although somewhat isolated, examples in Bohemia, Switzerland, and Spain. In England one finds the tradition of horned Moses firmly rooted and continuous. In an English psalter executed at Canterbury, ca. 1200 (Bibl. Nat. Lat. 8846),[22] Moses is pictured twice on folio 2^v, each time with horns and a halo (fig. 56). In the upper left square he stands next to a group carrying the ark; in the adjoining square he forms part of a group who stand with the grapes of the promised land. In another Bible of the early thirteenth century (Br. Mus. Add. 15452),[23] horned Moses in an initial to Deuteronomy, folio 54[r], is pictured teaching (fig. 57). An English statue from St. Mary's Abbey, York, of the period ca. 1200[24] (now in the Yorkshire Museum) also provides Moses with horns; he holds the tablets of the Law in one hand and a staff with a coiled serpent in the other (fig. 58).

It should be interjected at this point that during the Middle Ages Moses is very often represented in Old Testament scenes that foretold events in the New Testament; for perhaps the most completely developed aspect of biblical exegesis was that of relating the Old and New Testaments. This was gradually systematized into what is known as the typological method, where every notable event in the New Testament is shown to have had one or more prefigurations in the Old, and figures of importance in the latter—including Moses— were shown to be "types" of Christ. Thus Moses raising up the Brazen Serpent was a prefiguration of Christ on the Cross as the New Serpent; Moses striking the rock for water, a prefiguration of the blood that flowed from Christ's side; and so on. It will be evident that this principle is at work among the many examples of Moses' portrayal discussed later on.

The logical biblical sequence for giving horns to Moses was not always observed. Moses was often pictured with horns in events that took place *before* Exodus 34:29. An English psalter, dating before 1222 (Bayerische Staatsbibl. Cod. Lat. 835),[25] provides a good example. On folio 20[r] (fig. 59) Moses is depicted with horns in scenes representing events after the renewal of the Law: the miracle of Moses striking the rock for water and the raising of the Brazen Serpent; however, he is also horned in events that preceded Exodus 34:29, as on folio 18[r] (fig. 60) where he removes his shoes before the Burning Bush and again when he and Aaron stand before Pharaoh.

The early thirteenth century provides an example of horned Moses at almost the opposite end of the western Christian world in

Bohemia (or Moravia), in the *Cursus Sanctae Mariae* (Morgan Lib. MS 739), dated ca. 1215. His appearance in a Central European manuscript is remarkable evidence of the wide reach of the horned Moses image by the early thirteenth century. This manuscript is a Book of Hours probably executed in the Premonstratensian Monastery of Louka in Moravia, at the instance of the Margravine Kunegund, for presentation to her niece, Saint Agnes;[26] it was designed for private worship.[27] The text is in Latin; the rubrics (for the illustrations) are in a German dialect. On folio 15^v Moses is shown horned as he stands before the Burning Bush and when he and Aaron stand before Pharaoh; on folio 16^r (fig. 61) he is also horned as he strikes the rock for water, as he receives the initial tablets of the Law, and as he shatters the tablets. It has been suggested that this manuscript has possible ties with provincial products of the Salzburg school;[28] one may speculate about possible influence via the Gebhardt Bible of the earlier Salzburg school. Or, the horns may have derived from English influence, directly or by way of Cluny in Burgundy. A new type of reading Annunciate in the English St. Albans Psalter (ca. 1123) was found by Otto Pächt to have a parallel both in a Bohemian miniature of about 1085 and in a Lectionary from Cluny also around the end of the eleventh century.[29] Pächt thinks that the stimulus for both the English and Bohemian examples may have come from Cluny.[30] That Cluny may well have been an important intermediary for horned Moses is underscored by his appearance on the south portal of the Cathedral of Lausanne whose architecture and sculpture have been described as related to that of Burgundy.[31]

It is in the magnificent stained-glass windows of France, then achieving their full flowering, that the greatest impact of the horned Moses imagery can be observed in the first half of the thirteenth century. The first example that I am able to point out is at Chartres. Here, in one of the apsidal windows, probably dating in the first quarter of the thirteenth century, is horned Moses before the Burning Bush (fig. 62).[32] (It is of interest to observe that the portal sculpture of Moses at Chartres does not have horns.) The community of ideas regarding choice of subjects and interpretation is reflected in the continuity of the horned Moses imagery in the windows of other great Gothic cathedrals. The scenes with Moses are very richly and extensively developed in the very beautiful windows of Sainte-Chapelle in Paris,[33] and in all these he is depicted with horns. Moses can be seen in the north rose window of Notre-Dame of Paris[34] with horns, his rod, and the tablets of the Law; all three became integral parts of his iconography (fig. 63). In one of the symbolic windows around the Crucifixion at Le Mans,[35] horned Moses is shown striking a rock for water, and also raising up the Brazen Serpent. A similar grouping is found at Bourges, differing only in insignificant details. Figure 64 shows the scene of Moses and the Brazen Serpent at Bourges.

Thirteenth-century French manuscript illuminators modeled much of their composition and iconography on the programs of the stained-glass windows. It has been said that the first time this influence can be unequivocally detected is in the Psalter of Blanche of Castille (Bibl. de l'Arsenal MS 1186), dated ca. 1230.[36] The psalter contains miniatures in superimposed medallions, a device quite clearly borrowed from stained glass. See for example, folio 14ʳ (fig. 65): In the upper medallion a horned Moses receives the Law (the first time); and in the lower medallion the Israelites worship the Golden Calf.

The program and style of French stained-glass windows are nowhere more effectively reflected than in the production of the enormous *Bible moralisée* executed in the royal workshops about 1250.[37] Typology, discussed earlier, is here supplanted by moralizing. The enormous labor of actual artistic production was equaled by that of producing the textual extracts and the moral commentary.[38] Three copies still exist of several that were made. The *Bible moralisée* is a key document in our study of horned Moses, for here can be found several different iconographic traditions associated with Moses coexisting with that of the horns. For this reason several examples of how Moses is represented in this great Bible will be described, using illustrations from the copy that is divided and held in three different libraries: Oxford Bodleian 270b, Bibliothèque Nationale Lat. 11560, and British Museum Harley 1527.[39]

Moses is occasionally represented in this Bible without any special addition to the hair of his head—no horns, no rays, no halo. This can be seen, for example, on folio 52^r (fig. 66 a and b),[40] in both of the two top medallions and in the two medallions third from the top. Sometimes Moses' head is shown draped with a type of shawl as in folio 57^v (fig. 67)[41] in the top left medallion. But there is one representation in this Bible that is of immense interest, for it uses an artistic convention that much later (in the fourteenth and fifteenth centuries) came to be a kind of conventionalized device; two separate groupings of lines (or rays) placed on the head of Moses occurs on folio 56^r,[42] (fig. 68), on the right in the third medallion from the top, and so far as it has been ascertained, does not recur in the manuscript. This is possibly the earliest, or one of the earliest, pictorializations of the theologian's rationalization of Moses' horns as rays of light. The interpretations of the theologians will be discussed in the next chapter.

More often the portrayals of Moses in the *Bible moralisée* show him horned, as on folio 184^r (fig. 69) on the left in the second medallion from the top and folio 216^r (fig. 70) on the left in the fourth medallion from the top.[43]

How is this mixture of different iconographic motifs for Moses within the *Bible moralisée* to be explained? A partial answer might be found in the very size of the project. The several artists required perhaps each used the tradition he was conversant with. It is also possible that close supervision of the illuminations was difficult; consistency may not have been possible on a project of this scale. But whatever the reason, the Bible gives rich documentation of the overlap of iconographic traditions, a phenomenon that will be observed again in some later documents.

It is interesting to note that the *Bible moralisée* provides evidence that occasionally Moses was given horns for his appearance in the scene of the Transfiguration,[44] as on folio 32^v of Br. Mus. Harley 1527, where he has horns but no halo.[45] Folio 4^r of the early thirteenth-century English psalter (Br. Mus. Royal MS I.D.X.),[46] also portraying the Transfiguration, shows Moses with horns and a halo on one side of Christ; Elias on the other. (See top portion of fig. 71.) This iconography of horns for Moses was contrary to the more prevalent type based on the Byzantine formula in which Moses and Elias appear at either side of Christ with halos. Conventionalized rays proceeding from Christ toward the three Apostles are sometimes also shown streaming toward Moses and Elias. This is the type found, for example, in a stained-glass window at Chartres.[47]

During the thirteenth century the style of Paris as exemplified by the Psalter of St. Louis (Bibl. Nat. Lat. 10525), ca. 1253–1270 (fig. 72), spread throughout France, with horned Moses becoming more and more a standard feature. For example, in a Latin Bible from France (Morgan Lib. MS 109) ca. 1260, Moses reclining, eyes closed, appears to receive his horns from the hand of God (fig. 73); and Moses is horned even in a scene depicting the Crucifixion, as in folio 345^v (fig. 74) of the Psalter of Yolande de Soissons (Morgan Lib. MS 729), ca. 1275.[48] A number of the illuminated French versions of La Somme le Roy show Moses horned, as for example, folio 5^v of Br. Mus. Add. 54180 (fig. 75) where he receives the Law and then shatters the tablets.[49] This very popular compendium of Church doctrine was composed for Philip III by his confessor, the Dominican Frère Laurent in 1279, and will be discussed again later in this study.[50]

French influence carried the horns of Moses further north and south. For example, in an initial of a Bible of the second half of the thirteenth century, coming from Tournai,[51] Moses has both horns and a halo (fig. 76); and in a Spanish Bible of ca. 1293 (Br. Mus. Add. 50003),[52] on folio 61^v (fig. 77), Moses is horned but does not have a halo.

Horned Moses continued to be part of the artistic traditions of

England and France in the fourteenth century; and this imagery began to be more widely dispersed through German-speaking territories. It was still mainly in northern Europe that there was a widespread use of horns for Moses; as yet the motif did not gain much ground among Mediterranean artists. It seems only later, during the fifteenth and sixteenth centuries, that this motif seeped into the program of Italian artists.

Manuscripts of the fourteenth century reflect English fidelity to horned Moses. In the well-known Queen Mary's Psalter (Br. Mus. MS 2 B. VII), Moses has horns after the renewal of the Law, and is so pictured on all subsequent folios of this manuscript.[53] Although Old Testament illustration ends with Noah in the Holkham Bible (Br. Mus. Add. 47682), ca. 1330, horned Moses can be found on folio 10[r] in the first Tree of Jesse. [54] Moses appears horned on folio 85[v] in the English Humphrey de Bohun Psalter (Vienna Nationalbibl. MS 1826*), ca. 1372. This psalter has been described as showing strong, direct Italian influence,[55] but apparently not enough to change or remove the horns from Moses. As mentioned, horned Moses does not seem to have been part of the Italian repertoire at this time. For example, Giotto in his decoration of the chapel in Padua (ca. 1303–1308), depicts Moses bearded, with a halo like that of the Lord, but with neither horns nor rays.[56] An example of horned Moses in fourteenth-century France may be seen in the Bible of Rheims (Rheims MS 39).

Spread of the horned Moses motif throughout the German-speaking countries was aided by the *Biblia Pauperum*[57] and the *Speculum Humanae Salvationis*.[58] Both works utilized the typological method of the Middle Ages, described earlier.[59] The texts varied, but all copies showed the allegorical connection between events of the Old and New Testaments in groups of pictures. Usually the scene from the New Testament is in the center set between two Old Testament scenes.

The prototype for the *Biblia Pauperum* manuscripts is thought to go back to the middle thirteenth century;[60] surviving manuscripts begin with the fourteenth. About eighty manuscripts, partial and whole, still remain from the fourteenth century[61] and have been classified according to textual variations, sequence of the groups of pictures, and iconographical peculiarities.[62] The popular (but erroneous) idea that the *Biblia Pauperum* was produced for the poor has now been unequivocally dispelled.[63] In the thirteenth and fourteenth centuries these manuscripts were not written for laymen; rather they were intended for teaching purposes.[64] Generally they contained thirty-four groups of pictures, with two groups on every page. As with the thirteenth-century *Bible moralisée*,[65] the fourteenth- and very early fifteenth-century *Biblia Pauperum* manuscripts reveal a mixture of iconographic traditions for Moses. For example: Moses is sometimes represented with a halo and no horns;[66] occasionally he is shown wearing a type of mitre;[67] sometimes he is given no special attribute;[68] and only very rarely is Moses represented with horns.[69] (It will be shown that later this mixture disappears from the *Biblia Pauperum* manuscripts and horned Moses reigns supreme.)

The overlap of different iconographic traditions is strikingly demonstrated by an early fifteenth-century *Biblia Pauperum* (ca. 1414),[70] Bayerische Staatsbibliothek Cod. Lat. 8201. On folio 81r, Moses is horned in the scene of the Burning Bush (fig. 78). On subsequent folios, [71] however, Moses is given the double grouping of rays that we saw earlier in the *Bible moralisée*. Compare for example folio 89r of the Bayerische Cod. Lat. 8201 (fig. 79), where Moses receives the Law, with the folio from the *Bible moralisée* (fig. 68). Note that in the *Biblia Pauperum* manuscript the artist has employed the same conventionalized technique of a series of finely drawn lines to render the radiation of a cross nimbus for the head of Christ (figs. 78 and 79) as he did for Moses' rays (fig. 79).

A similar mixture of iconographic traditions is found in copies of the *Speculum Humanae Salvationis*.[72] For example, in the scene depicting the rain of manna, in Munich Clm. 146, Moses wears the kind of mitre described earlier with reference to the *Biblia Pauper-*

um;[73] but in another fourteenth-century copy of the *Speculum Humanae Salvationis,* now in Kremsmünster, Moses, in this same scene, is depicted with giant horns and a halo (fig. 80).

The middle of the fifteenth century saw a significant change in the format and iconography of the *Biblia Pauperum.* It was changed to a forty-page book with only one group to a page, and a highly important stage was marked by the appearance of woodcut editions. It is this version that became by far the most popular, probably bought by laymen as well as preachers.[74] Moses is consistently horned in this later forty-page version, as for example in a 1471 edition: figure 81 shows two figures of horned Moses—one at the top next to David, and at the right in the scene of the rain of manna.[75] These more readily available woodcut versions may have been a significant factor in the spread of horned Moses in the North.[76]

Fifteenth-century France retained the horn motif for Moses. It is revealing to observe its continuity in Burgundy where the powerful horned Moses sculpture by Claus Sluter at Dijon[77] (fig. 82), gives hint of a tradition going back to the now nonexistent horned Moses on the twelfth-century portal of Saint-Bénigne.[78] Contemporary with the Sluter Moses is an illumination in the beautiful Bible historiale de Guyart des Moulins (Bibl. de l'Arsenal MS 5212),[79] where on folio 128[v], as on many other folios in this manuscript, Moses is represented with large, fierce horns (fig. 83).

Horned Moses persisted in the art of the German-speaking areas of Europe. He appears with horns in a detail of the "Betrothal of the Virgin," painted by Robert Campin,[80] and in a detail of the "Presentation in the Temple," painted by Stefan Lochner of Cologne, ca. 1447.[81] By contrast, in Italy there still seems to be a scarcity of the motif. For example, Fra Angelico represented Moses with the two conventionalized groupings of rays (as found earlier in the *Bible moralisée* and *Biblia Pauperum*) in a fresco in San Marco, ca. 1446[82] depicting the Transfiguration.

Raphael and Perugino in the early sixteenth century followed the practice of Fra Angelico; Raphael painted Moses with the two groups of rays in the Loggia of the Vatican (ca. 1519);[83] Perugino did the same in work done in Perugia.[84] But Michelangelo gave Moses his most famous horns in the statue done about 1513, now in San Pietro in Vincoli, Rome (fig. 84).

Michelangelo, however, was not the only well-known Italian artist to give Moses horns in the sixteenth century. Bernadino Luini, with remarkable inconsistency, painted Moses in several different ways in frescoes originally executed for the Villa Pelucca near Monza, ca. 1520.[85] He gave him horns in the scene of Moses on Sinai (fig. 85); but in the scene of the passage through the Red Sea he depicted him with rays; and in the scene of Moses striking the rock, he gave him horns that seem to emit rays of light. In a fresco of slightly later date, the scene of the presentation in the Temple, Luini seems to have definitely settled on horns.[86] Horned Moses was even part of Titian's repertoire, appearing in his great *Pièta* (ca. 1573–1576), originally painted to hang over his own tomb.[87] Here Moses is horned, holds the tablets of the Law, and stands to the right of the group mourning Christ.

The prevalence of the horn motif begins to diminish during and after the sixteenth century; however, it is not completely eradicated. For example, one can see a delicately horned Moses depicted in the sixteenth-century French Bibl. Nat. Lat. 1429, on folio 45[r] (fig. 86); and horned Moses is represented twice on a sculptured relief done by the sixteenth-century German artist, Veit Stoss (fig. 87). Even Rembrandt suggested horns for Moses in the pictorial arrangement of the hair on his forehead in a painting of Moses shattering the tablets of the Law, ca. 1659.[88] Horned Moses on a Dutch tile of the late eighteenth or early nineteenth century is an indication of its tenacity (fig. 88).

The horns of Moses lingered on, or, perhaps one might say, they were partially revived in the twentieth century. Chagall, in his many biblical illustrations, usually depicted Moses with rays of light; however, in at least one of his illustrations, "Moses and the Plague of Darkness," the rays have been assimilated; they look like horns.[89]

More recently, Sorel Etrog,[90] the contemporary sculptor born in Romania, 1933, has dramatically revived the horned Moses image in a gigantic sculpture. While the sculpture is abstractly conceived, the horns form an easily distinguishable and fully integrated part of this monumental work now in the garden of the Los Angeles County Art Museum (fig. 89).

The survey in the preceding pages of this chapter, though not exhaustive, presents a body of material of sufficient variety and span in time and geography to focus an inquiry on the underlying iconographic problem. The tenacity of the imagery, particularly in the North, and the copious examples, indicate that horned Moses had significant meaning for medieval men. While the image depicted in manuscripts may only have been seen by the clergy, horned Moses as represented in the liturgical dramas, on sculptured cathedral facades, in stained-glass windows, and in woodcut editions of the *Biblia Pauperum*, were seen by the laity as well.

In the succeeding chapters of this study we shall try to see horned Moses through the eyes of both the learned and the ignorant. He may have meant one thing to learned theologians and scholars and something quite different to illiterates. Some impressions will be gathered from the writings of those who espoused Church dogma; it will be more difficult to ferret out what the horns may have meant to the ignorant. The man-on-the-street did not write books.

VII Commentary of the Theologians

"Horn" in the Bible is generally used metaphorically.[1]
It signifies glory, dignity, power, might, honor, victory, kingship,
courage, defense, safety, and salvation. Here are a few representative examples:[2]

Ezekiel 34:21.—[God reproving evil
            shepherds says:]
            Because you thrusted with sides and
            shoulders, and struck all the weak
            cattle with your horns, till they
            were scattered abroad.
Deuteronomy 33:17.—[Moses blessing the tribes, speaking of
Joseph:]
            His beauty as of the firstling of
            a bullock, his horns as the horns
            of a rhinoceros:[3] with them shall
            he push the nations even to the
            ends of the earth.
Luke 1:68, 69.—[With reference to the symbol of salvation:]
            Blessed be the Lord God of Israel;
            because he hath visited and wrought
            the redemption of his people: and
            hath raised up an horn of salvation
            to us, in the house of David his
            servant.
Psalm 17:3.—[Again with reference to the Lord as the horn of
salvation:]
            My God is my helper, and in him will
            I put my trust. My protector and
            the horn of my salvation, and my
            support.

Daniel 8:20, 21.—[Here representing kings or kingdoms:]
    The ram, which thou sawest with
    horns, is the king of the Medes and
    Persians. And the he goat, is the
    king of the Greeks, and the great
    horn that was between his eyes, the
    same is the first king.

These references are in keeping with the meaning of horns in the ancient world, as discussed at the beginning of this study.[4] It is within this same context that Jerome chose "horned" for Moses.

Jerome had two different translations for the Hebrew *qeren* (Exod. 34:29) available to him: "glorified" in the Septuagint, and "horned" in the Aquila version.[5] Familiar with both (he drew material from many different sources[6]), perhaps in his scholarly search for what he believed to be the original word, he chose "horned." (It should be emphasized that what in fact represents most accurately the original words and form of the Old Testament Scriptures, is not at stake here.) As we shall see, Jerome's own comments make it eminently clear that he made a conscious choice, not a simple translation error; and furthermore, that he thought of "horned" metaphorically.

Thus far I have found no indication in Jerome's writings that he believed Moses descended from Mt. Sinai with solid horns on his forehead.[7] Quite the contrary. Jerome says in his *Commentary on Ezekiel*:

unde et Moyses in nubem ingressus est et caliginem ut possit mysteria Domini contemplari, quae populus longe positus et deorsum manens uidere non poterat; denique post quadraginta dies, uultum Moysi uulgus ignobile caligantibus oculis non uidebat, quia "glorificata erat," siue, ut in hebraico continetur, "cornuta," facies Moysi;[8]

[Moses also went up into a cloud and a fog in order that he might contemplate the mystery of God, which the people left behind could not see. Finally after forty days the common people with their clouded eyes could not look at Moses' face because it had been "glorified," or as it says in the Hebrew, "horned";]

This brief allusion indicates that Jerome equates glorified with horned. And when Jerome's other references to horned are considered, it becomes increasingly certain that metaphorical usage is what he intended. Curiously enough, however, historians have neglected this aspect of Jerome's translation. Jerome's concept of horned is particularly striking in his *Commentary on Amos* when he compares Moses with the "just man" and contrasts men who pervert justice, with those who are truly just:

> Those who do that delight in no good word . . . except in vain . . . and puffed up in their pride, they say: "Did we not have horns in our courage . . ." While the just man will glory in God, and will say, as in Psalm 43:6 . . . "Through Thee we will push down our enemies with the horn. . . ." And in Exodus, in the Hebrew edition and Aquila edition, we read: "And Moses did not know that the face of his countenance was horned. . . ." Moses, indeed, could have said: "Through Thee I push down my enemies with my horn."[9]

Jerome, referring to men who are puffed up in their pride, is alluding to the sin of exalting one's horn, that is, to the exhibition of pride, for as described in Psalm 74, only the Lord can exalt the horn: Line 5:

> I said to the wicked: Do not act wickedly:
> and to the sinners: Lift not up the horn.

And then in line 11:

> And I will break all the horns of sinners:
> but the horns of the just shall be exalted.

Thus, the "just man" having humbly received this symbolic motif—the horns—would use them as in Psalm 43 to destroy the enemy in the name of the Lord. The passage in Jerome's *Commentary on Amos* shows, therefore, that Jerome's concept of a horned Moses was within the general metaphorical context of the Bible.

This is demonstrated again in Jerome's *Homily on Psalm 91* where he comments on the line, "But my horn shall be exalted like that of the unicorn," and he says:

> A horn is always set up in a kingdom. "Our foes through you we are struck down with the horn." As a matter of fact, no animal is immolated to the Lord in the temple unless it is horned. In the temple there are three animals sacrificed to the Lord: the bull, the ram, and the buck. Three are sacrificed and all three are horned. Unless one has a horn with which to rout his enemies, he is not worthy to be offered to God. That is why, too, the Lord is described as a horn[10] to those who believe in him; and it was with the horns of the cross that He routed His enemies. On the cross He confounded the devil and his entire army.[11]

Jerome is not saying that Christ is a *real* horn. He expressed a religious concept in language appropriate for the period in which he lived. Similarly, he did not imply that Moses had *real* horns. Both in the example of Christ, and that of Moses, "horn" and "horned" serve as metaphors. What is of essential importance here is that Jerome's choice of "horned" for Moses in Exodus 34:29 became the accepted phrasing in the standard Bible of the Latin West in the Middle Ages, later known as the Vulgate.[12] This phrasing was retained for hundreds of years, and remains to this day in the Bible used by Roman Catholics. In English versions the "horned" was retained at least until 1560.[13] Thus, it was this phrasing of Exodus 34:29 which formed the basis for biblical exegesis during the Middle Ages.[14]

It is Paul, of the New Testament, who can be thought of as the first commentator on Exodus 34:29. For in 2 Corinthians 3, Paul refers to the face of Moses and its glory. In verse 7, he says:

> Now if the ministration of death, engraven with letters upon stones, was glorious; so that the children of Israel could not steadfastly behold the face of Moses, for the glory of his countenance, which is made void.

(We shall recall that Jerome, in his *Commentary on Ezekiel,* speaks of Moses' face as being glorified.)[15] It is the whole of chapter 3 of the second Epistle to the Corinthians which provided one of the basic ideas of the Church of the Middle Ages, namely: what Moses covered with a veil[16] is unveiled by the teachings of Christ; the Old Law, the Law of Moses, is superseded and made complete by the New Law or era of Grace brought by Christ; the glory of the Lord can now be beholden with an open face by those who accept Christ. Thus the Old Testament resolves itself into the New, if interpreted after the manner of Paul.[17]

Paul's reference to the glorification of Moses in 2 Corinthians 3:7, and its relationship to Exodus 34:29, is alluded to repeatedly by Christian biblical commentators. For, whether they were commenting on the "horned" of the Vulgate, or the "glorified" of the Septuagint, it was always a reference to a mark of glorification symbolizing Moses' communion with God. The glorification of Moses is reinforced by his reappearance as the representative of the Old Testament Law at the Transfiguration of Jesus in Matthew 17:2,3:[18]

> And he [Jesus] was transfigured before them.
> And his face did shine as the sun: and
> his garments became white as snow.
> And behold there appeared to them
> Moses and Elias talking with him.

One of the earliest and most extensive commentaries on the glorification of Moses is found in the writings of Origen (ca. 185–254). Briefly summarized, he says:[19] Moses was only partially glorified in the Old Testament; indeed, it was only his face that had glory; the rest of his body such as his hands and his feet, were not glorified. The glory of Moses' face represented the Law, that is, the language or words of the Law, but the glory of that knowledge remained hidden behind a veil (and he refers to Paul). Only with conversion to the Lord can the veil be lifted. He continues saying that while Moses had nothing glorious in the Law except his face, in the Gospels he is completely glorified (i.e., his whole body) at the Transfiguration while talking with Jesus. Origen based his exegesis on *glorificata facies;*[20] however, it should be observed that many of Origen's ideas were woven into later commentaries using the *cornuta* of Jerome's Vulgate.

A remarkably early reference to horned Moses occurs in the writings of the British monk, St. Gildas of the sixth century. This appears in his *De Excidio et Conquestu Britanniae,*[21] a widely studied document as one of the few sources for the confused and uncertain history of Britain in the sixth century. Scholars have concerned themselves mainly with the first part of this text, which deals with the historical aspects of Britain.[22] The second part is denunciatory; it catalogs the sins of five British kings and of priests in general.[23] Gildas's charges are supported by a mass of scriptural quotations; in one of his invectives against bishops and priests, the allusion to horned Moses appears:

> quis in monte cum domino locutus et nequaquam concrepantibus tubis exinde perterritus duas tabulas cornutamque faciem aspectu incredulis inhabilem et horrendam tropico sensu, ut Moyses, advexit?[24]

> [Who is he that like Moses, speaking with our Lord in the mountain, and not there terrified with the sounding trumpets, hath in a figurative sense presented unto the incredulous people the two tables and his horned face which they could not endure to see, but trembled to behold?][25]

This passage is of additional interest because the scriptural quotations in the second part of *De Excidio* have been described "as having some value since their text is not that of the Vulgate."[26] It is possible, however, that Gildas was familiar with the Vulgate text. The facts of his life are very uncertain;[27] Jerome's version may have been accepted as the standard text in Ireland during the sixth century;[28] it could have come into Gildas's hands through the Irish Church.

What is of special importance here is that this passage demonstrates that Gildas wanted "horned face" unequivocally understood as a metaphor, and so adds, *tropico sensu*. This was, however, the extent of his comments on the horns of Moses. Does this early sixth-century allusion to horned Moses reveal an early and continuous literary tradition for him in England? Can one tie this in with his later appearance in art in eleventh-century England? The present state of the evidence makes it impossible to arrive at an answer. One might infer that Gildas's allusion to horned Moses suggests that, at least among the more learned in sixth-century England, Moses' horns were not interpreted as *real* horns. On the other hand, one might even more reasonably infer that Gildas added *tropico sensu* because he was afraid that the horned image might be taken literally; or that he had possibly encountered Englishmen and others who had already misinterpreted Jerome's Vulgate translation to mean that Moses had real horns.

One other very important aspect of this passage in Gildas's writings should be stressed; namely, that it may be the earliest *direct* allusion to the horns of Moses subsequent to Jerome's translation of Exodus 34:29.

Direct references to the horns of Moses do not seem to be present in early biblical exegesis. There is, however, an indirect, oblique allusion that appears in Isidore's (ca. 560–636) *Quaestiones in Vetus Testamentum*, a text summarizing many of the commentaries of the early Fathers, and influencing later ones. Isidore's comments on Exodus 34:29 reflect Paul's words in 2 Corinthians 3, and their elaboration by Origen. But something new has been added, or so it seems. Isidore says:

> Quod vero, descendente denuo Moyse cum tabulis, facies ejus glorificata videtur, sed tamen velamine tegitur, hoc significabat ut ostenderet eam legem mystico esse velamine co-opertam, tectamque infidelibus et occultam. Sermo quippe legis habet scientiae gloriam, sed secretam: habet et cornua

duorum Testamentorum, quibus contra dogmata falsitatis incedit armata.[29]

[When Moses descends again with the tablets, that his face is seen to be glorified, yet is covered with a veil, is meant to show that this law was covered with a mystic veil, covered and hidden from the unfaithful. Of course the word of the law has the glory of knowledge, but hidden: And it has the horns of the two Testaments, armed with which it goes forth against the dogmas of falsehood.]

It is possible that Isidore's reference to the horns of the two Testaments was an obtuse, if awkward, allusion to the horned face of Moses in the Vulgate text. It seems to me that Isidore builds on Origen in this way: Origen had said that the glory of Moses' face represented the Law, that is, the words of the Law, with the glory of its knowledge remaining hidden behind the veil.[30] Thus, the words of the Law represent one Testament (the Old), while that which is hidden would represent another Testament (the New). Therefore, if the glory of Moses' face is described as horned in the Vulgate by Jerome, a logical corollary could be drawn that the two Testaments are also described as horned. Although Isidore's allusion seems somewhat forced, the opinion that it is an indirect reference to the horns of Moses will be corroborated (in the following chapter) by evidence in William Durandus's prayer for the imposition of the bishop's mitre; he speaks there of arming the head of the bishop with the horns of the two Testaments, so that the bishop may go forth as Moses did.[31]

The interpretations contained in Isidore's *Quaestiones in Vetus Testamentum*, one of the essential links in the long chain of Church traditions, were repeated for centuries by medieval writers. The passage quoted above occurs almost word for word in the commentary on Exodus 34:29 by the English historian and theologian, Bede (ca. 673–735).[32] And Rabanus Maurus (ca. 784–856), educated under the direction of Alcuin, also reproduces Isidore's exposition without significant change.[33] The use of this unusual imagery by three great theologians (Isidore, Bede, and Rabanus Maurus), representing a considerable span of time (the late sixth century through the middle of the ninth), indicates how slowly biblical interpretations changed. The horns of Moses were not part of the visual imagery of this period; it is possible that their later appearance in art stimulated rethinking and reevaluation of them.

Probably the earliest exegete to directly refer to and interpret the horns of Moses was the renowned French Rabbi Shelomoh Ben Yiçhaq, called Rashi by the Jews (by means of the juxtaposition of his initials), and called Rabbi Salomon by the Christians. Rashi commented on the very passage that concerns us. He says with reference to Exodus 34:29:

> And it came to pass when Moses went down [from Mount Sinai]—when he brought the second tablets on the Day of Atonement . . . that the skin of his face beamed . . . is an expression connected with the word . . . "horns," and the phrase . . . the light-"horned," is used here because light radiates from a point and projects like a horn.[34]

Rashi's interpretation of the horns of Moses, I would suggest, was the source for much of later Christian exegesis. Rashi was born in Troyes in 1030.[35] His interpretation of the Old Testament achieved tremendous popularity among the masses of the Jews. Rashi's commentaries dominated western Judaism during the period between his lifetime (1030–1105) and that of Nicolas of Lyra (1270–1349), never losing their first place among devout Jews. Rashi was particularly appropriate as a focus for the Christian scholars seeking out Jewish interpretations, for he was the only Jewish commentator who covered the entire Old Testament.[36] Furthermore, Rashi had particular appeal to both Jewish and Christian scholars because his commentaries were more available and more understandable.[37] His ideas were simply stated and did not extend into the more complicated reasonings of an Ibn Ezra or Kimhi. The fact that Rashi's comments did not involve questions of faith added to his appeal to Christian scholars.[38] While it was Nicolas of Lyra (ca. 1270–1349), one of the most famous of the commentators on the Old and New Testaments, who made the greatest use of Rashi, there were other Christian scholars who were acquainted with Rashi's commentaries for more than 150 years before Lyra, as for example Hugh of St. Victor (d. 1141) and Andrew of St. Victor (d. 1175).[39]

It is my opinion that Rashi's rationalization of the horns of Moses, as described above, served as a source for Petrus Comestor's, interpretation in his *Historia Scholastica* of ca. 1167:

> And when he descended from the mountain with the tablets, his face appeared to be horned, and he himself did not know it, that is, wonderful rays of splendor emanated from his face, that struck [or blinded] the eyes of those who were watching.[40]

Comestor, like Rashi, was born in Troyes, possibly a few years before Rashi died, and he was very likely the "closest in personal touch with the individuals who made up the continuing school of Rashi."[41] Although there seems to be little evidence of direct quotations from Rashi in the *Historia Scholastica*, Hebrew exegesis influenced Comestor.[42] It has been shown that he used Andrew of St. Victor as a principal source,[43] and Andrew, we are told, was very much influenced by information he obtained from Jewish sources,[44] including Rashi's commentaries and ideas as well as those of the school of Rashi. Whether Comestor derived his ideas directly or indirectly, his explanation of horned as "wonderful rays of splendor" emanating from Moses' face substantially reflects Rashi's concept: "that the skin of his face beamed." And there can be little doubt that Petrus Comestor played an important role in popularizing the notion that horns meant rays. This was perhaps in no small measure due to the tremendous spread and influence of his *Historia Scholastica*. It became one of the most popular books of the Middle Ages, serving as a setbook in the schools, and as a classic for both clergy and laity.[45]

Rashi's explanation for the horns of Moses became the most generally accepted one during the Middle Ages, used by Nicolas of Lyra in his Commentaries. This is of particular interest since Lyra's writings summarized medieval biblical commentary up to his time[46] and strongly influenced commentaries of later theologians. Lyra's writings met with immediate success, eminent theologians of the fourteenth century contending for the purchase of his writings.[47] And it was his biblical commentary that was the first to be printed.[48]

Nicolas's principal work was his *Postillae perpetuae in universam S. Scripturam,* an elucidation of the text in verse succession (the same method as used by Rashi). In this text, Nicolas says that the horns of Moses are rays of wonderful splendor proceeding upward toward heaven in the manner of horns, which the Apostle (that is, Paul, in 2 Cor. 3:7) calls the glory of Moses' face.[49] Nicolas of Lyra not only describes the horns as rays of light in the manner of horns, but he gives various explanations for the initial gift to Moses by the Lord:

> Some say that he did not have as clear a cognition of God until afterwards—such rays appeared to denote this. . . .

> Others say that these rays appeared in order that the people who had sinned through idolatry would fear him the more and would tremble in awe. . . .

> Ra. Sa. [Rashi] says that they appeared because God put his hands over Moses' face.[50]

And Nicolas states that Moses finally knew that he was horned because of the hinting of others.[51]

Almost every commentator who wrote after the time of Nicolas of Lyra, paraphrases and elaborates on him. The only difference, perhaps, is that those who wrote after Lyra composed longer commentaries and were more verbose and repetitious. For example, the fifteenth-century commentator, Dionysius the Carthusian (Denys van Leeuwen), ca. 1402–1471, whose writings became especially popular in the century after his death,[52] writes an extensive commentary on Exodus 34, almost all of it just a longer version of that of Nicolas of Lyra.[53]

The Flemish biblical exegete, Cornelius à Lapide (1567–1637), also remains faithful to Nicolas of Lyra and reflects the same medieval exegesis:

> Cornutum is understood here metaphorically, for to be sure Moses did not have horns on his forehead as the painters give him, but so radiant was his face that it flashed forth rays of light as if they were in the shape of horns.[54]

Most of his other ideas are the same as those of Nicolas of Lyra, always stressing the concept that the horns were horns of light:

> Therefore these horns were not of bone, but of light, because the law which God was to give was light and it was heavenly and divine.[55]

Cornelius, however, keenly aware of the differences of interpretation justifies Jerome's choice, saying:

> Our translator [Jerome] very well translated *cornuta;* for the verb *karan* signifies properly to be horned, and not indeed to radiate as some make of it. In the same way, the noun *keren* signifies horn, and this is so in almost all languages.[56]

This last quotation, however, considered in conjunction with the other two referred to above, makes it certain that Cornelius meant horned figuratively, that is, horns of light, not horns of bones.

This concern with the "rays" or "horns," is part of the history of the English Bible too. The Aelfric Paraphrase had translated the *cornuta* directly into *gehyrned,* and this was followed in the Wycliffe Bible, where it was rendered:

> and he wiste not that his face was horned of the felouschipe of Goddis word.[57]

But by 1539, Coverdale, in the Great Bible, incorporates the traditional theological explanation for the horns as horned rays of light, thus rendering the passage:

and Moses wyst not that the skinne of his face shone in maner of an horne, whyle he talked with him.[58]

As late as 1624, Thomas Godwyn in England, in a marginal note, still referred to Rashi in Hebrew. On the page itself, he interprets Moses' horns saying:

And hence it is that *Moses* is painted with *horns*, which some of the Rabbins have interpreted (p) *horns of magnificence*: the errour grew from the doubtful signification of the *Hebrew* word, signifying *splendor* or *brightness*, and also *horns*.[59]

Although Rashi's concept of light emanating in a hornlike manner became the explanation generally preferred by Christian scholar-theologians for the horns of Moses, it was not, however, the only interpretation given during the Middle Ages. A surprising explanation for horned Moses can be found in the writings of the Premonstratensian, Adamus Scotus. In his treatise on the threefold sense of the tabernacle, written at the abbey of Dryburgh, Berwickshire, Scotland, in 1179 or 1180,[60] Adam includes a chapter where he describes the twofold image of Moses, explaining how that image when it is placed outside the tent designates Moses tropologically. He says:

As the entrance and exit of Moses are seen in our picture, we have depicted two representations of the same Moses: one outside the tabernacle at the entrance of the tent, but the other inside, to the right of the kindled altar. The image outside represents the right and proper form of Moses, who here exhibits his horned countenance to the people and appears standing in secular clothing, because to be covered with secular clothing and in common garb is to be concerned with earthly matters. But that image which is inside, especially as it is clothed in pontifical vestment, should properly express the High-Priest Aaron himself, but has the ability, nevertheless, in this place and according to this signification, to even designate Moses who is free here for the purity of contemplation in his innermost secret heart. And indeed careful attention must be given to this image for it does not represent Moses' form, either in garb or in countenance, that is represented outside the tabernacle at the entrance of the tent; for he has a very different state of mind who in his innermost secret heart contemplates heavenly and eternal matters than the one who mixed with the crowd and directed his attention to earthly and temporal things. Outside Moses both shows his horned countenance to the people and doesn't differ in his clothing from them, because however saintly one may be, as long as he dwells upon earthly actions, it is extremely difficult for him not to exhibit a somewhat animal-like [bestialem] countenance and a somewhat secular attitude in his dealings. But inside Moses is seen without the horned countenance and in priestly vestment, because when we dwell most deeply upon the contemplation of purity, then our activities adorned with holiness and our countenance unveiled, we gaze upon the glory of the Lord. And so the image of Moses outside designates the executor; that inside designates the contemplator; the one the active life, the other the contemplative life.[61]

We are informed that Adam consulted Comestor's *Historia Scholastica*;[62] however, Comestor's interpretaton is most certainly not reflected in Adam's comments on horned Moses.[63] Adam clearly states that the horned countenance of Moses is only portrayed or seen when Moses is outside the tent, occupied with earthly, secular, impure activities; he is without horns inside when concerned with heavenly, eternal, and pure thoughts. Adam even implies that Moses' countenance outside the tent partakes of something animal-like (*bestialem*).

Adam has been described as "learned in a solid, old-fashioned way,"[64] and his writings have been described as telling something of the mind of the Scottish twelfth-century canons, "a mind having much in common with the simplest of evangelical thought."[65] Does Adam reflect ideas current during this period in Scotland and in England? From what sources did Adam derive his unusual interpretation for horned Moses? It is hoped that historians devoted to the complex and difficult discipline of medieval exegesis[66] will provide illuminating answers to these questions. This study has been dependent on those texts in print; the bulk of medieval material remains in manuscript form.[67]

One also wonders how influential Adam's interpretation may have been. He later (ca. 1188) joined the Carthusian charterhouse at Witham in England, where he became a close friend of Hugh of Lincoln.[68] Adam's treatise on the threefold sense of the tabernacle seems to have been generally well known, yet it is difficult to determine what effect the particular passage about horned Moses had on later churchmen. Insofar as I have been able to ascertain, Adam's interpretation appears to be outside the main current of thought. It is assumed then, at least until further evidence changes our suppositions, that the most prevalent scholarly medieval explanation was that the horns of Moses were like rays of light—as described by Rashi, Comestor, Lyra, and later commentators. (This does not rule out, however, the possibility that secular interpretations were quite different.)

It remains to reconcile—if possible—the commentary of the theologians with the art of the theologian-directed artists. One may properly inquire: how may the artistic renderings of Moses described in chapter vi be squared with the general agreement of most theologians that the horns were not bone but rather rays of light—projecting in the manner of horns?

The evidence in chapter vi showed Moses with no special attribute (just his hair); with a halo; with horns and a halo; with a mitre; with a shawl-draped head; with horns only; and occasionally with two distinct groupings of rays. It is this last category that most distinctively reflects the artists' attempts to visually reveal the theological interpretation of horns as rays of light.[69] The earliest example of this convention was observed in the French *Bible moralisée* of ca. 1250 (fig. 68), discussed in chapter vi. So far this seems to be an isolated example in this period; perhaps further examples will be found by other students of this subject. Subsequently this artistic device was noted in a copy of the *Biblia Pauperum* of ca. 1414 (fig. 79), and in the paintings of Fra Angelico, Raphael, and Perugino. Yet there did not appear to be a smooth transition from horns to rays; sometimes they coexisted as in the *Bible moralisée*, the *Biblia Pauperum* or, later, the Luini frescoes. Furthermore, the two groups of rays did not achieve the popularity of the horns. It seems that only gradually, with the development of the Reformation and the Church of the Counter-Reformation, did the practice of depicting Moses with horns substantially decline.

Beyond the evidence of chapter vi, there was a middle ground—another artistic effort during the Middle Ages to graphically represent horns in the manner of rays, or rays in the manner of horns. It is closely allied with a popular[70] vernacular text, the *Weltchronik*, written by the versatile and prolific Rudolf von Ems, a Swiss-Austrian poet, between 1228 and 1254. This poem does not properly belong in this chapter, for it is part of the more general religious literature to be discussed in chapter ix. It is mentioned at this time, however, because occasionally illustrations in some of the copies reveal another artistic approach to the more general scholarly interpretations. The text of the *Weltchronik*, written in Middle High German (of which there are variant texts) has been edited.[71] The poem describes the appearance of Moses as he descended from the mountain the second time:

> Moses, the good man, then again came
> down from the mountain,
> and when he came there to the crowd,
> from all of this the people
> thought that he had been horned
> because seven beams [or rays] formed a
> ring around the chosen hero and
> encompassed his head and face.
> The beams shone like the sunshine,

gleamed with so much brilliance
that no one was able to look
with open eyes at the very
bright aspect of the rays.[72]

Comestor, one of Rudolf's sources, may have served as the basis
for Rudolf's elaboration.[73] Some of the artists who illustrated copies
of the *Weltchronik* occasionally depicted Moses with a semicircu-
lar grouping of seven or more horns radiating from his head. The
earliest example of this appears in a manuscript dated between
1255 and 1270,[74] Bayerische Staatsbibl. Cgm. 6406, folio 68[r] (fig.
90).

In another later illustrated copy of the *Weltchronik*, ca. 1340–
1350,[75] on folio 87[r] of Zürich Zentralbibliothek MS Rh. 15, again
an artist depicts Moses with radial horns (fig. 91).[76] It is noteworthy
that although Rudolf described the reality as beams or rays forming
a ring around the hero's head and face, the artists adapt the poet's
version of what the crowd thought, depicting a ring more of horns
than of rays of light. (See figs. 90 and 91.)

It seems then it was only in the relatively infrequent representations of the two groupings of rays that the scholar-theologian's concept of horns as rays was correctly reflected in art. This seems remarkable since the importance of the Church's supervision of all
artistic schemes has often been emphasized.[77] In the Middle Ages,
the guiding direction of the scholar and the theologian can be seen
everywhere, and Church doctrine is reflected in the visual arts:

There is little doubt that they superintended the decoration of
their cathedral, and themselves planned and drew up the
scheme. They must in many cases have provided the artists
with actual "livrets."[78]

One can only ask, what happened in the case of Moses' horns?

First of all, there is the possibility pointed out earlier with reference to the Aelfric Paraphrase, that men of the early Middle Ages
may not have found the horns of Moses offensive. It can at least be

conjectured that all of the negative associations with the horns of the devil, cuckold, and pagan divinities, were not as deeply rooted in the early part of the Middle Ages as they later became. The fact that devils, monsters, and other infamous creatures were depicted with horns did not seem to inhibit the artists' desires for giving Moses horns too.

Second, while one can say that the artists were directed by the clergy, or were even often clergymen themselves, not all bishops, cathedral clerics, and priests were scholars. And as we saw in the writings of Adamus Scotus, even learned men of the Church did not necessarily stay within the more dominant framework of biblical exegesis. And therefore it seems that the most generally accepted interpretation for the horns of Moses as horns of light, or rays of splendor, was not always expressed in the art of the religious book, or in the churches. Moses' horns were represented in medieval art—most of the time—as just plain horns.

VIII The Bishop's Mitre

THE SIGNIFICANCE of Moses' horns, and their symbolic meaning within the context of the medieval Church, is nowhere more vividly shown than when their meaning is transferred to the horns of the bishop's mitre. The horns of Moses grow—so to speak—upon the Christian bishop's mitre, so that it becomes a "helmet of salvation."[1] This is not to be literally construed; however, the evidence presented in this chapter will show that during the Middle Ages the scholar-theologians interpreted and related the horns of the mitre to the horns of Moses.

It is important to note that the bishop has horns on his mitre only in the Latin Church; and furthermore, attention is called to the immensely significant fact that the mitre, even in the Latin West, does not become a horned mitre until *after* Moses appears with horns in art. It is this extraordinary sequence of events that seems to have been overlooked. It is my contention that while later interpretations of the horns of the mitre are dependent upon horned Moses as expounded in the biblical text, the horned mitre itself does not appear among the Church vestments until after the date of the first attestable appearance of a horned Moses in art—that of the Aelfric Paraphrase (ca. 1050), discussed in the first part of this study.

One looks in vain for anything that resembles a mitre, that is, any kind of a specific liturgical headdress for a bishop, in the first 1000 years of Christianity.[2] And there is no specific liturgical mitre in the written or pictorial sources for the Greek rite even toward the end of the Middle Ages.[3] The origin of the mitre in the Western Church appears to be obscure.[4] It may have gradually evolved from the *camelaucum*, a low, round headgear shaped like a helmet[5] worn at the beginning of the eighth century as one of several imperial head coverings[6] and was later known as *mitra* or *regnum*. At some later time, perhaps around 950, this head covering was changed for the pope to a liturgical one thereby distinguishing it from the imperial head-dress.[7] Around 1000 there were probably two head coverings for the pope; a liturgical one for divine service; a worldly one for reigning, with the former becoming the mitre and the latter becoming the tiara.[8] The first written mention of the mitre is that of Pope Leo IV (1049–1054), conceding the privilege to Eberhard, Archbishop of Trier in 1049, with the understanding that the mitre would be worn according to Roman custom.[9] It is not at all certain what that custom was. There are very few pictorial works of the eleventh century in which the mitre is shown, but its oldest form seems to be a conical-shaped hat.[10] According to Joseph Braun, about A.D. 1100 the mitre begins to lose its pointed conical shape and becomes more rounded,[11] and after 1125 a side-horned mitre is found frequently on bishops' seals and in miniatures (figs. 92, 93, 94, 95).[12] Braun and others have suggested that this shape was perhaps achieved by pressing down on the top of the mitre from the forehead to the back of the head, a division that was occasionally emphasized by the addition of an ornamental band passed from front to back across the indentation.[13]

It is this side-horned mitre that may have been the direct descendant of the horns of Moses, appearing first probably around 1100. Later, the horns of the mitre are turned around so that they are at the front and the back, rather than at the sides, and so they have remained to this day. The changes through which the mitre has gone cannot be described by definite stages. They overlapped. One locale sometimes retained the older form while another place changed to the newer form (horns front and back). The side-horned mitre is thought to have been most prevalent between 1100 and 1175,[14] although in miniatures it occurs even in the thirteenth century.[15] The first reliable example of the later form—horns front and back—is toward the middle of the twelfth century.[16] We can follow this change on some English bishops' seals: very distinct side-horned mitres can be seen on the seals of Alexander of Lincoln, ca. 1123–1147 (fig. 92), Robert de Chesney of Lincoln, ca. 1148–1167 (fig. 93), Richard of Lichfield-Koven, ca. 1161–1182 (fig. 94), and Thomas Becket of Canterbury, ca. 1162–1170 (fig. 95). The change to the front-back horned mitre is represented on a seal of ca. 1167–1188 (fig. 96). [17]

The side-horned mitre is visually a more dramatic expression of horns than is the later type where the horns are juxtaposed front-back. A particularly striking illustration of a bishop wearing a side-horned mitre is in a manuscript now in the Bibliothèque de la ville d'Avranches, ca. 1160 (fig. 97). "The Donation of Richard II of Normandy to Bishop Manger of Avranches," is represented in this folio, and it is additionally interesting, because several typical head-dresses of the period can be observed: the twelfth-century head-dress of a king (at the right of the bishop), an abbot (at the left of the bishop), and the tonsured heads of the monks below. The visual impact of the horned mitre is lessened once the horns were turned around front to back. (See fig. 98 for Braun's diagram of the development of the mitre.)

Although the horned mitre was not part of the liturgical vestments of the first thousand years of Christianity, the artists, beginning in the twelfth century, often represented the mitre as though it were present in the early Christian period. Anachronistically, they depicted the early Church Fathers as wearing the horned mitres of contemporary Christian bishops. Thus we find for example, Gregory the Great dressed in a horned mitre (fig. 99), and Augustine similarly costumed (fig. 100).

Joseph Braun has stated that the horns of the mitre were first interpreted by Robert Paululus[18] of the early twelfth century. Paululus speaking of the mitre's horns says:

> Its two horns signify the defenses of the two Testaments by means of which the bishops must protect themselves and others against the enticements of the world, and by which the bishop must destroy the enemies of Christ.[19]

By the end of the twelfth century, Petrus Cantor comments on the horns of abbatial mitres (abbots were occasionally granted the prerogative):

> For if the horns of the mitre on the abbot's head signify the Old and New Testaments, then if any question arises as to its significance, should it not be referred to the bishop? For he seems to be the leader of the flock in such a way that he casts down the enemies with the horns of the Old and New Testaments. If it doesn't mean anything, then the mitre of the abbot is foolish, superfluous, puerile—like the mitre of a boy.[20]

Innocent III (ca. 1160–1216) had this to say:

> The pontifical mitre signifies the knowledge of both Testaments: for the two horns are the two Testaments, the two fringes are the spirit and the letter.[21]

The ideas utilized for these interpretations of the horns of the mitre may have been derived in part from the exposition of Exodus 34:29 by Isidore, Bede, and Rabanus Maurus:[22] that the word of the Law has the glory of knowledge and the horns of the two Testaments. Thus the horns of the two Testaments are now interpreted as the horns of the mitre. (Earlier it was suggested that the allusions by Isidore, Bede, and Rabanus Maurus to the horns of the two Testaments were oblique references to the horned countenance of Moses.[23])This becomes explicit later in the words of the prayer used in the imposition of the mitre at the consecration of a new bishop. By the end of the thirteenth century (ca. 1292), William Durandus, Bishop of Mende, the great canonist who made liturgical history with his *Rationale Divinorum Officiorum*,[24] included a prayer for the imposition of the mitre, still used in the very same form in the Roman Catholic Church of today. This prayer for the imposition of the bishop's mitre reads:

> Imponimus, Domine, capiti huius Antistitis et agonistae tui galeam munitionis et salutis, quatenus, decorata facie et

armato capite cornibus utriusque Testamenti, terribilis appareat adversariis veritatis; et, te ei largiente gratiam, impugnator eorum robustus exsistat, qui Moysi famuli tui faciem, ex tui sermonis consortio decoratam, lucidissimis tuae claritatis ac veritatis cornibus insignisti, et capiti Aaron Pontificis tui tiaram imponi iussisti. Per Christum Dominum nostrum. Amen.[25]

And in translation:

We, O Lord, set on the head of this thy Bishop and champion, the helmet of defense and of salvation, so that with comely face and with his head armed with the horns of either Testament he may appear terrible to the opponents of truth, and may become their vigorous adversary, through the abundant gift of Thy grace, who didst make the face of Thy servant Moses to shine after familiar converse with Thee, and didst adorn it with the resplendent horns of Thy brightness and Thy truth, and commandest the tiara to be set on the head of Aaron, the High Priest.

We see then that Durandus's prayer for the imposition of a mitre provides an interpretation that goes beyond those of Paululus, Petrus Cantor, and Innocent III. He illuminates the obscurity of the allusion to the horns of the two Testaments in the exposition of Isidore, Bede, and Rabanus; relating them not only to the bishop, but also to Moses.

A ceremony of consecration in which a mitre is given to the bishop goes back at least to the twelfth century,[26] and since about 1200 the ritual is mentioned repeatedly in the pontifical books.[27] V. Leroquais noted that the mitre mentioned in a twelfth-century pontifical of Avranches[28] was the first he had found in written sources, and that the prayer, as it is presently known, is not found earlier than that of Durandus.[29] It was Durandus's purpose, however, to arrange the pontifical as an authentic liturgical book for the use of bishops. His goal was to achieve this without innovations, and with respect for tradition;[30] this suggests that the ideas, and perhaps even the language of the prayer codified by Durandus, go back to an earlier period. Once Durandus's work was published, it became authoritative,[31] and even with the revisions of the pontifical begun under Pius XII, the words of this particular prayer remain the same today.[32] The importance of this ceremony of imposition of the mitre at an early period is testified to by a miniature in a French manuscript of the second half of the twelfth century, where one sees the newly ordained bishop receiving his mitre (fig. 101).[33]

Durandus, in the third book of his *Rationale Divinorum Officiorum*, devotes himself to a symbolic interpretation of all the sacred vestments, including the mitre. His interpretation is of special significance since it elaborates on the ideas included in his prayer, and provides additional clarification of the concept that the horns of the mitre should be thought of analogically as the horns of Moses:

> Now the Mitre betokeneth the knowledge of both Testaments; for its two horns are these same, the fore horn the New, the after horn the Old; and both these the Bishop ought to know by heart, and with them, as with a twofold horn, to smite the enemies of the Faith. Thus ought he to appear horned unto his flock, as did Moses in the eyes of Aaron and of the children of Israel from his companying with the Word of God, when bearing the two Tables of the Testimony he came down from Mount Sinai; as it is said in the thirty-fourth chapter of Exodus.[34]

The ideas expressed by Isidore, Bede, Rabanus Maurus, then by Robert Paululus, Petrus Cantor, Innocent III, and more fully expanded by William Durandus, are reflected in a later period in the writings of Dionysius the Carthusian (ca. 1402–1471). His explicit, detailed statements help in understanding how and why the symbolism of the horned mitre was associated with Moses.

> Lastly, through the light and rays of Moses' face, the truths are designated—and also, the mysteries and noble proper-

ties of the Scriptures of the Old Testament are designated. Through the veil there is difficulty and obscurity in understanding these Scriptures. But by the uncovering of Moses' face, the illumination of the Holy Spirit exposes it to us in order that through Christ we may understand the meaning of these Scriptures.

Through the horns of Moses' face we receive strong arguments from the Law and the Prophets with which we arm ourselves to refute the blinded Jews and others vying with sound doctrine and faith.[35]

It is also important to observe that from the early part of the twelfth century, the horns of the mitre were very well understood as horns—and were not referred to as points or humps or something else.

This is made clear by Hugh the Chantor in his *History of the Church of York* (1066–1127),[36] containing a somewhat bitter account of the archbishop of Canterbury's journey to Rome in 1116. (Hugh was concerned with maintaining the liberties of York as against Canterbury.) The passage is of great significance because it is a further demonstration of an understanding of the relationship between the horns of the mitre and those of Moses. Because it is so pertinent and is of such an early date, we quote it at length:

> As the archbishop set out, desiring to visit the threshold of the Apostles for his duty of prayer there, he said that he was going to Rome to buy horns, since at Rome everything was for sale. Whether he really meant to buy horns or something else, we know that though the temporalities of Canterbury are rich, and bring in a good income, he sold some of the treasure of the church for the sake of obtaining Thurstan's profession.[37]

(Hugh the Chantor is referring here to simony, and specifically to the purchase of bishoprics when he says "he was going to Rome to buy horns.") On this journey the archbishop and some of his companions fall sick, and Hugh says:

Perhaps God so willed in both cases, because both had proudly said they would buy horns, and were stiff-neckedly, and knowingly hastening to commit injustice.[38]

After they arrive in Rome:

He found no seller of horns there. The holy and true apostolic father, the vicar of Simon Peter, the adversary of Simon Magus, was then staying at Benevento.[39]

The archbishop was unable to obtain what he sought; the Pope would not grant him what he had tried to obtain "for his room full of gold and silver."[40] The Pope gave him a rather innocuous letter to help him save face, thereby really giving him nothing. When the archbishop returned to Normandy:

His face did not appear to have horns, like that of Moses, nor were many afraid when they saw him. But I have often thought over the question, what were the horns which he said he was going to buy. There are the horns of God, of which Habakkuk says, "And his brightness was as the light: he had horns coming out of his hand."[41] There are the devil's horns, of which, in the Revelation, the beast had "ten horns . . . and his tail drew the third part of the stars of heaven."[42] There are also the horns of the just and the horns of the wicked, of which the Psalmist speaks in the same verse, "All the horns of the ungodly also will I break: and the horns of the righteous shall be exalted."[43] Some of these horns are to be desired and bought at a great price, if they were for sale; others to be manfully broken and diligently avoided. The horns of the two former overcome evil; those [of the last] attack good.[44]

Thus at the very beginning of the twelfth century there was a sophisticated understanding of the horns of the mitre.

There is further and rich reference to the mitre as horned in the famous satire, *Speculum Stultorum*. This is a poem written in Latin by Nigel, a Benedictine monk, at Canterbury in 1180. It is a satirical animal allegory of great charm and humor. The poem tells of an ass, Burnel, who is ambitious. Burnel, in searching for the means of acquiring a longer and more luxuriant tail, is a religious in search of preferment. (While Nigel satirizes and criticizes certain aspects of Church life, he always does so with an unswerving devotion to his religion.) Burnel dreams of becoming a bishop. It is here that we find the mitre referred to as horned. Nigel criticizes the abbatial mitre as being powerless, having Burnel say:

> Mitra caput nostrum sine munere pontificali
> Nulla deaurabit, auxiliante Deo.
> Mitra nec ascendet caput hoc neque cornua sumam,
> Si non affuerit quod solet inde sequi.[45]

> [No mitre reft of pontiff's power shall gild
> My head (if God to me assistance yield).
> No mitre on my head, no horns for me,
> If in their power be no reality.][46]

And Burnel adds:

> Abbatum steriles mitras, quas nulla sequuntur
> Chrismatis officia, non probo, sintque procul.
> Gignere cum nequeat, sua sic genitalia gestat
> Mulus et est sterilis tempus in omne suum.
> Cum rem non habeant, sua sic insignia portant
> Hi qui nomen habent officioque carent.
> Absit ut ascendam vel talia cornua sumam,
> Qualia sumpserunt ille vel ille sibi. . . .

> Non ita Burnellus capiet sibi nomen honoris;
> Non sinet imponi cornua vana sibi,[47]

> [Never would I a sterile mitre take,
> Which cannot the anointing power awake.
> So bears a mule the limb of generation,
> Yet ever lacks the power of procreation.
> So they the emblems but no power possess,
> They bear the name but yet are functionless.

Never for me such horns of high position,
The aim of this or that man's high ambition. . . .

Burnel will no such title take, nor let
Horns without power upon his brow be set.][48]

The possibility that the mitre evolved from the horns of Moses
is given additional support by the fact that Aaron and other Jewish
high priests were often shown wearing the bishop's horned mitre.
The association of Moses (founder of the priesthood) and Aaron-
the-High-Priest, with that of the Christian bishop became part
of the interpretation of the Middle Ages.

The importance of the bishop as a descendant of the family of
Moses and Aaron is emphasized as early as the eighth century in
the pontifical of Archbishop Egbert, where the ordination of Aaron
as the first high priest by Moses is mentioned four times in the
prayers of the ordination of the Christian bishop.[49] This concept is
found later in a sermon by Wulfstan (d. 1023) preached at the consecration of a bishop,[50] although no mention is made of a mitre.[51]
Aaron-the-High-Priest was often mistakenly depicted in the vestments of a Christian bishop. While the Bible does describe the
vestments of Aaron, and includes a reference to a mitre (Exodus
28:39), no details of its shape are given. Thus, once again, in the
art of the Western Church, the association of ideas is responsible
for some new iconography. Aaron, as high priest, is often represented then with his censer, bells on the bottom of his tunic, and
with the horned mitre of the Christian bishop. There is, however,
no evidence that the Jewish priesthood ever had a unique headdress, and certainly not a horned mitre. For example, Aaron is
represented in a high rounded hat in one of the paintings of the
third-century Dura-Europos synagogue.[52] Nevertheless, the idea
that the Jewish high priest wore a horned mitre took hold, so that
for example, in the thirteenth-century stained-glass window at
Le Mans, in a scene where Joachim is driven from the Temple, the
Jewish high priest wears a side-horned mitre like those of the

early twelfth-century Christian bishops.[53] Or sometimes he wears the front to back horned types, as in a late twelfth-century northern French manuscript (fig. 54).

William Durandus, in his book on the sacred vestments referred to earlier, does distinguish between the Christian vestments and the "vestments of the law—or Old Testament."[54] He lists and describes the vestments of the Old Testament, as prescribed according to the Mosaic Law of Exodus 28, at the end of his book on the sacred vestments. When he describes the mitre of the high priest he adds substantially to the Exodus description:

> The fourth and last Vestment was that of the head, to wit, the Tiara or Mitre; this did end in a point, and had a golden circlet, with pomegranates and flowers; and from it there did hang down upon the brow a Plate of gold, in the shape of a half-moon, whereon was written *Anoth Adonai*, to wit, the Holy Name of the Lord, the Tetragrammaton or Four-lettered Name, whereof again below.[55]

Where did Durandus derive the "shape of a half-moon"? There is, of course, no description of the shape of the plate in Exodus. Durandus later interprets the Old Testament vestments allegorically, but unfortunately he does not specifically allude to the "shape of a half-moon." But he does say that the Golden Plate is a figure of wisdom, and that it foreshadows the sign of the Cross, which is made in the Office of Confirmation.[56] Thus, while the mitre of the Jewish high priest is not described by Durandus as horned like that of the bishop, the horn-crescent shape of the Golden Plate does perhaps suggest the horns of Moses.

Nicolas of Lyra (ca. 1270–1349) may have thought of the Jewish high priest in a similar way, perhaps having been influenced by Durandus. Lyra added diagrams to illustrate particular points in his commentaries.[57] He drew thirty diagrams in all, and among them was a drawing of the high priest officiating in his sacred vestments as described in Exodus 28. Our figure 102 reproduces the diagram from a fifteenth-century printed edition of Lyra's *Postillae*. While Lyra does not give the high priest the horned mitre, he does give him a high, helmet-shaped hat, with a crescent-shaped horn motif on the front part of the headdress (fig. 102). There is, of course, no more textual basis for the crescent-horn motif than there is for any other specific design. Lyra here seems to follow in the tradition of Durandus's description of the ancient high priest. In doing so, Lyra thus continues the idea of the horns of Moses by suggesting them in this crescent motif on a conical headdress of the high priest.

Lyra's diagrams were copied, along with his ideas and commentaries.[58] His diagrams are in many later Bibles. For example, the high priest turns up in Luther's Pentateuch printed in Wittenberg, 1523,[59] and we offer two examples from later Danish Bibles now in the Norwegian Folk Museum: one from Christian III's Bible of 1550 (fig. 103), and another from Frederic II's Bible of 1589 (fig. 104). In a nineteenth-century design for a glass church window in Glasgow, the priests carrying the holy ark through the desert wear the same kind of headdress that Lyra drew in his early fourteenth-century diagram.[60]

How rumor will travel and corrupt. The mistaken belief that the horned mitre descended from the Jewish high priest was so pervasive that occasionally it became part of Jewish tradition itself.[61] For example, Aaron is represented wearing the side-horned mitre (fig. 105) in an early eighteenth-century Hebrew book of the Zohar. And in the eighteenth century we find a spectacular side-horned mitre among the embroidered symbols of a Jewish ritual cloth denoting that its owner was a Levite (fig. 106).

It is suggested here that the whole mistaken idea that the Jewish high priest wore a horned mitre strengthens the possibility that the bishop's horned mitre evolved from Moses' horns. Perhaps it was thought that the horns descended first to Aaron, and then to other Jewish high priests, then to Christian bishops. In the next chapter it will be shown that Moses was thought of as the founder of the priesthood, so that the high priests prefigure, so to speak, the Christian bishops.[62]

In conclusion, then, it is suggested that the idea of horns for the bishop's mitre was stimulated by the appearance in art of horned Moses. This is based on the evidence presented in this chapter, in summary: that the horned mitre appeared among the liturgical vestments of the Church only *after* Moses appeared horned in art; that only in the Latin Church of the West was there ever a horned mitre (the Eastern Church had no horned Moses in biblical text or art, and no horned mitre); that the horns of the mitre appear first as horns at the sides thereby presenting a vivid impression of horns (only later are they turned front and back); that they were called horns and not something like peaks or humps; that the horns of the mitre were directly related to Moses' horns in the writings of medieval theologians; and that the mistaken depiction of Aaron and other Jewish high priests with horned mitres indicates a pattern of thinking that presupposes a descent of the horns from Moses to the bishops via the Old Testament high priests. This evidence I believe is convincing. The horns of the mitre, like those of Moses, were usually interpreted as symbols of honor serving on a helmet of salvation—at least among the Church scholars. This finds corroboration in some of the religious literature of the Middle Ages, discussed in the next chapter.

IX Religious Literature of the Middle Ages

THE RELIGIOUS literature of the Middle Ages did not ignore the horns of Moses. Much of it, written in the vernacular languages (as well as in Latin), was copied extensively. It reached a wider audience than the theological commentaries[1] and may have exerted considerable influence upon the thinking of men who could read their own language, if not Latin. It is explored here for this reason.

It was in the vernacular English paraphrase of Pentateuch and Joshua that Moses was described as horned by Aelfric.[2] This phrasing became traditional. The horned Moses of the Aelfric Paraphrase became the inheritance of the later English Bibles and of the literature based upon them. This was not, however, a tradition without an exception. For example, Moses is described differently in an English poem of ca. 1250, called *Genesis and Exodus*:

And sunne-bem bright son is wliten.[3]
[And as sun-beam bright shone his features]

The author of this poem was dependent upon Comestor's *Historia Scholastica* as his source where, as mentioned earlier, Moses' horns were described as those "wonderful rays of splendor emanating from his face."[4]

The older tradition of Moses as horned (in the Vulgate and the Aelfric Paraphrase) recurs in the *Cursor Mundi*, that famous and extremely popular poem written around 1300.[5] This is a very long poem of about 30,000 lines,[6] written in Northern Middle English. It tells the history of the world (biblical, of course) from its creation to doom. The poet in his prologue tells us that he composes this work in honor of the Virgin and that he writes it all in English, stating that although French rhymes are commonly found everywhere, there is nothing for those who know only English.[7] He adds that he writes for those who are unlearned so that the common folk can understand the wisdom therein, and can then mend their idle ways and be pardoned for their sins.[8] The Early English Text Society has published four of the many manuscripts of this poem still extant. In each of them Moses is described as horned—for example, one text reads:

> Quen moyses had broght þe lagh
> And his folk in þe face him sagh,
> þam thought him hornd apon farr,
> And duted þam to cum him nerr.[9]

The author of this long poem, while appealing to the unlearned, was himself a man of learning.[10] The *Cursor Mundi*, because of its great popularity, doubtless helped to spread the idea and image of a horned Moses among Englishmen. Its tremendous appeal is attested to by the large number of manuscripts in which it still survives.[11] The poem gives religious instruction skillfully by means of concrete examples and picturesque descriptions,[12] yet the poet does not explain the horns of Moses. We, therefore, can only surmise what its impact was upon those who read it or heard it recited, those unfamiliar with the theological explanations of the Church scholars. If nothing else, it may have served to reinforce whatever visual impressions these men had from viewing horned Moses in art or in liturgical dramas.

In chapter vii we spoke of Rudolf von Em's *Weltchronik*.[13] It is worth again mentioning the *Weltchronik* in the context of this chapter, because it was one of the most popular works in the medieval body of religious literature. Written in Middle High German, it influenced the thinking of laymen in the German-speaking territories from the time of its composition in the mid-thirteenth century through the fourteenth and fifteenth centuries, serving as one of the more important lay sources for a knowledge of Old Testament history.[14] It should be recalled that although the text explained that Moses appeared horned because seven beams formed a ring around his head and face,[15] artists often represented this concept as a group of radial horns (figs. 90 and 91), not as rays or beams. This leads one to speculate on whether readers came away convinced that Moses was horned or merely beaming.[16]

Neither the English *Cursor Mundi* nor the German *Weltchronik* provided lengthy explanations for horned Moses. It is in a French poem of a little later date (ca. 1330) that one finds a remarkably extensive interpretation of the horns of Moses. This is the poem written by Guillaume de Deguileville, a Cistercian monk of the Royal Abbey of Chaalis. It has been variously described as *Le pèlerinage de vie humaine, Le pèlerinage du corps humain,* and *Le pèlerinage de l'homme.*[17] We know very little about the life of this fourteenth-century monk of Chaalis, but we do know that he was not lacking in enthusiasm or perseverance. The poem is of immense length, yet because it was taken from Deguileville before he could put it in final shape (copies having been dispersed throughout France), he was displeased and began the gigantic task of rewriting and enlarging the first version. A second version was completed about twenty-five years later (ca. 1355), and this became the basis for John Lydgate's well-known version in English verse in 1426.[18] It is to Lydgate's English version that I will most often refer.

To some readers of today, Guillaume de Deguileville's poem is incredibly boring. It is filled with incidents somewhat absurdly strung together and when read does not always seem to make too much sense. Such observations, however, are in no way an indication of how the poem was received in its own time, or in the century following its composition.[19] The poem had an appreciative and widespread audience both in the fourteenth and fifteenth centuries, and even later.[20] It was translated into German, Dutch, and Spanish.[21] In addition to the many manuscript copies in French, a French prose version was made in 1464 for Jeanne de Laval, Queen of Jerusalem and Sicily.[22] Without making a judgment as to its aesthetic merit, one can emphatically say that it was extremely popular.[23] And it is interesting to learn that the poem was dramatized in the later half of the fifteenth century, performed at the Convent of St.

Michel at Huy, Liège.[24] Several English versions[25] were created other than the very important verse translation by Lydgate. (Even Chaucer was influenced, for he had translated Deguileville's A.B.C. prayer to the Virgin occurring in the *Vie*.)[26] It has even been argued that this poem is the model on which John Bunyan based his *Pilgrim's Progress*.[27]

Deguileville's poem is of great assistance in our task of finding out what the horns of Moses meant to the men of the Middle Ages: On the one hand it reflects the beliefs and the dogma of the Latin Church; yet it also reflects some of the concepts of the less learned clergy and laity. The amazing popularity of the poem, its very wide distribution, its long life, and its lengthy account of Moses—all make it worth while to consider at some length.

The poem is an allegory that treats of the pilgrimage of a man (really the author himself) who resolves to go to the Holy City. The Pilgrim begins his journey and meets Grace of God, personified by a woman of great beauty, who takes him to her house (the Church) where he hears the story of the Creation and the Fall of Man. Here he is baptized and confirmed. He meets Moses, Nature, Reason, and others. After a long journey beset with difficulties—always rescued by Grace of God—he ends up in the Ship of Religion (the monastery of the Cistercians), and there he sees that Death will await him. The poem not only mentions Moses and his horns, but describes how he got them, what they mean, and why the bishop has them too. Deguileville leaves little to the imagination. (Occasionally the manuscripts and printed editions of this poem were illustrated. Some of the folios from the fifteenth-century French MS 2 of the John Rylands Library, Manchester, England, are reproduced here and will be referred to when appropriate.)

Moses first appears in the poem after the Pilgrim has been baptized in the river and has entered the house of Grace of God. The Pilgrim sees a sign of the Tau, sprinkled with blood, and standing beside it a "master" of great authority, a vicar of Moses, or allegorically speaking, Moses himself. The Pilgrim says:

> And pleynly tho (as I be-held,)
> In hys hond a staff he held
> Crooked be-forn (I took good hed;)
> And hornyd also was hys hed.[28]

Moses makes the sign of the cross on the Pilgrim's forehead, confirming the Pilgrim. See figure 107 which shows Moses in the center of the illustration touching the Pilgrim's forehead, Grace of God standing to the right of the Pilgrim, and other pilgrims standing to the left of Moses. It should be noted at once, that here, and later in this poem, Moses (as the old vicar) functions like a Christian bishop. This is part of the allegorical method of the poet; his concept becomes increasingly clearer as the poem progresses. Moses is represented both in his ancient milieu, as the founder of the priesthood (appointing and instructing Aaron and the others via the word of God), but at the same time he demonstrates the qualities, duties, and services of a contemporary bishop of the Church.[29] The allegory is not always coherently and consistently presented, and since the poet is perhaps lacking in certain skills, one just has to jump about with the author in order to make sense of it.

Moses is next described in the poem as giving three ointments to the "official" (that is, the bishop). The Pilgrim describes this scene, saying:

> Affter al thys, I hadde a syht
> Off the mayster [Moses], wych of Ryht
> Made the holsom oynement,
> And after took yt of entent
> To the sayde offycyal [a bishop],
> And gaff to hym thys charg with-al[30]

See figure 108 where the official and Moses converse about the ointments.

Reason, personified as a woman, now arrives and admonishes both the bishop and Moses. She tells them to be gentle so that they do not through rudeness and cruelty injure those whom they would

111

cure. She reminds them that they are not to take vengeance, for
that is reserved only for God. Following this is a very long discourse
in which Moses, described here as the wondrously old vicar, asks
Reason what purpose his horns and sharp pointed staff serve. Moses speaks again, both for himself and for the bishop. Moses asks:

> Wherof sholde myn hornys serve?
> Thys staff ek [also], with the sharpë poynt,
> Telleth me fro poynt to poynt,
> Be they nat maad, by good resoun,
> For punysshynge and Correccioun;
> Myn hornys, for to takë wrak [vengeance]
> On shrewës, & putte abak?[31]

Reason answers Moses at great length. And in these verses we
realize that the response, though directed to Moses, is really directed to all of his vicars—who are, of course, the vicars of Christ—
the bishops of the Church. Thus, in speaking to Moses, Reason
speaks to the rulers of the Church of the day.[32] She says that although the horns and the point of the staff were given for chastis-
ing, men should first of all be given direction and corrected fairly.
Then, if they remain obstinate, they should be punished. But even
then, judgment should be tempered with mercy. Reason says:

> In thyn entent to be mor clene,
> Thogh thyn hornys be sharp & kene,
> To punysshe folk by ryhtwysnesse,
> Thow sholdest ay the poynt so dresse
> In thy Rygour of eguyte,
> Euere [ever] in hert [heart] to han [have]
>   pyte [pity]
> On hem that thow hast iustesyed [judged].
> Let mercy with ryht be so alyed,
> And thynk how many day to-forn,
> Or thow haddest any horn,[33]

In these verses just quoted, the comment made earlier about the
double role of Moses in the poem is particularly appropriate, for

112

these lines seem more addressed to bishops than to the Moses of old.

In the next verses the same is true. Reason speaks to Moses, but she is really speaking to the present-day bishops. She tells Moses (or the bishop) to remember that he was anointed before he was horned, and tells him to remember whose Vicar he is and to follow his example. Then what appears to be the real confusion, she tells him to follow the example of Moses, and here the poet means to follow the example of the original biblical Moses. Reason says:

> Remembre also ful wel, and se
> That he, of whom thow art vyker,
> And chose to be hys offycer,
> Was humble, meke, & debonayre [gentle],
> Charytable, & nat contrayre:[34]

Reason then notes that although Moses was horned in appearance, he did not use his horns with violence, but with his staff led the Israelites through the Red Sea. She tells him, therefore, to take this example and remember that although he is horned to the sight, that is, outwardly, he should be merciful within[35] and says:

> By wych exaumple han [have] in mynde,
> Thogh thow be hornyd on thyn hed,
> To shewe outward a tookne of drede
> Vn-to folk that be contrayre,
> Yet ay be inward debonayre [gentle].[36]

Thus the horns of Moses (or the horns of the bishop's mitre), are to serve as a token of intimidation for the contrary folks, yet those men who wear the horns should always be inwardly gentle.

But Reason hasn't finished the subject of horns. For after this moral lesson, Reason gives "Moses" (the old vicar), and the "bishop" (the official) an interesting bit of ancient history. She now fills in with some fascinating information as to how and when the horns were first given—all of which seems to fall outside of, and beyond anything, that the great Church theologian-scholars had to say about the horns of Moses. Reason again addresses herself to both

113

Moses and the bishop. She tells them that originally a horned beast dwelt here—here, meaning the house of Grace of God, implying the Church or perhaps heaven. Moses was given his horns and a staff to drive out this powerful monster. This is stunning and unique written evidence of some remarkable ideas about the horns of Moses, and their descendants, the horns of the bishop's mitre:

> Whylom [formerly] her ther dydë dwelle
> Thornyd best [the horned beast] wych lyeth in helle,
> Makynge here hys mansion
> And longe held her pocessyon,
> Lordshepe ek [also] & gouernaunce,
> Wych was gret dysplesaunce
> To Grace Dieu, that he so sholde
> Abyden her [here], as I the tolde.
> And Tavoyden [to drive out] fro thys place
> Thys hornyd best [beast], and tenchase [to drive away],
> She callede the, lyk as I fynde,—
> I trow [trust] thow haue yt wel in mynde,—
> Gaff [gave] the hornys in sentence [in effect]
> With hym to stonden at diffence.
> The staff also, wych I off telle,
> Sche [she] took to the [thee], hym to expelle;
> Armede the of entencioun
> (Lyk tamyghty champyoun,) [like the mighty champion]
> With thys hornys that I of spak,
> On thys beste to takë wrak [vengeance]
> To make hym fro thys hous to fle,
> By power that she gaff [gave] to the:
> The vntrewe false enherytour [untrue false inheritor]
> That was her lord & gouernour,
> And long tyme pocessyowner,
> Tyl thow dydest thy dever [duty],
> As Grace Dieu the tauhte a-ryht [taught thee right],
> To putte hym out by verray [true] myght,
> Thorgh hurtlyng of thyn hornys tweyne [two];
> And dyst also thy bysy peyne [endeavor],

> With thy staff to make hym flee,
> Maugre [in spite of] hys myght & hys powste [ability]
> Thogh he were sory to departe,
> Thow dyst that Feloun so coarte [coerce],
> That he durst nat abyde.[37]

Who is the horned beast who formerly dwelt here but who now "lyeth in helle?" Is it Lucifer cast down from heaven? Satan? Loki of the old Northern myths? The Fenris wolf? It somehow presents a picture of old pagan demonology mixed with the Christian Devil, then combined with the idea expressed in Psalm 43:6:

> Through Thee we will push down our enemies with the horn:

Since the time the beast was conquered by means of the horns of Moses, Grace of God has willed that all vicars (bishops) are also to be so armed. This is so that all may fear and remember how the foe was beaten, and so the House of Grace of God will always be defended:

> That thow be armyd offtë sythe,
> As a vyctor, they myght to kythe [make known],[38]

Reason thus tells them that the horns and staff are for the defense of the House of Grace of God—the Church. And if this defense is lacking in any way, then the horns and staff are only a mockery and the horns are no better than a snail's:

> Thyn hornys hiħ vp on thyn hed,
> Nor thy staff, (yt ys no dred,
> I dar pleynly specefye,)
> Ar but tooknes [tokens] of mokerye,
> Lych hornys of a lytell snayl,
> Wych seruë for noon avayl,[39]

Reason tells them to follow the example of St. Thomas and St. Ambrose in the defense of the Church. She says that they used their horns properly:

> Thys folk, to myn oppynyoun,
> Vsede ther hornys by Resoun [Reason],
> As I to the ha told ryht now.
> And, by exaumple, so sholdyst thow
> Bar thyn hornys for dyffence,
> And suffre that no vyolence
> Were ydon vn-to thy spouse [Grace of God, the Church].[40]

And thus, the moral of the story: if the horns are properly used, as a defense of the Church, then and only then, can bishops be truly called "Moses." Reason says:

> Than sholdestow (yt ys no les,)
> Be trewely callyd Moyses,[41]

Moses' horns are not discussed again in the poem; however, Moses appears repeatedly throughout the journey of the Pilgrim. For example, Moses shaves the crown of some of the other pilgrims, thereby giving them to the Church.[42] He is demonstrating that it is from him that the officers and servants of the Church are descended. So Moses appoints his officers[43] to aid the bishops, and subsequently he presents Grace of God to all of the newly ordained servants of the Church.[44] See figure 109 where Grace of God has been presented to the bishop and to the other newly appointed servants or officials of the Church.

Much later in the story the Pilgrim on his journey to Jerusalem is seen with Memory. The Pilgrim asks Moses for bread for his trip,[45] and Moses gives him this bread (fig. 110), which when eaten, makes the Pilgrim very strong. Moses, here, is giving the bread of eternal life, that of Christ, and not the manna of the Old Testament. Deguileville presented this same concept earlier in the poem where Grace of God had Moses change the bread and wine into Christ's flesh and blood.[46] This seems, at first, a very strange thing for Moses to be doing. If we bear in mind, however, that the teachings of the Church in the Middle Ages saw the Old Testament as nothing but a prefiguration of the New—the events of the Old, and the prophets of the Old, as mere predictions of things yet to come with the New

Testament of Christ—then Moses is really a type of Christ, and the bread that he offers is the body of Christ. The manna of Moses which was given to the Israelites was a prefiguration of the real bread of life to come. It is based on the passage from John 6:48–51:

> I am that bread of life:
> Your fathers did eat manna in the wilderness, and are dead.
> This is the bread which cometh down from heaven, that a man may eat thereof, and not die.
> I am the living bread which came down from heaven: if any man eat of this bread, he shall live forever: and the bread that I will give is my flesh, which I will give for the life of the world.

This concept of the manna of Moses as a prefiguration of the real bread of life—Christ—was an integral part of another religious work of the Middle Ages, the *Speculum Humanae Salvationis*.[47] It is told in a series of examples all using this concept of the Old Testament as a prefiguration of the New. The rain of the manna was thus pictured with the Last Supper. (See again fig. 80.)

An analogous method was followed by the *Biblia Pauperum*[48] where, as mentioned earlier, Moses was also represented with horns in some of the copies of this text. See figure 81 where the main scene —that of the Last Supper—is in the center; to our left is Melchizedek (whose offering of bread and wine to Abraham foreshadows the institution of the Eucharist), and to the right is Aaron and a horned Moses who are overseeing the collection of the manna.[49] Moses was thus honored as a prefiguration of Christ, and since these books were often illustrated with Moses as horned, they too contributed to the increasing popularity of this iconography. These works, along with such texts as the *Cursor Mundi*, the *Weltchronik*, Deguileville's *Le pèlerinage de vie humaine*, were copied extensively and distributed widely, helping to spread the image of horned Moses. Thus far, however, it seems that only in the poem of Deguileville do we find an extensive and novel interpretation of the horns of Moses.

The concept of a horned, but honorable and honored, Moses was most certainly part of the traditional doctrine of the Church. Some later documents, and their illustrations, underscore this observation. For example, a 1506 woodcut represents theologically complex Church dogma by means of a triumphal chariot motif, "The Triumph of Theology."[50] Theology is personified as a beautiful woman, pulled in a chariot by a team of horses, with horned Moses riding the lead horse (fig. 111). The chariot is also being pulled by other prophets and saints. Note that the four evangelists are represented at the four corners of what might be considered a building's foundation, probably that of the Church. And at the wheels of the chariot are found the four esteemed early Church Doctors: Ambrose, Jerome, Gregory, and Augustine. While the elements in the picture are at times difficult to decipher, the rubrics above the illustration make the ideas in the picture explicit (fig. 111). So we read in the upper right corner of the woodcut:

> This Chariot seeks again the triumph of the
> Sacred Scriptures:
> It carries the Fathers [of the Church],
> of whom no theologian can be ignorant,
> without being called foolish.

And in the upper left of the woodcut:

> They come to the throne of the supreme
> Thunderer [God]:
> They, the conveyors who pull with a swift hand
> the ropes of the golden chariot,
> Showing the saving approach [salvation] and
> the way to heaven.

Moses, horned, and on the lead horse, is clearly one of the most important of the "conveyors," and one who thus helps show the way to heaven.

All the ideas contained in this "Triumph of Theology" are represented in some unusual watercolor drawings that are part of a

118

French manuscript of about 1460. This manuscript, now in the Free Library in Philadelphia, contains a text by Jean Germain called, *Le chemin de paradis.* It has been suggested that the drawings may represent the composition of two tapestries, now lost, which the author, a bishop of Chalon-sur-Saôn had ordered for his cathedral.[51] The text was supposed to have explained the allegory in the two lost tapestries. We have reproduced two of the six drawings in the manuscript (figs. 112 and 113.) From these drawings it is clear that Germain's *Chemin de paradis*, is the well-traveled one of the Middle Ages. It is the only road that loyal and militant Christians can take to get to Paradise. It is the same road that the "conveyors" of the chariot of "Theology" take to show the way to heaven. (Compare fig. 111 with figs. 112 and 113.)[52]

The road to Paradise is the way of salvation and must be sought via the Church. One cannot reach the Heavenly City without the aid of the Church. Thus Germain's *Chemin de paradis* is really a variation on the old theme of the parallels between the Old and New Testaments that were found in the *Speculum Humanae Salvationis*, the *Biblia Pauperum*, and in *Le pèlerinage de vie humaine*. The Bible was presented by the Church of the Middle Ages as a succession of types of Christ, who formed a "Via Sacra" to Christ. Here on this road were all the men and all the ideas that any good Christian needed to know. Kings, philosophers, and such were excluded since they did not participate in the way to Christ, that is, the road to Paradise. Christ, is the key to the mystery of life, and since Moses prefigures and helps to reveal Christ, he too is to be studied and understood, for he guides the way to Paradise.

The drawings in the Germain text are a dramatic and unique illustration of some of the ideas of the Church's dogma and theology which have been discussed in Part II of this book. Note that a horned Moses rides on an animal, suggesting that he is pulling the Church (figs. 112 and 113). Furthermore, note that above Moses' horned head is a bishop's mitre (representing the continuity of the horns of Moses), and directly above the mitre is a crown, perhaps the crown of life promised to the elect in heaven. For we read in Apocalypse 2:10:

> Be thou faithful until death:
> and I will give thee the crown of life.

Thus the crown is the symbol of the future glory that awaits those who are elected to be saved. William Durandus had commented on the mitre and the crown, saying:

> And the two horns are the two precepts of charity: wherefore the Bishop taketh the Mitre in understanding that he ought to guard his five senses against the allurements of the world, so as to keep the laws of the two Testaments; and to fulfill the two precepts of Charity, that he may be counted worthy to receive an eternal crown.[53]

Durandus also says that the bishop, when he celebrates, puts off his clothes of everyday, and puts on garments pure and holy, and comments on each vestment, saying of the mitre:

> In the thirteenth place, the Mitre, that he so live as to be worthy of receiving the eternal crown.[54]

The sequence seems clear: The knowledge of the Old Testament (horns of Moses), plus the faith and grace brought by the New Testament and its Church (symbolized by the bishop's mitre), will lead the way to Paradise and to the Crown of Life in Heaven. (See again fig. 113.)

X Ambiguity of the Meaning of Horns: Horns of Dishonor as Well as Horns of Honor

It HAS been the intention of Part II of this study to determine what the horns of Moses meant to men of the Middle Ages. The thinking of the great Church theologians and scholars as revealed by their written commentaries, and the ideas reflected in religious literature of a more popular nature, have been discussed. It was concluded that most often the horns of Moses were interpreted as horns of honor, power, and glory, not as symbols of dishonor and humiliation. (Adamus Scotus's exposition of the horns as the worldly, secular, aspect of Moses appeared to be outside the mainstream of the written commentaries.) And when the horns appeared on the bishop's mitre, they were similarly interpreted as honorable attributes.

Except for esoterics, the honorable meanings associated with horns have gradually paled and almost disappeared, so that today most men interpret horns on heads as symbols of dishonor. During the Middle Ages and into the Renaissance, horned heads had both honorable and dishonorable meanings. Could these ambiguities have led to misunderstandings about the horns of Moses? First let us look at the range of meanings for horns during that period.

Horns were often interpreted as dishonorable attributes, connoting cuckolds,[1] demons, devils, and the "evil" pagan gods of the Mediterranean and North. Satan himself had inherited many of his features from horned pagan divinities. For example, he received his bull features from Dionysus, his goat attributes from Pan, and perhaps also inherited his horns from Thór and the ancient Cernunnos.[2]

121

The power of the horn or horns was vast and constant; it could be associated with good or with evil, and could be transferred to "good" gods or "bad" gods, "good" men or "evil" men. The ambiguous meaning of horns is reflected in Jerome's *Commentary on Amos* where he compares the prideful horns of sinners with those of the just.[3] Hugh the Chantor, too, was profoundly aware of the many different meanings, and shades of meaning, for horns. His comments contrast the horns of Moses, the horns of the bishop, the horns of God as mentioned in Habakkuk, with the horns of the Devil; he then adds that some horns are to be desired and others should be diligently avoided.[4]

Deguileville's poem, discussed in chapter ix, contains allusions to horns with both honorable and dishonorable connotations. We saw that the horns of Moses as well as those of the bishop were interpreted as honorable. It should be recalled, however, that Moses was described as originally being given his horns to drive an evil horned beast out of Grace of God's domain.[5] This poem contains another example of horns with a dishonorable connotation: Pride is personified and is described as wearing the horn of boasting. Pride says:

> And, therfore I bere thys horn
> Wych that callyd ys "bostyng,"[6]

And earlier, Pride's horn denotes cruelty:

> And I am she (yt ys no dred)
> That ber an horn in my forhed,
> Wych ys ycallyd "Cruelte,"[7]

A particularly striking figure of evil personified and horned occurs in Ambrogio Lorenzetti's painting, *Allegory of Evil Government*[8] (ca. 1337–1340). He is depicted here with two huge horns, gigantic werewolf teeth, and is attended by a goat and an ugly black centaurlike beast.

On the other hand, knights still wore horns in the Middle Ages, with the ancient connotation of victory.[9] That a horned knight still represented honor, courage, and victory in the fourteenth century is demonstrated by a folio in a manuscript of that period containing a copy of the *Speculum Humanae Salvationis* (fig. 114). Represented here is David with his three valiant soldiers, those who crossed the enemy camp to bring water (2 Kings 23:13–23). These are the valiant men of the biblical text, and two of these valiants are dressed in armor complete with helmets. One wears the horns of a bull on his helmet, the other, a deer's antlers. The artist, trying to convey the impression of brave soldiers, dressed them in medieval armor, and added horned crests to their helmets to stress their association with bravery, honor, and victory.[10]

Horns (by themselves or on a helmet) served as a family crest for Danish noblemen and are found on their seals, beginning at least as early as the thirteenth century,[11] and continuing at least through the sixteenth century.[12] The horn crest motif can be found also in the fifteenth, sixteenth, and seventeenth centuries carved as coats of arms on Danish family furniture.[13]

Horns kept their double connotation of honor and dishonor for some time. Shakespeare was aware of the multiple connotations of a horned head. In *As You Like It*, act IV, scene 2, we read:

Jaques

Which is he that killed the deer?

A Lord

Sir it was I.

Jaques

Let's present him to the duke, like a Roman conqueror; and it would do well to set the deer's horns upon his head for a branch of victory. Have you no song, forester, for this purpose?

Forester

Yes, sir.

Jaques

Sing it: 'tis no matter how it be in tune, so it make noise enough.

Forester
Song
What shall he have that kill'd the deer?
His leather skin and horns to wear.
   Then sing him home:
Take thou no scorn to wear the horn;
It was a crest ere thou wast born:
   Thy father's father wore it,
   and thy father bore it:
The horn, the horn, the lusty horn
Is not a thing to laugh to scorn.

In *Measure for Measure*, act II, scene iv, lines 16, 17, we read:

Let's write good angel on the devil's horn;
'Tis not the devil's crest.

Is it possible that the medieval man-on-the-street had difficulty separating the men with good horns from those with evil horns? How many among the uneducated masses were aware of the generally accepted theological interpretation of Moses' horns as symbols of honor and glorification, of horns of light, not *real* horns? The layman was handicapped by his illiteracy, receiving notions of the Old and New Testaments second hand,[14] and even more ignorant churchmen occasionally made awkward mistakes in interpretation.[15] What did ordinary men think when they saw a horned Moses in stained glass or in a religious drama? Their testimony is not available; they were the nonreading, nonwriting majority of the population, about whom one historian has said:

If historians are to attempt to write the history of mankind, and not simply the history of mankind as it was viewed by the small and specialized segments of our race which have had the habit of scribbling, they must take a fresh view of the records, ask new questions of them, and use all the resources of archaeology, iconography, and etymology to find answers when no answers can be discovered in contemporary writings.[16]

If there is little or no direct evidence to provide answers, do we have any way of searching out the secret of the horns of Moses; what they may have meant to the silent majority? Some ideas will be suggested, if not specifically about horned Moses, at least about the total environment that surrounded him. Ultimately any conclusions may have to remain in the realm of conjecture; nevertheless, whatever evidence is presented may provide a few hints of what horned Moses may or may not have meant to the ignorant men. Perhaps later research and discoveries will fill in the gaps and furnish definitive answers. For the present we must be satisfied with hypotheses.

As one of the determinants of the thinking of unlearned men about Moses' horns, it would seem useful to investigate the more general status of Moses (with or without horns) and of the Old Testament itself in medieval thought. Medieval attitudes toward the Old Testament can be described as confused, ambivalent, and often contradictory. As mentioned earlier, theologian-scholars taught that the Old Testament ought to be studied and revered because it prefigured the New. At the same time, it was also commonly understood that the New had replaced the Old. Gradually the Old Testament's importance greatly declined, and at times it seemed to be totally denigrated in its association with the Synagogue and the Jews. This puzzling ambivalence and contradiction in attitudes toward the Old Testament was perhaps nourished by Paul's comments on the Law in 2 Corinthians 3. In verses 3–11 Paul contrasts the tables of stone (Old Law) with the fleshy tables of the heart (New Law of Christ): the letter which killeth with the spirit that giveth life; the ministration of death written on stones and the glory of Moses, "which glory was to be done away," with the ministration of the spirit. Then in verses 12 and 13 he contrasts his own speech with that of Moses:

Seeing then that we have such hope, we use great plainness of speech:

125

And not as Moses, which put a veil over his face, that the children of Israel could not steadfastly look to the end of that which is abolished.

Paul continues (verses 14 and 15): that this veil remains in the present reading of the Old Testament, that even when Moses is read today (in the Old Testament) the veil is "upon their heart" (i.e., of the Jews): and then in verse 16, when "it" (the Jews) shall turn to the Lord, the veil will be taken away. It seems that Paul provided a basis for what later became an unglorious association of Moses with the tablets of the Law ("the letter which killeth"), with the Old Testament (to be superseded by Christ's New Testament), and with the Synagogue and its unconverted Jews.

Synagogue and Church, personified as women, were frequently represented in medieval art. Church was shown as victorious, wearing a crown, holding a standard with flying banner in one hand, a chalice in the other. By contrast, Synagogue, whose iconography seems to have evolved from about the ninth century,[17] was most commonly represented with a veil across her eyes, a broken staff, and a drooping banner. Negative associations were inevitable. As anti-Semitism grew, so did the number of unpleasant attributes given to Synagogue,[18] and she was shown as well with the tablets of the Law slipping from her hands; occasionally she was shown holding the head of a goat or ass,[19] or represented as riding on one of these animals.

The association of Moses with this unhappy figure of Synagogue occurs frequently in medieval art. Here are a few examples. Earlier it was mentioned that Moses was depicted in the English Bible, Lambeth Palace Library MS 3, dated ca. 1150.[20] On folio 198r (fig. 52) upper right, note that Synagogue's veil is being pulled away by a hand, presumably the hand of God, while horned Moses and Synagogue look intently and sadly at each other. Most of the other figures in this folio, except for the four virtues in the center medallions, point or look upward toward Christ.

Synagogue is uniquely portrayed in an illuminated copy of Hil-

degard of Bingen's *Scivias*,[21] of about 1170, in folio 35 (fig. 115).
Moses is shown holding the tablets of the Law in the bosom of
Synagogue; the other prophets are in Synagogue's belly. The
miniatures in this manuscript are closely allied with the text, clari-
fying the exposition of Hildegard's visions. Here Hildegard describes Synagogue[22] as sightless, pale from head to lap (because she
is the true mother of the Son of God); but black from lap to feet
(because she has been defiled by her transgression of the testament
of her fathers). Moses and the other prophets are described as look-
ing longingly at the beauty of the Church which they had foretold.
Hildegard predicts that when Antichrist is thrown down, Synagogue will be called back to the true faith.

The English Psalter of Robert de Lindesey, ca. 1214–1222,[23] in
its portrayal of the Crucifixion on folio 35^v, also shows a horned
Moses paired with Synagogue, while St. Peter is paired with
Church (fig. 116). Horned Moses and Synagogue can be found
similarly grouped together in the fourteenth-century Queen Mary's
Psalter.[24]

In the examples given thus far, no definite negative associations
about Moses can be drawn from his depictions with Synagogue.
There is, however, some remarkable artistic evidence to show that
the close association of Moses and Synagogue was sometimes mis-
understood; for occasionally Synagogue replaces Moses, and sometimes Moses replaces Synagogue. This process of thought can be
observed first by comparing several copies of *La Somme le Roy*,[25]
all executed at about the same time (ca. 1295). The scene of horned
Moses shattering the tablets of the Law occurs in folio 5^v of Br.
Mus. Add. MS 54180 (fig. 75): Moses is portrayed in the same way
in folio 1^v of Br. Mus. Add. MS 28162; and again in folio A^v
of Bibl. Mazarine MS 870. But, in folio 7^v (fig. 117) of Bibl. de
l'Arsenal, MS 6329, Moses has been replaced by Synagogue: here
Synagogue stands in the upper right corner of the miniature, the
very same place that Moses held in the other three copies. (Compare figs. 75 and 117.)

At least in the thinking of some, Moses seems to have become guilty by association or transferred identity. This contamination from a close association with Synagogue reaches its apogee in a late fifteenth-century missal from Poitiers,[26] where Church is seen substituting the New Sacrifice for the Old Law (fig. 118). Church with her crown, holding the chalice and the Host, is no longer opposed by Synagogue; a horned Moses not only has taken Synagogue's place, but he even is portrayed with some of her usual attributes: the broken standard, the drooping banner, and the slipping tablets turned upside down. A saddened Moses, his eyes cast down, is excluded; the Lord looks toward Church and blesses her.

Negative associations of this same nature may also have arisen from the fact that Moses was sometimes represented wearing the *Judenhut*, the pointed medieval Jew's hat. This hat became the outstanding feature of Jewish costume as mirrored in medieval art, ultimately taking a place among the official infamous badges Jews were required to wear during the Middle Ages. The Fourth Lateran Council called by Innocent III in 1215 first established the requirement (canon 68) that Jews and Saracens be distinguished from Christians by a difference in their clothes.[27] This was interpreted in different ways in various countries.[28] By 1267 the pointed Jewish hat was made obligatory for Jews in provincial Church councils at Breslau[29] and Vienna,[30] where it was referred to as the *pileum cornutum* (horned cap). The shape of this hat varied somewhat; some of the hats were conical; some were pointed and terminated with a knob; some were spiked; most common were those hats that can be described as funnel-shaped. The Judenhut was represented in art as early as the twelfth century, although not officially prescribed until the thirteenth.

Biblical Israelites and Old Testament prophets were pictured wearing the Judenhut. See for example, figs. 59, 61, 64, 65, 73, 75, 78, 79, 80, 90, 91, 117.[31] Most of the time it is difficult to discern whether definite negative connotations are intended when the Old Testament figures are so represented.[32] In the context of the New

Testament, however, figures depicted wearing the Judenhut did have a derogatory association, for they included those who scoffed at, tortured, and executed Christ.[33] See for example the depictions of those hats on the Jews, including Malchus whose ear is partly cut off by Peter, in the scene of "The Kiss of Judas" on the thirteenth-century choir screen of Naumburg Cathedral (fig. 119). Even Joseph, husband of Mary, was occasionally shown with the Judenhut,[34] but the Apostles, who were also Jews, were never seen with this hat.

There is some remarkable evidence that occasionally the Judenhut was used in the context of the Old Testament to draw an important distinction between good and evil. In another miniature in the already discussed Bohemian *Cursus Sanctae Mariae* of ca. 1215,[35] folio 9ᵛ (fig. 120), the sacrifice offered by Cain and Abel, and the slaying of Abel by Cain are portrayed. In each case, Cain wears the Judenhut; Abel does not. This reflects the thought contained in the system of medieval typology where Abel was a type of the future Messiah, with his death a prefiguration of the Crucifixion; Cain, however, in his killing of Abel, was considered a symbol of the Jews who killed Jesus.

Jews shown wearing Judenhuts were often depicted as the principal enemies of the Church,[36] and infidels and heretics were often shown under the guise of Jews wearing their Judenhuts. This occurs, for example, in the miniatures of *La Somme le Roy*. In folio 97ᵛ of Br. Mus. Add MS 54180 (fig. 121), Humility and a penitent sinner can be seen opposed to Pride and a hypocrite. The hypocrite wears a pointed hat. And again in folio 14ᵛ, a figure labeled hypocrite wearing a Judenhut is seen worshiping the Beast of the Apocalypse (fig. 122). Even Synagogue herself, as early as the twelfth century, was portrayed wearing a Judenhut instead of the toppling crown.[37]

Evidence of the negative associations of the pointed hat can even be found in the portrayal of contemporary Jews. Although individual portraiture is indeed rare in medieval art, some does exist.

In a rare and possibly the oldest caricature of a group of English Jews, some of whom can be identified by name,[38] a remarkable portrayal is found at the head of a roll of the Issue of the Exchequer of 1233[39] (fig. 123). In this caricature, with its very sinister overtones, one of the men, Mosse-Mokke, wears a version of the characteristic pointed Jewish hat.

Biblical Moses did not escape the Judenhut. Note that in the *Scivias* miniature discussed earlier,[40] Moses, in the bosom of Synagogue, wears a Judenhut (fig. 115). It was not uncommon to portray Moses, along with other Old Testament figures, in this distinctive hat. Another example is in the Klosterneuburg Altar of Nicholas of Verdun (ca. 1181), where although Moses has a halo in scenes such as the reception of the Law, and the crossing of the Red Sea,[41] he is strangely depicted wearing a funnel-shaped Jew's hat in the scene where he returns to Egypt accompanied by his wife and sons.[42] Moses also wears this hat in the title page of a twelfth-century manuscript containing the *Antiquitates Judaicae* (fig. 124).[43] Here with his serpent he probably represents one of the stages in the Fall and Redemption sequence. (Note Adam and Eve at the top, then Noah and the Ark, then Moses, then the Crucifixion.)

Moses is depicted wearing the Judenhut in the scene of the crossing of the Red Sea in folio 15ᵛ of the *Cursus Sanctae Mariae* of ca. 1215,[44] the very same manuscript in which Cain wore a Judenhut and Abel did not (fig. 120).

The *Weltchronik* manuscripts of the thirteenth and fourteenth centuries, discussed earlier,[45] also show Moses wearing the Judenhut in scenes portraying the crossing of the Red Sea.[46] But even more significant is the miniature discussed with reference to the circlet of horns for Moses in the folio of the thirteenth-century Munich *Weltchronik* (fig. 90). In this scene Moses seems to be doubly identified: as the biblical Moses by his horned headdress and as a Jew by the Judenhut held on his shoulder by a cord.

Although it is difficult to determine with any degree of certainty whether the Old Testament prophets depicted with Jewish hats were

often, rarely, or ever, regarded as figures of evil, what is emphasized here is that the image of the pointed Jewish hat was negative
in the context of Jews who wore it as a Jew-badge in contemporary
medieval life; it was negative in the context of the New Testament;
it was negative as a headdress for Synagogue;[47] it was negative as a
hat for figures denoted as heretics and infidels; and occasionally its
negative implications were vividly depicted as in the case of Cain
and Abel discussed above. It should be added that the Judenhut was
also used for publicly pillorying Christian usurers and persons who
had had relations with Jews.[48] It seems to us that the overwhelm-
ingly negative context surrounding the Judenhut may have led to
unpleasant associations when it appeared on Old Testament figures,
Moses included. Although smear tactics may not have been intended, human nature being what it is, the ugly overtones may have
been unwittingly transferred to all figures wearing this hat.

An ambiguous attitude toward Moses and the Old Testament is
further demonstrated by the denigration of the two tablets of the
Law, It has already been mentioned that they became part of Synagogue's representation, allied with her so to speak, and even occasionally shown upside down, slipping from her hands as in figure
117[49] (or from Moses' hand, fig. 118). In a portrayal of a dignified
burial of Synagogue over which Christ presides, in a fifteenth-
century manuscript,[50] Synagogue is shown in a sarcophagus with
her toppled crown, holding the tablets of the Law. The implication
intended here is that both Synagogue and the Old Law as represented by the two tablets, are now dead, to be buried and done away
with by the New.

A negative attitude toward the tablets of the Law is further demonstrated by the information that in England the Jew-badge was
prescribed as a shape imitative of the two tables of stone, that is, the
tables of the Law, the very Law received by Moses on Mount Sinai.
It was decreed as early as 1217 by Henry III that Jews should wear
this badge made of white linen or parchment on the front of their
upper garment.[51] In 1222 the Council of Oxford required that each

131

of the tablets be two fingers broad and four long, and that the color differ from that of the garment.[52] Under Edward I, in 1275, the white color was changed to yellow, the length to six inches, the width to three inches.[53] Several illustrations of this practice can be noted. In a manuscript chronicle of the reign of Edward I, Br. Mus. Cottonian MS Nero, D 2., where it is used to illustrate a regulation forbidding the practice of usury by English Jews, folio 180ʳ shows a bearded Jew wearing a flat hood and this Jew-badge of the two tablets on his outer garment.[54] Again, a sketch in the margin of an Essex Forest Roll of 1277 in the Public Record Office (fig. 125), caricatures a Jew depicted with the two tablets and labeled Aaron, Son of the Devil.[55] Another example of this badge can be found on the exterior of Lincoln Cathedral where statues of Church and Synagogue each stand on a sculptured corbel. Church is upheld by an angel issuing from a cloud; Synagogue rests on the shoulders of a bearded male figure wearing on his breast the Jewish badge in the conventional form of the two tablets.[56]

How are these negative contexts for the two tablets of the Law —as part of Synagogue's iconography and as a Jew-badge in England—to be reconciled with the fact that the two tablets were perhaps the most important part of Moses' iconography throughout medieval, Renaissance, and later periods of art? (See figs. 49, 50, 53, 54, 55, 58, 59, 63, 66, 67, 69, 70, 72, 73, 75, 79, 88, 90, 91, 113, 115.) One can hardly do less than suggest that these contradictory contexts indicate ambivalence and confusion in the attitudes of medieval men toward the Old Testament the two tablets and, possibly then toward Moses. Perhaps the key to this puzzle is found in a thirteenth-century Latin hymn, "De lege Moisis et de lege Jesu Christi," which in translation reads:

> The Law was an unbearable burden to those
> established under it—
> Grace now grants to those freed from the yoke
> of servitude [the Old Law]

132

The impossibility [that which they were not able
earlier to comprehend, i.e., the inner mystery]
of the Law—[the New Law]
Now Moses is shut out from the earth which
is divided among those who follow Jesus
as their leader.[57]

Moses is clearly associated here with those who have not converted
to Christianity, namely, the Jews who are still tied to the unbearable
burden of the Old Law. This is also what was indicated in the late
fifteenth-century miniature discussed earlier[58] (fig. 118).

Thus, though one of the central figures of the Bible, even a prefiguration of Christ, Moses while a preeminent Jew was nonetheless
a Jew. In this connection it is significant to note that the position of
the Jews within the Christian community steadily deteriorated
from a relatively more favorable status in the early Middle Ages.[59]
The Old Testament had not only been appropriated by Christianity, it had been completely absorbed, losing its separate identity. It
ultimately became little more than prophecies of Christ and Mary
or prefigurations of their Acts. Paradoxically, it seems that its inclusion by the New, doomed it to exclusion, except perhaps within
the minds of the few very learned scholar-theologians. As the position of the Jews worsened during the twelfth and thirteenth centuries, it is paralleled with a similar slippage of the Old Testament,
which reaches a low point at the waning of the Middle Ages. It
would seem that gradually Moses, the Old Testament, the tablets of
the Law, blind Synagogue, and the stubborn unconverted Jews
were all lumped together in common degradation. Some evidence
of this deterioration can be found in late German folksongs of the
sixteenth, seventeenth, and eighteenth centuries about Old Testament figures. (Although this is indeed late evidence, it is a common-
place that folk material is rarely documented until long after an oral
tradition has been established. One can often infer that collected
folk material dates to a much earlier period.) In these songs, then,

Old Testament figures were often mocked and caricatured. For example, there are songs about Adam and Eve, who are presented as stupid people, described in extremely vulgar language.[60] There was a very popular game of pretending to pull Abraham's beard (the beard also being thought of as a typically Jewish characteristic in the medieval period).[61] There was a song with several variations about Abraham and Isaac fighting over a piece of rusk,[62] and a mocking song about the three patriarchs, Abraham, Isaac, and Jacob.[63] Moses was also prey for this kind of mockery. For example, one song pokes fun at Moses saved from the Nile through the words of a crocodile who says:

> "Moses sei nur still;"
> Sprach das Krokodil,
> "Denn ich fress nur Christe,
> Judde ich kei will."[64]

Jeering songs parody the birth of Moses; he is described as the son of Pharaoh's daughter, and saved from the Nile only for that reason.[65] In another song, Moses and the crossing of the Red Sea are mocked by the use of contemporary Jewish jargon.[66] The profanation of Moses is vividly revealed in a very vulgar rhyme that had many variations:

> "Moses und die Propheten
> Seeten achtern Busch un scheeten.
> Seggt Moses: Pup
> Dor neih'n all de Propheten ut."[67]

The fact that living Jews often carried the same names as Old Testament figures, as for example Moses, led to additional mockery and caricature.[68] The thinking of ordinary men as reflected in these folk rhymes and songs, indicates that either they did not comprehend the subtle concepts espoused by the Church about the Old Testament or that they ignored them. Unevenness in levels of education and differing levels of comprehension may have contributed to contradictory concepts among the learned on the one hand, and the ignorant on the other—a phenomenon not unique to the Middle Ages.

A contradictory attitude toward the Jews themselves resulted from an unresolved tension. Purely theological reasons (not humane ones) were given for the protection of Jews: that their existence was proof of the truth of the story of Jesus; that though they fail to understand their Scriptures, yet they are its guardians; that Jesus asked that their conversion be awaited patiently; and that at least a remnant of them will be saved.[69] But although men such as Saint Bernard (1090–1153) preached that "The Jews are not to be persecuted, killed, or even put to flight," for "we are told by the Apostle that *when the time is ripe all Israel shall be saved*,"[70] the increasingly vicious attacks on Jews, their wholesale expulsion from various countries, and the steady worsening of their position in Christendom, stands in direct contradiction to any theological or pious pronunciations. Hostility toward the Jews increased in the post-Crusade period, gathering force with each century. The Jew became the personification of evil and nothing less than an agent of the Devil.[71] The Jews and the Devil were thought of as allied in their opposition to Christ, and thereby to contemporary Christian civilization. While this concept may have originally arisen as vilification, it became an actuality in the minds of the uncritical. Recall the superscription on the Forest Roll of Essex of 1277 (fig. 125) where Aaron is described as the son of the Devil, an early visual depiction and verbalization of this concept.

The Jew was thought to have certain physical characteristics, setting him apart from human beings, and identifying him with the Devil—and horns were an integral part of this image.[72] The firmly rooted popular belief that Jews had horns has even persisted into the present. Joshua Trachtenberg reported that on a trip through Kansas a farmer refused to believe that he was Jewish because he lacked horns on his head.[73] Others have testified to similar beliefs.[74]

Artistic evidence for this incredible fantasy can be found in later documents. For example, Lucas Cranach executed a woodcut for the title page of Luther's *Von den Jüden und Iren Lügen* in 1543; it features a Jew with a horned headdress (fig. 126). And in a satirical caricature, "Der Jüden Ehrbarkeit," of 1571, horned devil figures are identified as Jews by means of the best known of the Jewish badges, the *rouelle*, also known as the circular or wheel badge (fig. 127). Jews depicted with horns occur in a scurrilous seventeenth-century print,[75] and in an almost completely similar picture at the beginning of the eighteenth century, where the artist has added, with what seems to be gratuitous literalness, "Dieses ist der Juden Teuffel" (fig. 128). It is pertinent to recall in this context that the pointed Jew's hat, discussed above, was often referred to as a horned hat (*pileum cornutum*); and there is evidence that Philip III required the Jews of France to attach a horn-shaped figure to the customary Jew-badge.[76]

Is it possible that the preposterous fantasy that Jews had horns influenced the interpretation of horned Moses among those who held such attitudes? Perhaps the horned image of Moses, who in some circles was thought of as the Jew par excellence, even served as confirmation for the belief that all Jews had horns.

It is difficult to believe that Moses' horns were always understood as symbols of honor. We have seen that even in Adamus Scotus's comments, the horns of Moses appeared only when he stood outside the inner sanctum, partaking of the earthly, the secular, and the impure.[77] And we have seen that the position of Moses in medieval thought was not completely stable; he was associated with Synagogue, with a denigrated concept of the tablets of the Law, with the Judenhut, and with the unconverted Jews. The caricatures of Moses in later folksongs indicate a gradual slippage from his more revered place in early Christian and early medieval thought.

It is suggested here, as hypothesis only, that while learned men of the Church had no difficulty distinguishing between the Devil's horns, the horn of Pride, the horned hat of the Jews, the horns of the bishop's mitre, and the horns of Moses, it is possible that the great majority of men were not so clear in their understanding of these differences.[78] For by the time we reach the twentieth century, the original intention of the horns for Moses is lost. The connotations of the horns are mostly negative, except to those who are familiar with the scholarly commentaries of the Church of the Middle Ages. The idea of a horned Moses may be acceptable on the paperback cover of Freud's *Moses and Monotheism* (fig. 129) that appeals to men of intellectual interests, as does the recent sculpture of Moses by Sorel Etrog (fig. 89), but for the most part, the horns of Moses are horns of dishonor, something to be explained away. They have become symbols of ignominy, particularly for Jews. Is it any wonder that a Los Angeles cemetery advertises for Jewish patronage with a dehorned, commercialized rendition of Michelangelo's Moses (fig. 130)? The draftsman and his employers were certainly correct in the assumption that for their purposes the image of a horned Moses would seem strange, scary, ugly, and totally unappealing to a twentieth-century mourner—and particularly to a Jew. But out of the past comes paradox to rekindle our fascination with medieval iconography: the ancestor of this modern rendition, Michelangelo's sculpture of horned Moses (fig. 84), was planned as funerary sculpture to honor the memory and adorn the tomb of Pope Julius II.

Summary and Conclusions

THE ENIGMATIC image of a Judaic-Christian prophet with horns on his head becomes far less puzzling when the changing cultural contexts of different periods of history are taken into consideration. The horns of Moses entered the biblical text of the Old Testament through Jerome's translation of Exodus 34:29 in which the Hebrew, *qeren*, was translated, *cornuta*. This appears to have been a conscious choice on Jerome's part and in keeping with the context and meaning of "horned" in the ancient world as well as the metaphorical meaning of "horn" and "horned" in the Bible. It meant strength, honor, victory, power, divinity, kingship, and salvation. While Jerome's translation was made at the end of the fourth century, no artistic representation of the horns thus far found is earlier that the eleventh century, a gap partially explained by an early established iconography for Moses without horns, which remained fairly constant through the Carolingian period. Moses was never given horns in the art of the Eastern Church which retained the Septuagint biblical text.

The present evidence shows that the horns of Moses first became visual in eleventh-century England, a time and place of originality and innovation, where perhaps through the stimulation of a vernacular text, the Aelfric Paraphrase of Pentateuch and Joshua (British Museum Cotton Claudius B. IV), the Old English *gehyrned* was given a literal, concrete representation—a kind of word-illustration. In this manuscript Moses is depicted wearing a horned headdress or hat. While it is possible that the liturgical drama may have stimulated the innovation in the illuminations, there is not sufficient evidence to conclude that this was so. In either case, the horned headgear on Moses may reflect the ancient custom of adorning helmets with horns, tusks, and other animal motifs. The examination of a number of fragmentary survival forms of the concept of the horned helmet leads us to believe that the Aelfric Paraphrase represents a transposition of an ancient Anglo-Saxon-Scandinavian motif implying the great honor, power, and dignity of a "great commander" onto the Judaic prophet-leader, Moses.

The horns of Moses became increasingly popular in the art of the Western Church. They were retained in England throughout the Middle Ages, spread through northern Europe during the twelfth through the fourteenth centuries, and seem to have reached Italy during the fifteenth and sixteenth centuries.

Once the horns of Moses became visual they were usually interpreted by most of the scholar-theologians of the Church as horns of light, or light emanating in the manner of a horn—an interpretation first suggested by Rashi, the famous eleventh-century Jewish biblical commentator. The Rashi interpretation became the predominant one, for it was followed by Petrus Comestor and subsequently by Nicolas of Lyra; both had tremendous influence on other biblical commentators. The one outstanding exception to this was Adamus Scotus who, in the twelfth century, presented an equivocal concept of the horns being related to earthly, secular, impure activities.

Medieval theologians related the horns of the bishop's mitre to the horns of Moses. It is significant that only after Moses was given horns in art, and only in the Latin Church, was there a horned mitre. The Eastern Church had neither a horned Moses in text or art nor a horned mitre. It is my opinion that the horns of the mitre were the offspring of the horns of Moses, an interpretation emphasized by their earlier form, the side-horned mitre, and by the prayer of imposition of the mitre on the bishop. Both the horns of Moses and the horns of the mitre were generally interpreted by the Church scholars as symbols of honor, station, and power. And they were so described and interpreted in some of the religious vernacular literature of the Middle Ages, a literature reflecting Church concepts.

Because horns were occasionally thought of in a context of dishonor, and because the Old Testament began to lose its position of importance during the later Middle Ages, it is possible that the ignorant people confused Moses' horns with those of the Devil, the cuckold, or other symbols of evil. The error may have been compounded by the notorious fantasy held by some of the people of the Middle Ages (and later) that Jews had horns and were in league with the Devil. Thus while learned men could distinguish between horns of honor and horns of dishonor, the great majority of untutored men may not have made such fine distinctions.

By the time we reach the twentieth century the original meaning of the horns of Moses is lost to most people, appearing to some as an enigmatic motif, to others as an artistic accident, and to more as an infamous and defamatory attribute.

Notes to the Text

1. See Louis Réau, *Iconographie de l'art chrétien*, 6 vols. (Paris: Presses Universitaires de France, 1955–1959), vol. 2, pt. 1, p. 177, who says: "La Vulgate, assimilant les rayons lumineux à des cornes d'or. . . . C'est cette traduction fautive qui a donné naissance au type du Moïse cornu"; and see Karl Künstle, *Ikonographie der Christlichen Kunst*, 2 vols. (Freiburg im Breisgau: Herder, 1928), 1:288, "Da Moses später gehornt dargestellt wurde, behruht auf der ungeschickten Vulgataübersetzung von Exod. 34, 29"; and André Neher reflects this attitude in his book, *Moses and the Vocation of the Jewish People*, trans. Irene Marinoff (New York: Harper Torchbooks, Longmans, 1959), pp. 8–9, "A mistake due to a translator's error on the part of St. Jerome has now for more than a thousand years given the features of Moses a satanic cast." This concept is similarly reflected in a general textbook by John Ives Sewall, *A History of Western Art* (New York: Holt, 1953), pp. 540, 742.

2. From *The Pentateuch and Haftorahs*, Hebrew text, English trans. and comm., ed. by the late chief rabbi, Dr. J. H. Hertz, C.H., (London: Soncino Press, 1952), p. 368. The translation reads: "And it came to pass, when Moses came down from mount Sinai with the two tables of the testimony in Moses' hand, when he came down from the mount, that Moses knew not that the skin of his face sent forth beams while He talked with him."

3. *Ibid.*, under n. 29, p. 368, the interpretation is: "The Heb. קרן either means, 'a ray of light' or, more commonly 'a horn.'" See also *Dictionnaire de la Bible*, ed. F. Vigouroux, 5 vols. (1st printing, 1899; Paris: Librairie Letouzey, 1926), under *corne* (col. 1007), described as: "hébreu: qérén"; under *cornes* (col. 1010), described as: "rayons de lumière. . . . Le verbe qâran signifies 'rayonner.' . . . Quand Moïse descendit du Sinai, sa face 'rayonnait,' qâran."

See also the Septuagint at Exod. 34:29, which reads: . . . οὐκ ἤδει ὅτι δεδόξασται ἡ ὄψις τοῦ χρώματος τοῦ προσώπου αὐτοῦ ἐν τῷ λαλεῖν αὐτὸν αὐτῷ, from *Septuaginta*, ed. Alfred Rahlfs, 2 vols. (Stuttgart: Privilegierte württembergische Bibelanstalt, 1952), vol. I, under Exod. 34:29. Here, Moses is described as having been "glorified." It has been pointed out to me by Philip Levine that while some later translators of the Septuagint have translated this "irradiated with glory," or "radiant," the correct translation is, "glorified." See *A Greek-English Lexicon*, compiled by Henry George Liddell and Robert Scott (Oxford: Clarendon Press, 1867–1939), vol. I, under: δοξάζω.

4. Quoted from *Biblia Sacra iuxta Latinam Vulgatam Versionem ad codicum fidem*, iussu Pii PP. XI, cura et studio monachorum Sancti Benedicti Commissionis pontificae a Pio PP. X institutae sodalium praeside Aidan Gasquet, S.R.E. Cardinale edita (Rome: Typis Polyglottis Vaticanis, 1926, et seq.), vol. 2 (Exodus and Leviticus), 1929, Exod. 34:29, p. 259. This is the critical edition of the Vulgate initiated in 1907 by Pius X who appointed G. A. Gasquet president of The International Commission for the Revision of the Vulgate, to work on the project. Publication began with Genesis in 1926, and other volumes have followed, with more still to be published. A check of this passage in this edition shows no variations on *cornuta* in any of the manuscripts and editions collated, including that in the still most commonly used Sixto-Clementine version (1592). See, for example, *Biblia Sacra, Vulgatae editionis Sixti V Pontificis Maximi iussu recognita et Clementis VIII*, editiones Paulinae (Rome, 1957), under Exod. 34:29.

5. Note that the Authorized Version (1611) reads: "And it came to pass, when Moses came down from mount Sinai with the two tables of testimony in Moses' hand, when he came down from the mount, that Moses wist not that the skin of his face shone while he talked with him." The Revised Version (1881–1885) is almost identical. For a brief summary of the changes in Exod. 34:29 in English Bibles, see James Strachan, *Early Bible Illustrations* (Cambridge: Cambridge University Press, 1957), p. 14. Strachan points out that it was not until after 1560 that the concept of a horned Moses is completely eliminated from this passage.

6. *Oxford Dictionary of the Christian Church*, ed. F. L. Cross (London: Oxford University Press, 1958), under *Vulgate*.

7. Berthold Altaner, *Patrology*, trans. Hilda C. Graef (Freiburg: Herder; London: Thomas Nelson, 1960), pp. 468–469.

8. The horned god motif in religious history has been summarized by I. Scheftelowitz, "Das Hörnermotiv in den Religionen," *Archiv für Religionswissenschaft*, XV (1912), 451–487. And see the brief but excellent survey in the *Encyclopaedia of Religion and Ethics*, ed. James Hastings (1st imp., 1913; 4th imp., Edinburg: T. and T. Clark; New York: Scribner's, 1959), vol. 6, under *horns*.

9. *Encyclopaedia of Religion and Ethics*, p. 792.

10. *Ibid.*, p. 793. See also Scheftelowitz, "Das Hörnermotiv," pp. 471–473. And see Erwin R. Goodenough, *Jewish Symbols in the Greco-Roman Period*, 12 vols. (New York: Pantheon, 1953–1965), 7:3–28.

11. For the Ethiopic legends of Alexander see E. A. Wallis Budge, *The Life and*

Exploits of Alexander the Great (London: Clay, 1896), 2:46, 188, 355, 387, 388. In the Koran, he is referred to also as the "two-horned one" (Dhū l–Qarnain), Surah 18:82, 85, 93.

12. E. Douglas Van Buren, "Concerning the Horned Cap of the Mesopotamian Gods," *Orientalia*, XII (1943), 318.

13. *Ibid.*, p. 324.

14. Henri Frankfort, *Art and Architecture of the Ancient Orient* (Baltimore: Penguin, 1954), p. 43.

15. *Encyclopaedia of Religion and Ethics*, p. 795.

16. *Ibid.*, p. 795.

17. *Ibid.*, p. 794.

18. *Ibid.*, p. 795.

19. *Ibid.*, p. 794.

20. So dated by Frankfort, *Art and Architecture*, p. 41.

21. Hammurabi of Babylon is dated ca. 1792–1750 B.C., *ibid.*, p. 59.

22. Biblical usage is discussed in Part II which is concerned with interpretation, see pp. 76 ff.

23. See pp. 76–79.

24. See p. 2, for a description of the sequence of events in Exodus.

25. For a good resumé of the early iconography of Moses, see *Dictionnaire d'archéologie chrétienne et de liturgie*, ed. Fernand Cabrol and Henri Leclercq (Paris: Librairie Letouzey, 1907, et. seq.), under *Moïse*. See also Réau, *Iconographie de l'art chrétien*, vol. 1, pt. 1, under *Moïse*.

26. For good reproductions of this damaged painting in the Dura-Europos synagogue, see Goodenough, *Jewish Symbols*, vol. 11, fig. 324, and color pl. V. This damaged fresco shows the bottom portion of a man's torso. He appears to be standing on a mountain, his shoes removed and placed at the side.

27. Only a few examples are offered here; the development of the variations as well as the exact chronology are beyond the scope of this book. One must look to the Byzantinists for a full-scale study.

28. Kurt Weitzmann has pointed out that the first illustrators of the Septuagint were very creative, but that once the scenes were created, later generations copied them closely (unless a new text needed illustrating); and he says, "This explains why all Septuagint representations in manuscripts as well as other media which depend on manuscripts can be reduced to a very few archetypes," *Illustrations in Roll and Codex* (Princeton, N. J.: Princeton University Press, 1947), pp. 130–131.

29. This is reproduced in Cabrol and Leclerq, *Dictionnaire d' archéologie*, cols. 1655–1656.

30. This is reproduced in André Grabar, *Byzantine Painting*, (Lausanne and Geneva: Skira, 1953), p. 170. And see Hugo Buchthal, *The Miniatures of*

the Paris Psalter (London: Warburg Institute, 1938), for a discussion of the Byzantine iconography of Moses Receiving the Tables of the Law, pp. 33–39.

31. My examination of this theme has been cursory. Whether or not this scene of a "glorified" Moses had an earlier model—extant or hypothetical—I have thus far not been able to ascertain. Again, I must leave this interesting problem for the Byzantine specialists.

32. The fifth Octateuch, Athos Vatopedi 602, is lacking Genesis and Exodus; see Kurt Weitzmann, *The Joshua Roll* (Princeton, N. J.: Princeton University Press, 1948), p. 61.

33. See D. C. Hesseling, *Miniatures de l'octateuque Grec de Symrna* (Leyden, Sijthoff, 1909), fig. 204.

34. The dating of these manuscripts is from Weitzmann, *The Joshua Roll*, p. 61.

35. See Wilhelm Koehler, *Die Karolingischen Miniaturen*, vol. I, pts. 1 and 2 (1st ed. 1930 and 1933; reprint, Berlin: Deutscher Verein für Kunstwissenschaft, 1963), text I:1, 194–209; I:2, 22–26.

36. *Ibid.*, I:1, 250–255; I:2, 39–45.

37. Albert Boeckler, *Abendländische Miniaturen* (Berlin and Leipzig: de Gruyter, 1930), text: pp. 37, 109. Carl Nordenfalk argues in favor of Charles the Bald, *Early Medieval Painting* ([Lausanne]: Skira, 1957), p. 151; and see Ernest H. Kantorowicz, "The Carolingian King in the Bible of San Paolo fuori le Mura," *Late Classical and Mediaeval Studies in honor of A. M. Friend* (Princeton, N. J.: Princeton University Press, 1955), pp. 287–300, who convincingly attributes this Bible to Charles the Bald, dating it to 870.

38. Wilhelm Neuss, *Die katalanischen Bibelillustration um die Wende des ersten Jahrtausends* (Bonn and Leipzig: Kurt Schroeder, 1922), pp. 16–29.

39. *Ibid.*, p. 46. Neuss notes that the initial reception of the Law, fol. 82ʳ, was apparently fitted into the binding at some later time; and see p. 17, where Neuss points out that this Bible is something of a compilation with perhaps ten artists having contributed to it.

40. *Ibid.*, p. 46.

41. *Ibid.*

42. This presents many fascinating possibilities that cannot be dwelt upon here. However, see Origen in *Pat. Graeco-Latina*, vol. 12, col. 384, where Origen interprets the leprous arm of Moses as the imperfect execution (or working) of the Law.

43. This is the only example I have found thus far of this unusual iconography of a mask for Moses.

44. See Hugo Gressman, *Moses und seine Zeit* (Göttingen: Vandenhoeck and Ruprecht, 1913), sect. 18: Moses Maske, pp. 246–251; and see Julian Morgenstern, "Moses with the Shining Face," *Hebrew Union College Annual*

II (1925), 1–27, especially p. 4 n. 9. And for a more recent assessment of this problem see Martin Noth, *Exodus—a Commentary*, trans. J. S. Bowden from the German ed. of 1959 (Philadelphia: Westminster Press, 1962), p. 267.

45. For a discussion of the frescoes of Saint-Savin see Henri Focillon, *Peintures romanes des églises de France* (Paris: Hartmann, 1938), pp. 19–34; and see Georges Gaillard, *The Frescoes of Saint-Savin* (New York and London: Studio Publications, 1944), pp. 3–9.

CHAPTER I

1. This manuscript is one of seven surviving manuscripts that are copies of Aelfric's biblical translation. It is the only one remaining that is illustrated. Of the seven, two are pre-Conquest, one about the time of the Conquest, and four post-Conquest; see Raymond Wilson Chambers, "The Continuity of English Prose from Alfred to More and his School," in *The Life and Death of Sir Thomas More* (London, New York, Toronto: Early English Text Society, 1932), p. xci.

For studies and comments on the Aelfric Paraphrase: See Francis Wormald, *English Drawings of the Tenth and Eleventh Centuries* (London, Faber and Faber, 1952), pp. 39–49; Margaret Rickert, *Painting in Britain: the Middle Ages* (Baltimore: Penguin, 1954), p. 47; Montague Rhodes James, "Illustrations of the Old Testament," in *A Book of Old Testament Illustrations of the Middle of the Thirteenth Century*, ed. Sidney C. Cockerell (Cambridge: Roxburghe Club, 1927), pp. 21–26; Hanns Swarzenski, *Monuments of Romanesque Art* (1st ed. 1954; Chicago: University of Chicago Press, 1967), pp. 21–22; Edward Maunde Thompson, "English Illuminated Manuscripts—A.D. 700–1066," *Bibliographica*, I (1895–1896), 153–155; J. O. Westwood, *Paleographica Sacra Pictoria* (London: Bohn, n.d.), pp. 143–145; Carl Nordenfalk, *Early Medieval Painting* ([Lausanne]: Skira, 1957), pp. 186–187; Eric G. Millar, *English Illuminated Manuscripts from the Xth to the XIIIth Century* (Paris and Brussels: Van Oest, 1926), p. 22; T. D. Kendrick, *Late Anglo-Saxon and Viking Art* (London: Methuen, 1949), p. 24.

2. Émile Mâle, *L'art religieux du XIIᵉ siècle en France* (Paris: Librairie Armand Colin, 1928), p. 146.

3. Louis Réau, *Iconographie de l'art chrétien*, 6 vols. (Paris: Presses Universitaires de France, 1955–1959), vol. 2, pt. 1, p. 177.

4. See p. 1.

5. Arthur Watson, *The Early Iconography of the Tree of Jesse* (London: Oxford University Press, 1934), p. 26. The possible influence of liturgical drama will be considered later in this study.

6. Chaps. iv and v are based on hypotheses that were evolved from this important detail.

7. See James, "Illustrations of the Old Testament," p. 22.

8. Wormald, *English Drawings*, p. 40.

9. James, "Illustrations of the Old Testament," p. 22.

10. *Ibid.*, pp. 3, 4.

11. Swarzenski, *Monuments of Romanesque Art*, p. 21.

12. Otto Pächt, *The Rise of Pictorial Narrative in Twelfth Century England* (Oxford: Clarendon Press, 1962), p. 5.

13. See Bede, *Lives of the First Five Abbots of Wearmouth and Jarrow*, trans. Peter Wilcock (Sunderland: Hills, 1910), pp. 52–57.

14. See F. M. Stenton, *Anglo-Saxon England* (1st ed., 1943; Oxford: Clarendon Press, 1947), pp. 455–457.

15. Israel Gollancz has said, "In dealing with the extant remains of Anglo-Saxon art, we have constantly to remind ourselves that our evidence is very limited, and that we are dealing with the mere wreckage of time," in *The Caedmon Manuscript of Anglo-Saxon Biblical Poetry, Junius XI in the Bodleian Library* (London: Oxford University Press, 1927), p. xxxvii.

16. David Talbot Rice, *English Art, 871–1100* (Oxford: Clarendon Press, 1952), p. 206; see also James, "Illustrations of the Old Testament," p. 22; and see also *The Old English Version of the Heptateuch*, ed. S. J. Crawford (London: Early English Text Society, 1922), p. 2.

17. Rice, *English Art*, p. 2.

18. *Ibid.*, p. 206; see Thompson, "English Illuminated Manuscripts," p. 155.

19. Thompson, "English Illuminated Manuscripts, p. 153.

20. Wormald, *English Drawings*, p. 39.

21. Rice, *English Art*, p. 206.

22. For a stylistic description of the illuminations see Rice, *English Art*, p. 206; Thompson, "English Illuminated Manuscripts," p. 154; and Wormald, *English Drawings*, p. 39. The color of the horns on Moses in the Aelfric Paraphrase vary. From folio 105^v through 128^r they are yellow or uncolored; folios 136^v, 137^r and 138^v have horns of a brick-red color; in folio 139^v the horns are blue.

23. O. Elfrida Saunders has described some of these in *A History of English Art in the Middle Ages* (Oxford: Clarendon Press, 1932), p. 34.

24. See C. R. Morey, "The Illustrations of Genesis," in C. W. Kennedy, *The Caedmon Poems* (London: Routledge; New York: Dutton, 1916), pp. 177–195; and see Gollancz, *The Caedmon Manuscript* for a good facsimile of the illuminations. Dating varies on this manuscript. For example, Kendrick dates it 1030–1050, in "The Viking Taste in Pre-Conquest Art," *An-

tiquity, XV (1941), 137, while Nordenfalk, *Early Medieval Painting*, dates it to the second half of the tenth century, p. 187.

25. Corpus Christi College MS 23; Richard Stettiner was the first to comprehensively deal with the illustrated "Psychomachia" manuscripts, *Die Illustrierten Prudentius-Handschriften im Mittelalter*, 2 vols. (Berlin: Grote, 1895 and 1905), and listed the sixteen manuscripts according to a system of abbreviated designations. The above described manuscript is designated by him as C, see pp. 17–22; and pls. 31–34, 49–66. See Millar, *English Illuminated Manuscripts*, pp. 20, 21; see Helen Woodruff, "The Illustrated Manuscripts of Prudentius," *Art Studies*, vol. 1 (Cambridge: Harvard University Press, 1929), pp. 38–39; and see Adolph Katzenellenbogen, *Allegories of the Virtues and Vices in Medieval Art*, (first pub., 1939; New York: Norton, 1964), p. 7.

26. See Wormald, *English Drawings*, pp. 50–52, and see Nordenfalk's description of this manuscript, *Early Medieval Painting*, p. 186, and the color plate of folio 14ʳ, "The Harrowing of Hell," p. 184.

27. Nordenfalk, *Early Medieval Painting*, p. 228.

28. Thompson, "English Illuminated Manuscripts," p. 155.

29. On folio 103ʳ Moses is shown receiving the first tablets of the Law (Exod. 31:18); he holds a tablet in each hand—but quite in keeping with the biblical text, he does not as yet have horns.

30. The folios on which horned Moses appears are: 105ᵛ, 107ʳ, 107ᵛ, 108ᵛ, 110ᵛ, 111ʳ, 111ᵛ, 112ʳ, 113ᵛ, 114ʳ, 115ʳ, 115ᵛ, 116ʳ, 116ᵛ, 117ᵛ, 118ᵛ, 119ʳ, 119ᵛ, 120ʳ, 121ʳ, 121ᵛ, 122ᵛ, 123ʳ, 123ᵛ, 124ʳ, 124ᵛ, 125ʳ, 128ʳ, 136ᵛ, 137ʳ, 138ᵛ, 139ᵛ.

31. The representations of horned Moses in later periods will be discussed in pt. II, chap. vi.

CHAPTER II

1. Meyer Schapiro, in a book review of J. C. Webster, *The Labors of the Months in Antique and Medieval Art to the End of the Twelfth Century*, *Speculum*, XVI, no. 1 (Jan., 1941), 137. Interesting technological innovations in England of this period have also been pointed out; see Lynn White, jr., "Eilmer of Malmesbury, an Eleventh Century Aviator," *Technology and Culture*, II (1961), 97–111.

2. Arthur M. Haseloff writing in *Histoire de l'art*, ed. A. A. Michel, vol. 1:2 (Paris, 1905), p. 737. Similar sentiments are echoed later by H. P. Mitchell in, "Flotsam of Later Anglo-Saxon Art," *Burlington Magazine* XXXXII (1923–pt III), 304.

3. Adolph Goldschmidt, "English Influence on Medieval Art of the Continent," *Medieval Studies in Memory of A. Kingsley Porter*, 2 vols. (Cambridge: Harvard University Press, 1939), 2: 715–719.

4. Meyer Schapiro, "The Image of the Disappearing Christ—the Ascension in English Art Around the Year 1000," *Gazette des Beaux-Arts*, XXIII (March, 1943), 148; see also Carl Nordenfalk, *Early Medieval Painting* ([Lausanne]: Skira, 1957), p. 191; and see Schapiro, *Speculum*, p. 137.

5. See Dimitri Tselos, "English Manuscript Illustration and the Utrecht Psalter," *Art Bulletin*, XLI, no. 2 (June, 1959), 139.

6. Goldschmidt, "English Influence," pp. 720, 721.

7. Nordenfalk, *Early Medieval Painting*, p. 191; see O. Elfrida Saunders, *A History of English Art in the Middle Ages* (Oxford: Clarendon Press, 1932), p. 33; and see Goldschmidt, "English Influence," p. 721, who points out that the twelfth-century tale of the Irish knight, Tundalus, who saw this view of hell as a vision, can only be a parallel, and not the genesis, of its artistic portrayal, since it is recorded much later. Goldschmidt further points out that this motif can be traced in its influence on northern Germany. Otto Pächt has suggested that one possible stimulus for this monster concept might have come from the earlier images of Grendel in the heroic poem of *Beowulf*; see his *St. Albans Psalter* (London: Warburg Institute, 1960), p. 56, n. 6.

8. See Eric G. Millar, *English Illuminated Manuscripts from the Xth to the XIIIth Century* (Paris and Brussels: Van Oest, 1926), p. 19; and see Saunders, *History of English Art*, p. 33.

9. See C. R. Morey, "The Illustrations of Genesis," in C. W. Kennedy, *The Caedmon Poems* (London: Routledge; New York: Dutton, 1916), pp. 199 and 206 for reproductions of these two folios; or see Israel Gollancz, *The Caedmon Manuscript of Anglo-Saxon Biblical Poetry, Junius XI in the Bodleian Library* (London: Oxford University Press, 1927), for facsimile copies.

10. Nordenfalk, *Early Medieval Painting*, pp. 187, 188.

11. Francis Wormald, "Late Anglo-Saxon Art: Some Questions and Suggestions," *Studies in Western Art: Arts of the XX International Congress of the History of Art*, ed. M. Meiss, 1 (Princeton, N.J.: Princeton University Press, 1963), 20.

12. Nordenfalk, *Early Medieval Painting*, p. 186.

13. Saunders, *A History of English Art*, p. 34.

14. George Henderson, "Cain's Jaw-Bone," *Journal of the Warbug and Courtauld Institutes*, XXIV (1961), 108–114.

15. *Ibid.*, p. 108. The author believes that the innovation occurred possibly because of a misunderstanding on the part of the artist who may have

seen a representation of Samson slaying the Philistines and then confused it with the scene of Cain killing Abel.

16. Schapiro, "The Image of the Disappearing Christ." pp. 135–152.
17. Mitchell, "Flotsam of Later Anglo-Saxon Art," (1923–pt. II), pp. 167–168.
18. See pp. 7–9.
19. See, for example, Gerhart Ladner, "Die Italienische malerei im 11. Jahrhundert," *Jahrbuch der Kunsthistorischen Sammlungen in Wien*, new series, V (1931), 33–160, especially the description of the Sakramentary of Ivrea (ca. 1002), pp. 130–151.

CHAPTER III

1. See Charles W. Kennedy, *Beowulf, the Oldest English Epic* (1st ed., 1940; New York, London, Toronto: Oxford University Press, 1966), pp. xlix–liv; and see Raymond Wilson Chambers, *Beowulf*, with a supplement by C. L. Wrenn (1st ed., 1921; Cambridge: Cambridge University Press, 1963), pp. 121–128, 508–523.
2. For example, the Junius artist was the first to give the Ark the additional aspect of a ship, deriving this motif from the poem's text and reflecting the Anglo-Saxon familiarity with the sea; see C. R. Morey, "The Illustrations of Genesis," in C. W. Kennedy, *The Caedmon Poems* (London: Routledge; New York: Dutton, 1916), pp. 192–193.
3. R. H. Hodgkin, *A History of the Anglo-Saxons*, 2 vols., (1st ed., 1935; London: Oxford University Press, 1959), p. 457.
4. *Ibid.*, p. 458.
5. *Ibid.*, p. 159.
6. Albert Stanburrough Cook, ed., *The Old English Elene, Phoenix and Physiologus* (New Haven: Yale University Press, 1919), p. lxii. The editor points out that while the standard form of the *Physiologus* had 49 chapters, of the whole, Old English poetry has made use of only three—the "Panther," the "Whale," and the "Partridge,"—four if the "Phoenix" is included. It is uncertain whether or not they were originally part of a longer Old English poetical *Physiologus*. See also, Charles W. Kennedy, *Early English Christian Poetry* (New York: Oxford University Press, 1952), pp. 217–220, and his translation pp. 226–230.
7. Cook, *The Old English Elene*, p. lviii. Florence McCulloch, *Medieval Latin and French Bestiaries* (Chapel Hill: University of North Carolina Press, 1960) says that a Latin translation was made around the fourth century, p. 71.
8. *Beowulf* will be discussed in another context later in this book, see pp. 47–48.

9. *Oxford Dictionary of the Christian Church*, ed. F. L. Cross (London: Oxford University Press, 1958), under *Alfred the Great*; see F. M. Stenton, *Anglo-Saxon England* (1st ed., 1943; Oxford: Clarendon Press, 1947), pp. 267–270.

10. Stenton, *Anglo-Saxon England*, p. 445; see also Peter Hunter Blair, *An Introduction to Anglo-Saxon England* (Cambridge: Cambridge University Press, 1962), pp. 359, 360.

11. Stenton, *Anglo-Saxon England*, pp. 453–454.

12. See Cyril L. Smetana, "Aelfric and the Early Medieval Homiliary," *Traditio*, XV (1959), 163, who stresses Aelfric's virtuosity; see also Stenton, *Anglo-Saxon England*, pp. 452–453.

13. For the chronology of Aelfric's works, see Peter Clemoes, ed., *The Anglo-Saxons* (London: Bowes and Bowes, 1959), pp. 212 ff.

14. See *Dictionary of National Biography* (London: Oxford University Press, 1917, et seq.), under *Aelfric, abbot, called Grammaticus*.

15. *Ibid.*

16. Stenton, *Anglo-Saxon England*, p. 453.

17. *Ibid.*

18. See *The Old English Version of the Heptateuch*, ed. S. J. Crawford (London: Early English Text Society, 1922), p. 76; Blair, *Introduction to Anglo-Saxon England*, p. 358; and see also Stenton, *Anglo-Saxon England*, p. 453.

19. *Old English Heptateuch*, bottom of p. 32 where Aelfric refers to the fact that he had earlier translated some of the Scriptures into English. See also p. 76 for Aelfric's "greeting" to Aethelweard in his Preface to Genesis. See also Stenton, *Anglo-Saxon England*, p. 453. It is this same Aethelweard who was himself the author of a Latin chronicle—Latin which Blair and others have described as difficult and at times unintelligible, see A. Campbell, ed., *The Chronicle of Aethelweard* (London: Thomas Nelson, 1962).

20. *Old English Heptateuch*, p. 15.

21. This is the 1623 William L'isle translation, reproduced in *Old English Heptateuch*, p. 16.

22. Stenton, *Anglo-Saxon England*, p. 454.

23. This modern translation is from the *Dictionary of National Biography*, under *Aelfric*. See *Old English Heptateuch*, for the Anglo-Saxon, p. 80.

24. See Raymond Wilson Chambers, "The Continuity of English Prose from Alfred to More and his School," in *The Life and Death of Sir Thomas More* (London, New York, Toronto: Early English Text Society, 1932), p. lxviii.

25. See p. 145, n. 1.

26. Caroline Louisa White, *Aelfric, a New Study of His Life and Writings* [Yale Studies in English] (Boston, New York, and London: Lamson, Wolffe, 1898), pp. 72–75.

27. *Ibid.*, p. 72.
28. *Ibid.*
29. *Ibid.*, p. 146.
30. Aelfric, *The Homilies of the Anglo-Saxon Church*, ed. Benjamin Thorpe, 2 vols., (London: Aelfric Society, 1844), 2:466.
31. See p. 142, n. 4.
32. *Old English Heptateuch*, p. 285.
33. Beryl Smalley, *The Study of the Bible in the Middle Ages*, (repr. of 2d ed., 1952; Notre Dame, Ind.: University of Notre Dame Press, 1964), p. 119.
34. Meyer Schapiro, "The Image of the Disappearing Christ—the Ascension in English Art Around the Year 1000," *Gazette des Beaux-Arts*, XXIII (March, 1943), 152.
35. Otto Pächt, *The Rise of the Pictorial Narrative in Twelfth Century England* (Oxford: Clarendon Press, 1962), p. 57.
36. *Ibid.*, p. 58.
37. *Ibid.*, p. 55. This does not imply that such concrete and literal imagery was reserved only for England; see p. 21.

CHAPTER IV

1. Émile Mâle, *L'art religieux du XIIe siècle en France* (Paris: Librairie Armand Colin, 1928), p. 146, where he says: "Il me parait donc certain que Moïse apparut pour la première fois, avec des cornes d'or sur le front, dans le Drame des prophètes." For an edited text of this play (Bibliothèque municipale de Rouen MS 384), see Gustave Cohen, *Anthologie du drame liturgique en France au moyen-âge* (Paris: Les éditions du Cerf, 1955), pp. 120–136, or see Karl Young, *The Drama of the Medieval Church*, 2 vols. (Oxford: Clarendon Press, 1933), 2:154–165.
2. Arthur Watson, *The Early Iconography of the Tree of Jesse* (London: Oxford University Press, 1934), p. 27.
3. See Young's edition of this manuscript, *Drama of the Medieval Church*, 2:156; see also p. 154 which contains a photograph of one of the folios of the Rouen manuscript (fol. 33r).
4. Watson, *Early Iconography*, p. 26. However, Mâle, *L'art religieux du XIIe*, p. 138, n. 5, argues: "Le manuscrit est du XIVe siècle, mais le texte est certainement beaucoup plus ancien."
5. Paul Studer, *Le mystère d'Adam* (1st ed., 1918; Manchester: Manchester University Press, 1949), p. xi. And see, Gustave Cohen *Le théâtre en France au moyen-âge* (Paris: Presses Universitaires de France, 1948), pp. 7–8; see O. B. Hardison, Jr., *Christian Rite and Christian Drama in the Middle Ages* (Baltimore: Johns Hopkins Press, 1965), especially his chapter, "The Early

151

History of the *Quem quaeritis*," pp. 178–219. Hardison argues that this originated as a ceremony associated with the vigil Mass, not as an Easter trope, p. 219.

6. Gustave Cohen, "The Influence of the Mysteries on Art in the Middle Ages," *Gazette des Beaux-Arts*, XXIV (July–Dec., 1943), 329.

7. *Regularis Concordia*, trans. Thomas Symons (London: Thomas Nelson, 1953), pp. 44–45. The Latin text can be followed on parallel pages; see pp. 49–50 for the *Quem quaeritis*.

8. Young, *Drama of the Medieval Church*, 2:410.

9. *Ibid.*, p. 411.

10. *Ibid.*, p. 414.

11. See p. 30.

12. *Regularis Concordia*, pp. 49–50.

13. Young, *Drama of the Medieval Church*, 2:397; and for a comprehensive study of English religious drama throughout the sweep of the Middle Ages, see Hardin Craig, *English Religious Drama of the Middle Ages* (Oxford: Clarendon Press, 1955).

14. Hardison, *Christian Rite*, on p. 227 says, "Because the major forms of liturgical drama, including cyclic combinations, are found in thirteenth-century manuscripts and references to dramatic productions, we may assume that by the year 1300 the 'development' of Latin religious drama was complete."

15. Young, *Drama of the Medieval Church*, p. 401.

16. Hardison, *Christian Rite*, p. 12.

17. *Ibid.*, pp. 253 ff.

18. A. Lukyn Williams, *Adversus Judaeos* (Cambridge: Cambridge University Press, 1935), p. 321. See also Studer, *Mystère d'Adam*, p. xii.

19. Quoted in full by Marius Sepet, "Les prophètes du Christ," *Bibliothèque de l'École des Chartes*, XXVIII (1866–1867), 3–8; and see Williams, *Adversus Judaeos*, p. 321.

20. See p. 28.

21. Young, *Drama of the Medieval Church*, 2:166. Young has described most of the extant MSS containing a *Drama of the Prophets* in this chapter; see also, Hardison, *Christian Rite*, pp. 220–221.

22. This hatlike headdress with horns will be considered in detail in the section following this one within a different context, but it will not exclude the possible hypothesis that such a headdress for Moses might have occurred first in liturgical drama as a costume.

23. See *A Concise Anglo-Saxon Dictionary*, ed. John R. Clark Hall and Herbert D. Meritt (4th ed., Cambridge: Cambridge University Press, 1960), under *hraegl*; or see Joseph Bosworth, *An Anglo-Saxon Dictionary*, ed. and enl.

by T. Northcote Toller (London: Oxford University Press, 1898) as well as its supplement by Toller, (Oxford: Clarendon Press, 1921), both under *hraegl*.

24. Otto Pächt, *The Rise of the Pictorial Narrative in Twelfth Century England* (Oxford: Clarendon Press, 1962), pp. 33–59.

25. *Ibid.*, p. 41.

26. *Ibid.*, p. 42.

27. *Ibid.*

CHAPTER V

1. *Encyclopaedia of Religion and Ethics*, ed. James Hastings (1st imp. 1913; 4th imp., Edinburg: T. and T. Clark; New York: Scribner's, 1959), p. 793.

2. *Ibid.*

3. See pp. 3–4; and see again figs. 1, 2, 3, 4.

4. I. Scheftelowitz, "Das Hörnermotiv in den Religionen," *Archiv für Religionswissenschaft*, XV (1912), 465.

5. James H. Turnure, "Etruscan Ritual Armor: Two Examples in Bronze," *American Journal of Archaeology*, vol. 69, no. 1 (Jan., 1965), pp. 39–48, pls. 8, 9.

6. *Ibid.*, p. 45.

7. *Ibid.*, p. 46.

8. Scheftelowitz, "Das Hörnermotiv," p. 477.

9. *Paulys Real-Encyclopädie der Classischen Altertumswissenschaft* (Stuttgart: Metzler, 1894, et seq.), under *corniculum*. See also Scheftelowitz, "Das Hörnermotiv," p. 465.

10. See Mårten Stenberger, Det forntida Sverige (Uppsala: Almqvist and Wiksells, 1964), pp. 228–248 and bibliography relating to the rock carvings on pp. 860–861. Also see Stenberger's *Sweden*, trans. Alan Binns, vol. 30 in the series, *Ancient Peoples and Places* (London: Thames and Hudson, 1962), p. 99 where Stenberger mentions the difficulty of dating these carvings: "There can be no doubt that the great majority of the rock-carvings in southern and central Sweden—the stylized carvings as distinct from the naturalistic north Scandinavian ones—were produced during the Bronze Age, but exactly when the custom began and ended it is more difficult to say. They were probably produced over the whole period, with the greatest activity in the middle and later parts of it." Carl-Axel Moberg has dated the ones with the horned figures in them in the late Bronze Age, comparing them with the Viksø helmets (in a letter in 1966 to Marija Gimbutas). For extensive interpretations of the religious symbolism of these rock carvings see Peter Gelling and Hilda Ellis Davidson, *The Chariot of the Sun* (Lon-

don: J. M. Dent and Sons, 1969), pp. 9–116. I am indebted to Walter Horn for calling my attention to this recent interesting study.

11. See Stenberger, *Det forntida* for photographs of some of these rock carvings, figs. 102–112 (pp. 230–245).

12. Stenberger, *Sweden*, pp. 98–99.

13. E. O. G. Turville-Petre, *Myth and Religion of the North, the Religion of Ancient Scandinavia* (New York: Holt, Rinehart and Winston, 1964), p. 84.

14. Carl-Axel Moberg in a letter to Marija Gimbutas in August, 1966, stated: "Of course, the obvious comparison is with the Viksø helmets, even if I am convinced that human representations with horns on rock-carvings actually represent such helmets, this does not need to be the *only* explanation for *all* these rock-carvings; one has to think of the possibility of antler ornamented headdresses as an alternative—in the same way as the horned helmets themselves may be representations of such." (I am indebted to Marija Gimbutas for this correspondence.)

15. See Johannes Brøndsted, "A Survey of Danish Prehistoric Culture," in catalog, *The Arts of Denmark* (1960–1961), p. 23. See also H. Norling-Christensen, "The Viksø Helmets, a bronze-age votive find from Zealand," *Acta Archaeologica*, XVII (1946), 99–115.

16. Brøndsted, "Danish Prehistoric Culture," p. 25.

17. See Brøndsted, *Danmarks Oltid*, 3 vols. (København, 1957–1960), 2:188.

18. See Ole Klindt-Jensen, *Denmark before the Vikings* (London: Thames and Hudson, 1957), pp. 74–78.

19. Klindt-Jensen, "Foreign Influences in Denmark's Early Iron Age," *Acta Archaeologica*, XX (1949), 146.

20. *Ibid.*

21. *Ibid.*, p. 147.

22. See Cyril Fox, *Pattern and Purpose: A Survey of Early Celtic Art in Britain* (Cardiff: National Museum of Wales, 1958), p. 49.

23. I am indebted to Milton Anastos for calling my attention to this article: Andrew Alföldi, "Cornuti: A Teutonic Contingent in the Service of Constantine the Great and Its Decisive Role in the Battle at the Milvian Bridge," *Dumbarton Oaks Papers*, XIII (1959), 173; see also Hans Peter L'Orange and Armin von Gerkan, *Der Spätantike Bildschmuck des Konstantinsbogens*, [Studien zur spätantiken Kunstgeschichte], 2 vols., 10 (Berlin: de Gruyter, 1939), text and plates, see text, pp. 41 ff.

24. Alföldi, "Cornuti," p. 177.

25. *Ibid.*

26. *The Complete Works of Tacitus*, trans. Alfred John Church and William Jackson Brodribb (New York: Random House, 1942), see Germania 45, p. 731. Jaan Puhvel has suggested that these Aestii were probably a Baltic, i.e., an Old Prussian-Lithuanian-Lettish tribe.

27. *Ibid.*, p. 731.
28. Joachim Werner, "Eberzier von Monceau-Le-Neuf (Dép. Aisne)—ein beitrag zur Entstehung der völkerwanderungszeitlichen Eberhelme," *Acta Archaeologica*, XX (1949), 248–257.
29. *Ibid.*, p. 252.
30. *Ibid.*, p. 253.
31. Alföldi, 'Cornuti," p. 176, and see p. 177 where he points out: "Since in the social and religious life of primitive nations both the standard and the headgear denoted the sacred origins of a tribe or clan, it is not surprising that the *cornuti* should have identified themselves by such meaningful symbols."
32. Brian Branston, *Gods of the North* (New York: Vanguard Press, [n.d.]), p. 132.
33. Turville-Petre, *Myth and Religion of the North*, p. 151.
34. *Ibid.*, p. 95.
35. *Ibid.*, p. 175.
36. *Ibid.*
37. C. L. Wrenn has stressed the importance of a close-working arrangement in the study of Anglo-Saxon culture between historian, philologist, and archaeologist, saying: "Too many professed Anglo-Saxon archaeologists are out of touch with what is known of the runic inscriptions and early documents; and both the historian and the student of the Anglo-Saxon language too often work along parallel lines that never meet," *Anglo-Saxon Poetry and the Amateur Archaeologist* (London: Lewis, 1962), p. 5.
38. D. Elizabeth Martin-Clarke, *Culture in Early Anglo-Saxon England* (Baltimore: Johns Hopkins Press, 1947), p. 59.
39. See Haakon Shetelig and Hjalmar Falk, *Scandinavian Archaeology*, trans. E. V. Gordon (Oxford: Clarendon Press, 1937), p. 259, pl. 42B; see also Knut Stjerna, "Helmets and Swords in *Beowulf*," *Essays on Questions Connected with the Old English Poem of Beowulf*, trans. and ed. John R. Clark Hall (London: Viking Club Society for Northern Research, 1912), figs. 6, 7, 8 on p. 9, as well as fig. 9 on p. 11; and see Hjalmar Stolpe and T. J. Arne, *La nécropole de Vendel* [Kungl. Vitterhets Historie och Antikvitetsakademien, mono. no. 17] (Stockholm, 1927).
40. David M. Wilson, *The Anglo-Saxons* (London: Thames and Hudson, 1960), p. 217 where Wilson dates it seventh century; Stjerna, "Helmets and Swords," dated it ca. A.D. 500, see style B., p. 17.
41. Wilson, *Anglo-Saxons*, pls. 28, 29.
42. For additional details about the construction of this helmet see Herbert Maryon, "The Sutton-Hoo Helmet," *Antiquity*, XXI (Sept., 1947), 137–144, and see pls. I, II, III, IV. There are actually two horned figures on the Sutton Hoo helmet. It has been suggested that these represented twin gods,

and that they can possibly be linked with similar twin horned figures on helmet plates of the Vendel period and those on the Danish gold horns from Gallehus of about A.D. 500 (unfortunately destroyed, but known from eighteenth century drawings); see Gelling and Davidson, *The Chariot of the Sun*, pp. 176–179.

43. See *The Sutton Hoo Ship-Burial*, a provisional guide (1st ed., 1947; 8th imp.; London: Trustees of the British Museum, 1961.)

44. Charles Green, *Sutton Hoo.* (London: Merlin Press, 1963), p. 132.

45. Sonia Chadwick Hawkes, H.R. Ellis Davidson, and Christopher Hawkes, "The Finglesham Man," *Antiquity*, XXXIX (1965), 17–31. Mrs. Hawkes says that it "should probably not be dated too early in the 7th century," and suggests a date either in the middle or second half of the century, pp. 18–19.

46. *Ibid.*, pp. 18, 22.

47. *Ibid.*, pp. 26–27.

48. The Sutton Hoo helmet has been variously dated in the sixth and seventh centuries. See, for example, Rosemary J. Cramp who has dated it "probably sixth-century," in "*Beowulf* and Archaeology," *Medieval Archaeology*, I (1957), 59; J. L. N. O'Loughlin also dates this helmet in the sixth century in, "Sutton Hoo—The Evidence of the Documents," *Medieval Archaeology*, VIII (1964), 15–16. The date of the burial itself, ca. A.D. 650, however, is of particular importance to our study, for it indicates the time during which the helmet was available and seen.

49. See Raymond Wilson Chambers, *Beowulf* with a supplement by C. L. Wrenn, (3d ed.; Cambridge: Cambridge University Press, 1963), especially Wrenn's chap. i of the supplement, "Sutton Hoo and Beowulf," pp. 508–523; see also Cramp, "*Beowulf* and Archaeology," pp. 57–77; and see A. T. Hatto, "Snake-swords and Boar-helms in *Beowulf*," *English Studies*, XXXVIII, 4 (1957), 145–160.

50. *Beowulf* will be discussed further, see pp. 47 ff.

51. Green, *Sutton Hoo*, pp. 138–139. And see Nora K. Chadwick who says, "Perhaps it was the East Anglian royal family, the Wuffingas, who introduced the original story relating to their ancestors in Gautland, and naturalized it among their own subjects in East Anglia," in "The Monsters and Beowulf," *The Anglo-Saxons*, ed. Peter Clemoes (London: Bowes and Bowes, 1959), p. 203.

52. See Stenberger, *Det forntida Sverige*, pp. 810–815; Otto v. Friesen, *Sparlösastenen* [Kungl. Vitterhets Historie Och Antikvitets Akademiens Handlingar, Del 46:3] (Stockholm, 1940); Sven B. F. Jansson, *Runinskrifter i Sverige* (Uppsala: Almqvist and Wiksell 1963), pp. 32–37; and see Sven B. F. Jansson, *The Runes of Sweden*, trans. Peter G. Foote (London: Phoenix House 1962), pp. 11–17.

53. Stenberger, *Det forntida*, pp. 810–815 and Jansson, *The Runes*, p. 11.

54. Stenberger, *Det forntida*, pp. 814–815.

55. See Bjorn Hougen, "Osebergfunnets billedev," *Viking: tidsskrift for norrøn arkeologi* (Oslo, 1940), pp. 85–124, pls. V–IX. The tapestries from the Oseberg boat burial were reconstructed by Mary Storm at the Universitets Oldsaksamling in Oslo, under the supervision of Bjorn Hougen.

56. See Wilhelm Holmqvist, *Germanic Art during the First Millenium A. D.* [Kungl. Vitterhets Historie och Antikvitets Akademiens Handlingar, Del 90] (Stockholm, 1955), pl. LX.

57. Bjorn Hougen in a letter to me, summer of 1967, said: "However, it can be added with assurance that the motive must be a man wearing a helmet with horns." This same assurance was offered by Mrs. Mary Storm who did the actual reconstruction; similarly by Thorleif Sjøvold.

58. See A. W. Brøgger and Haakon Shetelig, *The Viking Ships* trans. Katharine John (Oslo: Dreyers 1951), p. 91; see also David M. Wilson and Ole Klindt-Jensen, *Viking Art* (London: George Allen and Unwin, 1966), pp. 48–49.

59. Wilson and Klindt-Jensen, *Viking Art*, p. 48; and see Holger Arbman, *The Vikings*, vol. 21 in series *Ancient Peoples and Places* (London: Thames and Hudson, 1961), p. 118.

60. Wilson and Klindt-Jensen, *Viking Art*, p. 48.

61. *Ibid.*, p. 83; see also Anders Hagen, *The Viking Ship Finds* (Oslo: Universitetets Oldsaksamling, 1960), p. 12.

62. Turville-Petre, *Myth and Religion of the North*, see caption under fig. 31.

63. *Ibid.*

64. See Holger Arbman, *Birka I, Die Gräber* [Kungl. Vitterhets Historie och Antikvitets Akademien], (Uppsala, 1943), p. 185 and Taf. 92, fig. 9. For a brief description of this important Viking metropolis see Arbman, *The Vikings*, pp. 37–47.

65. See Agnes Geijer, *Birka III, Die Textilfunde aus den Gräbern* [Kungl. Vitterhets Historie och Antikvitets Akademien] (Uppsala, 1938), p. 162. The Stockholm Historical Museum also dates this figurine tenth century.

66. Hilda R. Ellis [Davidson] discusses this stone in "Sigurd in the Art of the Viking Age," *Antiquity*, XVI (1942), 216–236; however, she does not mention this aspect of the carving; similarly this is true in Hilda R. Ellis Davidson, "Gods and Heroes in Stone," *The Early Cultures of North-west Europe*, ed. Cyril Fox and Bruce Dickens (Cambridge: Cambridge University Press, 1950), pp. 123–127.

67. Hatto, "Snake-swords and Boar-helms," pp. 145–160.

68. Klaeber, ed., *Beowulf and the Fight at Finnsburg* (3d ed.; Boston, New York, and Chicago: Heath, 1936), lines 333, 334.

69. Hatto, "Snake-swords and Boar-helms," p. 159.

70. *Ibid.*, p. 155.
71. *Ibid.*, p. 159.
72. *Ibid.*
73. I have checked the photographs of these reliefs in the Stockholm Historical Museum as well as the helmet itself, and the tusk is certainly convincing. This observation was confirmed by Bengt Schönbäck of the museum.
74. *The Oldest English Epic*, trans. Francis B. Gummere (1st ed. 1909; New York: Macmillan, 1923), lines 304, 305; hereafter this will be cited as Gummere. For another trans. see Charles W. Kennedy, *Beowulf, the Oldest English Epic* (1st ed. 1940; New York, London, Toronto: Oxford University Press, 1966), p. 12. While the language of the Gummere translation is archaic, it is used in my study because its language is painstaking and close to the original text. Compare the original Anglo-Saxon in Elliott van Kirk Dobbie, ed., *Beowulf and Judith* (New York: Columbia University Press, 1953), lines 304–305. And for another recent verse trans. see Edwin Morgan, *Beowulf* (Berkeley and Los Angeles: University of California Press, 1966), lines 304–305.
75. Hatto, "Snake-swords and Boar-helms," pp. 145–160 for a discussion of the boar-emblem as a protective device.
76. Gummere, lines 1448–1454; and cf. same lines in Kennedy, *Beowulf*; Dobbie, *Beowulf*; and Morgan, *Beowulf*.
77. Stjerna, "Helmets and Swords," pp. 1–18.
78. David Wright, *Beowulf, a prose translation* (1st ed. 1957; Baltimore: Penguin, 1964), p. 109.
79. *Ibid.*, pp. 109, 110.
80. J. M. Kemble, trans., *The Poetry of the Codex Vercellensis* (London: Aelfric Society, 1843), lines 150, 151.
81. *The Poetry of the Codex Vercellensis*, lines 511–517; and see Charles W. Kennedy, *An Anthology of Old English Poetry* (New York: Oxford University Press, 1960), p. 27, who translates it this way:

> Then was easily seen
> Woven mail on many an eorl
> Choicest of blades, bright battle-byrny,
> Visored casque and fair boar-crest;

82. See Albert Stanburrough Cook, ed., *The Old English Elene, Phoenix, and Physiologus,* (New Haven: Yale University Press, 1919), p. vii, where we are told this manuscript contained twenty-three homilies and six poems interspersed; the latter included: *Andreas, Fates of the Apostles, Address of the Soul to the Body, Falsehood of Men, Dream of the Rood,* and *Elene.*
83. *Ibid.*

84. Dated in the eleventh century by Charles W. Kent, *Elene an Old English Poem* (Boston and London: Ginn, 1889), p. 2.
85. Klaeber, *Beowulf and the Fight at Finnsburg*, p. 238.
86. Kemp Malone, trans., *Ten Old English Poems* (Baltimore: Johns Hopkins Press, 1941), p. 26, lines 28–30.
87. Klaeber, *Beowulf and the Fight at Finnsburg*, p. 246, line 30.
88. See *A Concise Anglo-Saxon Dictionary*, ed. John R. Clark Hall and Herbert D. Meritt (Cambridge: Cambridge University Press, 1960), under *bān*. Rosemary Cramp also believes the *bānhelm* in this poem means "horned helmet," "*Beowulf* and Archaeology," p. 73. See comments on this in Bruce Dickens, ed., *Runic and Heroic Poems of the Old Teutonic Peoples* (Cambridge: Cambridge University Press, 1915), p. 68.
89. Horns themselves were greatly treasured and were important in drinking toasts to the gods. Many Anglo-Saxon ornamented horns still survive, see Suse Pfeilstücker, *Spätantikes und Germanisches Kunstgut in der Frühangelsächsischen Kunst* (Berlin: Deutscher kunstverlag, 1936), pls. 21, 25. The importance of horns in the society is further demonstrated by one of the old Anglo-Saxon riddles that has for its answer, "Horn" and reads:

> Time was when I was weapon and warrior;
> Now the young hero hoods me with gold,
> And twisted silver. At times men kiss me.
> At times I speak and summon to battle
> Loyal companions. At times a courser
> Bears me o'er billows, brightly adorned.
> At times a fair maiden fills me with breath;
> At times hard and headless I lie on the board,
> Bereft of beauty. At times I hang
> Winsome on wall, richly embellished,
> Where revelers drink. At times a warrior
> Bears me on horse, a battle adornment,
> And I swallow, bright-shining, the breath
> > from his bosom.
> At times I win back
> Spoil from the spoiler, with sounding voice
> Put foemen to flight. Now ask what I'm called.

This translation by Kennedy, *An Anthology of Old English Poetry*, p. 43; see also Paull F. Baum, *Anglo-Saxon Riddles of the Exeter Book* (Durham, N.C.: Duke University Press, 1963), p. xii. Baum translates the first part of the riddle: "I was an armed fighter. Now a young home-dweller covers me proudly with twisted wires." p. 43.

90. Shetelig and Falk, *Scandinavian Archaeology*, p. 402.
91. Green, *Sutton Hoo*, p. 13.
92. *Ibid.*
93. See p. 43.
94. See Wrenn, *Anglo-Saxon Poetry*, p. 4 who emphasizes how the finds from Sutton Hoo have strikingly revolutionized our ideas of the historicity of the *Beowulf* civilization.
95. Francis Wormald, "Late Anglo-Saxon Art: Some Questions and Suggestions," *Studies in Western Art: Acts of the XX International Congress of the History of Art*, ed. M. Meiss, 4 vols. (Princeton, N.J.: Princeton University Press, 1963), i:41.
96. *Ibid.*
97. *Ibid.*, p. 39.
98. T. D. Kendrick, "The Viking Taste in Pre-Conquest Art," *Antiquity*, XV (1941), 137.
99. Wilhelm Holmqvist, "Viking Art in the Eleventh Century," *Acta Archaeologica*, XXII (1951), 14, 15.
100. *Ibid.*, p. 22.
101. See Francis Wormald in *The Bayeux Tapestry*, gen. ed. Frank Stenton (1st ed., 1957; London: Phaidon Press, 1965), pp. 30, 31; see also Roger Sherman Loomis, "The Origin and Date of the Bayeux Embroidery," *Art Bulletin*, VI (1923), 4.
102. Shetelig and Falk, *Scandinavian Archaelogy*, p. 258.
103. Gummere, lines 2760–2764; and cf. Kennedy, *Beowulf*, pp. 88, 89; also Morgan, *Beowulf*, 2759–2764.
104. Stjerna, "Helmets and Swords," p. 7.
105. Gummere, lines 180–184; and cf. Kennedy, *Beowulf*, p. 8; and see Dobbie, *Beowulf*, especially line 182.
106. F. M. Stenton, *Anglo-Saxon England* (1st ed., 1943; Oxford: Clarendon Press, 1947), p. 103 ff.
107. Bede [Ecclesiastical History], *A History of the English Church and People*, trans. Leo Sherley-Price (Baltimore: Penguin, 1955), pp. 86–87.
108. Wilson, *The Anglo-Saxons*, p. 155. See also Philip Webster Souers, "The Magi on the Franks Casket," *Harvard Studies and Notes in Philology and Literature*," XIX (1937), 249–254.
109. Brian Branston, *The Lost Gods of England* (London: Thames and Hudson, 1957), p. 5; and see fig. 1, p. 7. For other discussions of other sides and aspects of this casket see Eleanor Grace Clark, "The Right Side of the Franks Casket," *Publications of the Modern Language Association*, XLV (1930), 339–353; Souers, "The Top of the Franks Casket," *Harvard Studies and Notes in Philology and Literature*, XVII (1935), 163–179 and his "The Franks Casket: Left Side," *Harvard Studies*, XVIII (1935), 199–209.

110. For an excellent study of pagan survivals in England see William A. Chaney, "Paganism to Christianity in Anglo-Saxon England," *Harvard Theological Review*, LIII (1960), 197–217; see also Francis P. Magoun, "On Some Survivals of Paganism in Anglo-Saxon England," *Harvard Theological Review*, XL (1947), 33–46, who discusses the concept of mana in Old-English charms as well as Christianized personal mana in *Beowulf*; see R. Lowe Thompson, *The History of the Devil* (London: Kegan Paul, Trench, Trubner, 1929), p. 88; and see J. S. Ryan, "Othin in England," *Folklore*, 74 (1963), 460–480.

111. Bede, *A History of the English Church*, pp. 106–107.

112. *Ibid.*

113. *Ibid.*, p. 197.

114. *Ibid.*, p. 128.

115. Translated by Branston, *The Lost Gods*, p. 23; and see his reproduction of the catechism in Anglo-Saxon and Latin, a folio from MS Vat. Palat. nro. 557.

116. *Aelfric's Lives of the Saints*, ed. Walter W. Skeat, 2 vols. (London: Early English Text Society, 1881–1900), vol. II, Homily XXXI, "St. Martin, Bishop and Confessor," lines 710–717 (Anglo-Saxon on parallel pages).

117. Caroline Louisa White, *Aelfric, a New Study of his Life and Writings*, [Yale Studies in English] (Boston, New York, and London: Lamson, Wolffe, 1898), p. 85.

118. *Ibid.*

119. Turville-Petre, *Myth and Religion of the North*, p. 95. Also see Hilda R. Ellis Davidson, *Gods and Myths of Northern Europe* (Baltimore: Penguin, 1964), p. 90, who says that this stone may have been part of a cross, but that it is now built into the wall of the church in Cumberland. For a description and brief review of the many interpretations of the decoration of the tenth-century Gosforth cross, which is also full of pagan mythology, see Knut Berg, "The Gosforth Cross," *Journal of the Warburg and Courtauld Institutes*, XXI (1958), 27–43.

120. *Aelfric's Lives of the Saints*, "On Auguries," 1:364–382.

121. Aelfric, *The Homilies of the Anglo-Saxon Church*, ed. Benjamin Thorpe, 2 vols. (London: Aelfric Society, 1844), 2:30–36.

122. *Ibid.*, p. 240.

123. *Old English Version of the Heptateuch*, ed. S. J. Crawford (London: Early English Text Society, 1922), p. 21, 315.

124. White, *Aelfric, A New Study*, pp. 76 and 77.

125. *Old English Heptateuch*, p. 21.

126. *Ibid.*, p. 315.

127. *Ibid.*

128. *Aelfric's Lives of the Saints*, pp. 282–283.

129. *A Concise Anglo-Saxon Dictionary*, see *heretoga*. The *Oxford English Dictionary* says re *heretoga*, that in Old English history it meant: "The leader of an army; the commander of the militia of a shire or district."

CHAPTER VI

1. See Margaret Rickert, *Painting in Britain: the Middle Ages* (Baltimore: Penguin, 1954), p. 72; see also Otto Pächt, *The Rise of Pictorial Narrative in Twelfth Century England* (Oxford: Clarendon Press, 1962), pp. 12–13.
2. Pächt, *The Rise of Pictorial Narrative*, p. 13.
3. Recently dated 1135 by C. M. Kauffmann, "The Bury Bible," *Journal of the Warburg and Courtauld Institutes*, XXIX (1966), 60–81. C. R. Dodwell had previously dated it 1130–1140 in *The Great Lambeth Bible* (London: Faber and Faber, 1959), p. 8. See also Rickert, *Painting in Britain*, pp. 84–85 and T. S. R. Boase, *English Art, 1100–1216* (Oxford: Clarendon Press, 1953), pp. 161–164.
4. For a description of this psalter, its style and its relationship to other MSS, see Rickert, *Painting in Britain*, pp. 83–84; Mary Ann Farley and Francis Wormald, "Three Related English Romanesque Manuscripts," *Art Bulletin*, XXII (1940), 157–161; Wormald, "The Survival of Anglo-Saxon Illumination After the Norman Conquest," *Proceedings of the British Academy*, XXX (1944), 139; Eric G. Millar, *English Illuminated Manuscripts from the Xth to the XIIIth Century* (Paris and Brussels: Van Oest, 1926), p. 28, and pls. 32, 33 for examples of other folios; and see Boase, *English Art*, pp. 108–110.
5. For a description of this Bible, see Georg Swarzenski, *Die Salzburger Malerei*, 2 vols. (Leipzig: Hiersmann, 1913), text pp. 71–83; figs. 92–113. Swarzenski dates it ca. 1131, p. 79; Carl Nordenfalk, *Romanesque Painting* (Lausanne and Paris: Skira, 1958), dates it first half of the twelfth century, p. 218.
6. In another of the surviving folios of this Bible, fol. 70r, a Frontispiece to Numbers, Moses has a halo but no horns; see Kauffmann, "The Bury Bible," pl. 14. For a description of what illustrations are extant, see *ibid.*, p. 63.
7. See Rickert, *Painting in Britain*, p. 83.
8. Otto Pächt, *St. Albans Psalter*, (London: Warburg Institute, 1960), p. 59.
9. And of course, there is certainly the possibility that I may have overlooked some others.
10. For a description of this Bible, see Millar, *English Illuminated Manuscripts*, p. 32; Boase, *English Art*, pp. 165–169; Dodwell, *The Canterbury School of Illumination, 1066–1200* (Cambridge: Cambridge University Press,

1954); Dodwell, *The Great Lambeth Bible*; and Rickert, *Painting in Britain*, pp. 91–92.

11. See Rickert, *Painting in Britain*, pp. 93 ff. This psalter is also known as the Psalter of St. Swithin's Priory and as the Winchester Psalter. For other comments on it see Francis Wormald, "The Development of English Illumination in the Twelfth Century," *The Journal of the British Archaeological Association*, 3d series, VIII (1943), 41–42; and also his "The Survival," pp. 140–141; Boase, *English Art*, pp. 172–174; and see Fritz Saxl, *English Sculptures of the Twelfth Century*, ed. Hanns Swarzenski (Boston: Boston Book and Art Shop, [1952]) for a comparison with English twelfth-century sculpture, pp. 60, 66, 67, 69 n. 10, 73 nn. 25, 26, 74 n. 29; figs. 7, 27, 47, 48.

12. See Jean Porcher, *French Miniatures from Illuminated Manuscripts* (London: Collins, 1960), pp. 17–22, 37–38.

13. Urbain Plancher, *Histoire génerale et particulière de Bourgogne*, 4 vols., tome I (Dijon, 1739–1781), p. 498. This portal drawing has also been reproduced by Émile Mâle, *L'art religieux du XIIe siècle en France*, (Paris: Librairie Armand Colin, 1928) fig. 154, p. 217. Moses holds the tablets of the Law and is the second figure from the right; his horns are quite visible even in this poor reproduction.

14. Porcher, *French Miniatures*, p. 21.

15. *Ibid.*

16. *Ibid.*, pp. 17–19; see Millar, *English Illuminated Manuscripts*, p. 44; and see Nordenfalk, *Romanesque Painting*, p. 141.

17. See Philippe Lauer, *Les enluminures romanes des manuscrits de la Bibliothèque Nationale* (Paris: Éditions de la Gazette des beaux-arts, 1927), pl. XLV, pp. 126–127. For other brief comments on this MS, see A. Boutemy, "Les manuscrits enluminés du nord de la France," *Scriptorium*, III (1949), 117, n. 3; "De quelques enlumineurs . . ." *Scriptorium*, IV (1950), 248.

18. Porcher, *French Miniatures*, p. 33.

19. See Otto Pächt and J. J. G. Alexander, *Illuminated Manuscripts in the Bodleian Library Oxford, I* (Oxford: Clarendon Press, 1966), p. vii.

20. See Rickert, *Painting in Britain*, p. 109; Millar, *English Illuminated Manuscripts*, pp. 35, 36, 86; and see Porcher, *French Miniatures*, p. 41.

21. For some examples of Moses in Mosan art, see Hanns Swarzenski, *Monuments of Romanesque Art* (1st ed. 1954; Chicago: University of Chicago Press, 1967), Moses with the tablets of the Law (a bronze cast from the Lorraine) fig. 537; Moses as shown on the Foot of the Cross of Saint-Bertin, figs. 397, 399.

22. For a description of the manuscript see Millar, *English Illuminated Manuscripts*, p. 46, who describes its style as that of the end of the twelfth cen-

tury; see also Nordenfalk, *Romanesque Painting*, p. 117, and see Rickert, *Painting in Britain*, pp. 108–109.

23. See Boase, *English Art*, p. 285.

24. See O. Elfrida Saunders, *A History of English Art in the Middle Ages* (Oxford: Clarendon Press, 1932), pp. 90–91. There is a fascinating sculpture of horned Moses on a Norman font at Southrop (Gloucestershire), not precisely dated, but generally described as late twelfth century. For a reproduction see M. D. Anderson, *The Imagery of British Churches* (London: John Murray, 1955), Figure 3; for comments on the dating see M. D. Anderson, *Drama and Imagery in British Churches* (Cambridge: Cambridge University Press, 1963), p. 81, and also, Francis Bond, *Fonts and Font Covers* (London, New York and Toronto: Henry Frowde, 1908), pp. ix, 157, 181. See also Lawrence Stone, *Sculpture in Britain: the Middle Ages* (Baltimore: Penguin Books, 1955), p. 89, who dates the font in the 1170's.

25. Presumably from Gloucester, and dated by Rickert, *Painting in Britain*, p. 112; see also Francis Wormald's comments in "The Development of English Illumination," p. 47.

26. See Meta Harrsen, *Cursus Sanctae Mariae* (New York: Pierpont Morgan Library, 1937), title page, and see p. 7 for dating.

27. John Plummer, *Liturgical Manuscripts* (New York: Pierpont Morgan Library, 1964), p. 45.

28. See Harrsen, *Cursus Sanctae Mariae*, p. 27; and see Harrsen, *Central European Manuscripts in the Pierpont Morgan Library* (New York, 1958), p. 34.

29. Pächt, *St. Albans Psalter*, p. 66.

30. *Ibid.*, p. 67.

31. Joseph Gantner, *Kunstgeschichte der Schweiz von den anfängen bis zum beginn des Jahrhunderts*, Vol. II (Frauenfeld, 1947), fig. 150, p. 189; and see pp. 186–199 for a description of the portal and program.

32. See Y. Delaporte, *Les vitraux de la cathédral de Chartres*, 4 vols. (Chartres: Houvet, 1926), text vol., pp. 5–18.

33. These have been dated ca. 1243–1248, see Marcel Aubert, Louis Grodecki, Jean Lafond, and Jean Verrier, *Les vitraux de Notre-Dame et de la Sainte-Chapelle de Paris* [Corpus Vitrearum Medii Aevi] (Paris: Le comité international d'histoire de l'art, 1959), pls. 19, 25, 31, and color pl. II.

34. This part of Notre-Dame of Paris has been dated ca. 1250, *ibid.*, p. 35.

35. Reproduced in Émile Mâle, *The Gothic Image*, trans. Dora Nussey (1st ed. 1913; New York: Harper Torchbooks, 1958), fig. 79, p. 145.

36. See Jacques Dupont, *Gothic Painting* (Geneva: Skira, 1954), p. 27 and see pp. 28, 29 for color reproductions of some of the folios; see also Porcher, *French Miniatures*, p. 48.

37. Porcher, *French Miniatures*, p. 45.

38. This may have been done by Hugues de Saint-Cher, a Dominican who died in 1262, see *ibid.*

39. This copy has been reproduced in Alexandre comte de Laborde, *La Bible moralisée illustrée,* 5 vols. (Paris, 1911–1927).

40. Oxford Bodl. 270b, and see also fol. 7ᵛ of Bibl. Nat. lat. 11560 and fol. 120ᵛ of Br. Mus. Harley 1527.

41. Oxford Bodl. 270b; and see fol. 41ʳ of Br. Mus. Harley 1527.

42. Oxford Bodl. 270b.

43. Oxford Bodl. 270b; and see also fols. 40ʳ, 73ᵛ, 74ʳ, 105ᵛ. See also fols. 150ʳ of Bibl. Nat. Lat. 11560; and see fols. 32ᵛ, 112ᵛ, 151ᵛ of Br. Mus. Harley 1527. Moses is horned as well in some of the other copies of the *Bible moralisée*; see Laborde, *La Bible moralisée,* pls. 635, 660, 668. Moses with a halo, but no horns, can be found on fol. 194ʳ of Vienna Bibl. Impérial, cod. 1179, pl. 690 of Laborde.

44. Mark 9:1–12; Matthew 17:1–13; Luke 9:28–36.

45. See Laborde. *La Bible moralisée,* vol. 3, pl. 503.

46. See J. A. Herbert, "A Psalter in the British Museum (Royal MS I.D.X.) Illuminated in England early in the Thirteenth Century," *The Walpole Society,* III (1913–1914), 47–56.

47. See Louis Grodecki, *Chartres* (Paris: Draeger et Verve, 1963), picture opposite p. 28. See also two examples of this in Mosan art, Swarzenski, *Monuments,* figs, 389, 390.

48. See Erwin Panofsky, *Early Netherlandish Painting,* 2 vols. (Cambridge: Harvard University Press, 1953), p. 140.

49. For other examples see Eric G. Millar, *An Illuminated Manuscript of La Somme le Roy* (Oxford: Roxburghe Club, 1953), fol. 1ᵛ of Br. Mus. Add. MS 28162 on pl. XXVII; fol. Aᵛ of Bibl. Mazarine MS 870 on pl. XXIII. All date ca. 1295.

50. See p. 128.

51. Part of the H. P. Kraus collection, New York.

52. This Bible was written by Johannes Poncii, and the style of decoration seems to be mostly French. See George Warner, *Descriptive Catalogue of Illuminated Manuscripts in the Library of C. W. Dyson Perrins,* 2 vols. (Oxford: Oxford University Press, 1920), pp. 262–265; see also T. J. Brown, G. M. Meredith-Owens, and D. H. Turner, "Manuscripts from the Dyson Perrins Collection," *British Museum Quarterly,* XXIII (1961), 33-34.

53. George Warner, *Queen Mary's Psalter* (London: Trustees of the British Museum, 1912), pls. 45, 47, 48.

54. See W. O. Hassall, *The Holkham Bible Picture Book* (London: Dropmore Press, 1954) where all of the folios have been reproduced.

55. Rickert, *Painting in Britain,* pp. 168–169.

56. Curt H. Weigelt, *Giotto des Meisters Gemälde* (Stuttgart: Deutsche ver-lags-anstalt, 1925), pl. 96.

57. See Henrik Cornell, *Biblia Pauperum* (Stockholm: [Thule-tryck], 1925); Gerhard Schmidt, *Die Armenbibeln des XIV. Jahrhunderts* (Graz-Köln: Böhlaus Nachf., 1959), an extremely important and thorough study; Franz Unterkircher and Gerhard Schmidt, *Die Wiener Biblia Pauperum Codex Vindobonensis 1198*, 3 vols. (Graz, Wien, Köln: Verlag Styria [1962]); and for a concise summary of the recent studies on the *Biblia Pauperum*, see *Biblia Pauperum, The Estergom Blockbook of Forty Leaves*, introd. and notes by Elizabeth Soltész (Budapest: Corvina Press, 1967).

58. See *Speculum Humanae Salvationis*, texte critique, traduction inédite de Jean Mielot (1448), ed. J. Lutz and P. Perdrizet (Mulhouse: E. Meininger, 1907–09); Edgar Breitenbach, *Speculum Humane Salvationis*, eine typen-geschictliche untersuchung [Studien zur Deutschen Kunstgeschichte, Heft 272] (Strassburg, 1930); *The Miroure of Mans Saluacionne*, a fifteenth-century English trans. of the *Speculum Humanae Salvationis*, printed from a manuscript in the possession of Alfred Henry Huth (London: [privately printed], 1888).

59. See p. 66.

60. Schmidt, *Die Armenbibeln*, p. 87.

61. *The Estergom Blockbook*, p. v.

62. Schmidt, *Die Armenbibeln*, pp. 5–7.

63. *The Estergom Blockbook*, pp. vi-vii.

64. *Ibid.*

65. See pp. 68–69.

66. See Unterkircher and Schmidt, *Die Wiener Biblia Pauperum*, Abb. 5, which is fol. 1ᵛ of Bayerische Staatsbibl. Cod. lat. 23426; and see Cornell, *Biblia Pauperum*, pl. 22, which is fol. 7ʳ of the same MS, where in the upper por-tion Moses is shown with a halo; pl. 26b which is fol. 33ᵛ of Wolfenbüttel Landesbibl. Cod. 5.2. Aug. 4° (second half of the fourteenth century); pl. 27a which is fol. 1ᵛ of Weimar Grossherzogl. Bibl. Cod. Max 4 (first half of fourteenth century).

67. See Cornell, *Biblia Pauperum*, pl. 22, where in the bottom portion of fol. 7ʳ of Bayerische Staatsbibl., Cod. lat. 23426, Moses wears an early type of mitre; and see Unterkircher and Schmidt, *Die Wiener Biblia Pauperum*, bottom part of fol. 2ᵛ.

68. Unterkircher and Schmidt, *Die Wiener Biblia Pauperum*, fols. 4ʳ, 7ʳ, 9ᵛ of Codex Vindobonensis 1198, and see Abb. 4 which is fol. 1ᵛ of Bayerische Staatsbibl. Cod. lat. 4523 (first quarter of the fourteenth century); and see Cornell, *Biblia Pauperum*, pl. 23, which is fol. 1ᵛ of Berlin, Kupferstich-kabinett, 78 D.2.Hs. 121 (mid-fourteenth century).

69. Codex Vindobonensis 1198 shows only one horned Moses: fol. 3ᵛ where

horned Moses guides the Israelites through the Red Sea, as reproduced in Unterkirche and Schmidt *Die Wiener Biblia Pauperum*; see also Cornell, *Biblia Pauperum*, pl. 23, where on fol. 2ᵛ of Berlin Kupferstichkabinett, 78 D.2. Hs. 121, Moses is depicted with gigantic horns as he stands before the Golden Calf.

70. Cornell, *Biblia Pauperum*, p. 89.

71. *Ibid.*, see pls. 30, 35, 39, and 44.

72. This was written in 1324 by a German, Ludolphe, who became prior of the Dominicans of Strasbourg, see Louis Gillet; *Histoire artistique des ordres mendicants* (Paris: Laurens, 1912), p. 161.

73. See p. 72.

74. *The Estergom Blockbook*, p. viii.

75. For a facsimile edition, see *Biblia Pauperum—Deutsche Ausgabe von 1471* (Weimar: Gesellschaft der bibliophilen, 1906).

76. The iconographic importance and influence of the *Biblia Pauperum* and the *Speculum Humanae Salvationis* has been outlined by Émile Mâle, *L'art religieux de la fin du moyen-âge*, (Paris: Librairie Armand Colin, 1931), pp. 232-246, and see p. 292.

77. See Henri David, *Claus Sluter* (Paris: Éditions Pierre Tisné, 1951), text pp. 81–106 re the Puits de Moïse, especially pp. 96–97; and for reproductions of all the sculptures, see pls. 18–21.

78. See p. 64.

79. See Henry Martin, *La miniature française, XIIIᵉ au XIVᵉ siècle* (Paris and Brussels: Van Oest, 1924), p. 95 for bib.; and see Henry Martin and Philippe Lauer, *Les principaux manuscrits à peintures de la Bibliothèque de l'Arsenal à Paris* (Paris, 1929), pp. 28–29.

80. In the Prado, Madrid.

81. See Otto H. Förster, *Stefan Lochner ein Maler zu Köln* (Köln: Prestel, 1941), pl. 24 and detail on pl. 53.

82. See John Pope-Hennessy, *Fra Angelico* (London: Phaidon Press, 1952), pl. 93, and a color detail of it.

83. See Paul Adolf Oppé, *Raphael* (London: Methuen, 1909), for a reproduction, pl. CXCI.

84. See Karl Künstle, *Ikonographie der Christlichen Kunst*, 2 vols. (Freiburg im Breisgau: Herder, 1928), vol. 1, fig. 117, p. 291.

85. All of these frescoes are now in the Brera Gallery, Milan. See Angela Ottino della Chiesa, *Bernadino Luini* (Novara: Instituto geografico de Agostini, 1956), pp. 98–101 for a description.

86. These frescoes are in the Church of Santa Maria dei Miracoli in Saronno. For reproductions see della Chiesa, *Bernadino Luini*, fig. 148, and an enlarged detail, fig. 151.

87. Now in Venice, Accademia.

88. In the Kaiser-Friedrich Museum, Berlin.

89. See *Illustrations for the Bible by Marc Chagall*, appreciation by Meyer Schapiro (New York: Harcourt, Brace, 1956), pl. 31; for other types, see pls. 27, 28, 29, 30, 33, 34, 37, 39, 41.

90. Etrog studied art in Romania, then went to Israel and continued his work there; in 1958 he went to New York, and is presently in Canada. See W. J. Withrow, "Sorel Etrog," *Canadian Art*, no. 97 (May/June, 1965), pp. 20-22.

CHAPTER VII

1. See *Oxford English Dictionary* (Oxford: Clarendon Press, 1961), under *horn*, no. 8; See *Encyclopaedia of Religion and Ethics*, ed. James Hastings (1st imp. 1913; 4th imp., Edinburg: T. and T. Clark; New York: Schribner's, 1959), under *horns (Biblical)*; see *Dictionary of the Bible*, ed. William Smith, 2 vols. (2d. ed.; Boston: Little, Brown, 1861), vol. 1, under *horn, II. Metaphorical*; see *The Westminster Dictionary of the Bible*, ed. John D. Davis, rev. by Henry S. Gehman (5th ed.; Philadelphia: Westminster Press, 1944), under *horn*; and see *Harper's Bible Dictionary*, ed. Madeleine S. Miller and J. Lane Miller (6th ed.; New York: Harper, 1959), under *horn*.

2. Biblical quotes, unless otherwise noted, are taken from an English version of the Catholic Vulgate Bible: *The Holy Bible translated from the Latin Vulgate*, Douay version of 1609 (Los Angeles, 1914).

3. The Authorized Version refers to them as horns of unicorns.

4. See pp. 3–5.

5. See quote from Jerome's *Commentary on Amos*, p. 78, where Jerome alludes to the Aquila edition. The Aquila was a Greek version of the Old Testament written by a proselyte to Judaism in the second century, probably ca. 140, and was extremely literal, see *Oxford Dictionary of the Christian Church*, ed F. L. Cross (London: Oxford University Press, 1958), under *Aquila*.

6. See Beryl Smalley, *The Study of the Bible in the Middle Ages*, (repr. of 2d ed., 1952; Notre Dame, Ind.: University of Notre Dame Press, 1964), pp. 20–23.

7. The mistaken idea that Jerome truly believed that Moses descended from Sinai with solid horns has been passed down to this era: Frederick Thomas Elworthy in his book, *Horns of Honour* (London: John Murray, 1900), p. 23, argues that Jerome believed in actual horns for Moses. Note Elworthy's further confusion: He mistakenly ascribes the horning of Moses to the Jews—thinking that after their deliverance from Egypt, freshly familiar with the horns upon the heads of the Egyptian gods, they put horns on

Moses, see p. 22. Elworthy, like others, was unaware of the very late appearance of the motif in art.

8. S. Hieronymi Presbyteri Opera, *Commentariorum in Hiezechielem*, in *Corpus Christianorum*, Series Latina, LXXV (Turnholti: Typographi Brepols Editores Pontificii, 1964), p. 557, lines 262–264.

9. Translation based on Jacques Paul Migne, *Patrologiae cursus completus*, series Latina (Paris, 1844–1864), vol. 25, col. 1067 (hereafter cited as *Pat. Lat.*).

10. As in Psalm 17:3.

11. Translation here is by Sister Marie Liguori Ewald, in *The Homilies of Saint Jerome*, vol. 1 of *The Fathers of the Church* (Washington: Catholic University of America Press, 1964), pp. 170, 171. The metaphorical meanings of horn are similarly elaborated on by Jerome in his Homily on psalm 97, *ibid.*, pp. 200–201:

> "In Scripture, the horn properly signifies kingship and power just as it is written: 'He has raised up a horn of salvation for us,' and in another place: 'Our foes through you we struck down with a horn.' See, then, what the psalmist means here? Have two trumpets, one of silver and one of horn: the silver for speech, and the horn for strength.
>
> "Would you have proof that the horn is used always in a favorable sense? . . . We, therefore, as long as we have a horn, are worthy to be dedicated holocausts of God, but if our horn has been broken, we are like feeble men and cannot enter the priesthood of God."

12. Speaking of Jerome, Smalley, *Study of the Bible*, p. 21, says: "As a Hebrew scholar and humanist he brought the Bible closer to the Latin-speaking world. The Old Latin was an unliterary translation from the Septuagint; the Vulgate was based on the 'Hebrew Truth' as St. Jerome lovingly calls it." The Old Latin version of the Old Testament appears to be of little importance as compared with the New Testament. In the former it is only a version of a version, being made from the Septuagint; in the latter it is one of the earliest translations of the original Greek which we possess; see Frederic Kenyon, *Our Bible and the Ancient Manuscripts* (4th ed. rev.; London: Eyre and Spottiswoode, 1939), p. 83.

13. See James Strachan, *Early Bible Illustrations* (Cambridge: Cambridge University Press, 1957), p. 14, where he says: "It was not until the Geneva version of 1560 that Moses' irrational horns were withdrawn from English Bibles."

14. Speaking of the Vulgate, Kenyon, *Our Bible*, p. 85, has said: "Its historical importance is enormous, especially for the churches of Western Europe; for as we shall see in the progress of our story, it was the Bible of these Churches, including our own Church of England, until the time of the Reformation"; and see also H. Wheeler Robinson, ed., *The Bible in Its*

Ancient and English Versions (Oxford: Clarendon Press, 1940), p. 117.

15. See p. 77.

16. For some nineteenth- and twentieth-century assessments of Moses' veil (and his countenance), see George Rawlinson, *Moses: His life and Times* (London: James Nisbet, 1887); Hugo Gressman, *Moses und seine Zeit* (Göttingen: Vandenhoeck and Ruprecht, 1913), pp. 246–251; Julian Morgenstern, "Moses with the Shining Face," *Hebrew Union College Annual*, II (1925), 1–27; Bernardus Dirk Eerdmans, *The Covenant at Mount Sinai viewed in the Light of Antique Thought* (Leiden: Burgersdijk and Niermans, 1939), p. 22; and see Martin Noth, *Exodus—a Commentary*, trans. J. S. Bowden (Philadelphia: Westminster Press, 1962), p. 267.

17. This concept will be discussed further in chap. x.

18. See also Mark 9:1–12 and Luke 9:28–36. And see p. 70.

19. See Jacques Migne, *Patrologiae cursus completus*, series Graeco-Latina (Paris, 1857–1902), vol. 11, Homily XII, cols. 382–387.

20. *Ibid.*, col. 382.

21. I am indebted to Meyer Schapiro for calling my attention to Gildas and this fascinating early reference to horned Moses. Gildas's *De Excidio et Conquestu Britanniae* was probably written between 516 and 547; see James F. Kenney, *The Sources for the Early History of Ireland* (New York: Columbia University Press, 1929), p. 151.

22. C. E. Stevens, "Gildas Sapiens," *English Historical Review*, LVI (1941), 353–373.

23. Stevens has described the second part as "almost unreadable," *ibid.*, p. 353.

24. From Gildas's *De Excidio et Conquestu Britanniae*, in *Monumenta Germaniae Historica*, Auctores Antiquissimi, XIII (1896), 65.

25. Trans. from John A. Giles, *Old English Chronicles* (London: Bell, 1908), p. 348.

26. See C. E. Stevens in his article on Gildas in *Encyclopaedia Britannica*, 1966 ed., under *Gildas*.

27. See *Oxford Dictionary of the Christian Church*, under *Gildas* for some bibliography; see also, Kenney, *Sources for the Early History of Ireland*, pp. 150–151.

28. See Kenney, *Sources for the Early History of Ireland*, p. 627.

29. *Pat. Lat.* vol. 83, cols. 309–310.

30. See p. 80.

31. See p. 98.

32. *Pat. Lat.*, vol. 91, col. 332.

33. *Ibid.*, vol. 108, col. 239.

34. As translated in *Pentateuch with Targum Onkelos, Haphtaroth and Rashi's Commentary*, trans. M. Rosenbaum and A. M. Silbermann (New York: Hebrew Publishing, [1935]), p. 196; see also a similar translation that

reads: "for the light glistened and projected like a horn," in *The Pentateuch and Rashi's Commentary*, a linear translation by Abraham Ben Isaiah and Benjamin Sharfman (Brooklyn, N. Y.: Jewish Publication Society of Philadelphia, 1949), p. 436.

E. G. Suhr, in "The Horned Moses," *Folklore, 74* (1963), 387–395, has attempted to rationalize the "shining" and the "horned" by ascribing to "horned" a quality of the skin like that which Siegfried is said to have received after slaying the dragon Fafnir; see *Das Nibelungenlied*, ed. Karl Bartsch (Wiesbaden, 1956), p. 22. It is an interesting approach, but does not in any way help to solve the basic problem of the appearance of the horns in art, nor what they meant to medieval men.

35. Herman Hailperin, *Rashi and the Christian Scholars* (Pittsburgh: University of Pittsburgh Press, 1963), p. 25.

36. *Ibid.*, p. 104. Rashi's influence went beyond that of medieval exegesis, affecting later Latin translations, as well as translations into vernacular tongues in the sixteenth and seventeenth centuries; see Erwin I. J. Rosenthal, "Rashi and the English Bible," *Bulletin of the John Rylands Library*, XXIV (1940), 138–167.

37. Rosenthal, "Rashi and the English Bible," pp. 138–167.

38. *Ibid.*

39. *Ibid.*, pp. 105–134; and see Smalley, *Study of the Bible*, p. 190.

40. *Pat. Lat.*, vol. 198, col. 1192.

41. Hailperin, *Rashi*, p. 111.

42. *Ibid.* See also Esra Shereshevsky, "Hebrew Traditions in Peter Comestor's Historia Scholastica," *The Jewish Quarterly Review*, LIX (April, 1969), 268–289, who indicates many specific correspondences between Rashi and Comestor.

43. Smalley, *Study of the Bible*, p. 179.

44. *Ibid.*, chap. iv, esp. pp. 149–185.

45. *Ibid.*, pp. 178–179.

46. *Ibid.*, p. 355, says, "But already it is plain that Lyre represents the culmination of a movement for the study of Hebrew and rabbinics."

47. Hailperin, *Rashi*, p. 138.

48. *Oxford Dictionary of the Christian Church*, under *Nicolas of Lyra*.

49. *Biblia Latina* [cum postillis Nicolai de Lyra et expositionibus Guillelmi Britonis in omnes prologos S. Hieronymi et additionibus Pauli Burgensis replicisque Matthiae Doering] Venice. [Bonetus Locatellus, for Octavianus Scotus, Aug. 8, 1489], see Exod. 34.

50. Translation based on the *Biblia Latina*, see n. 49 above.

51. *Ibid.*

52. *Oxford Dictionary of the Christian Church*, under *Dionysius the Carthusian*.

53. *Denis le Chartreux, Doctoris ecstatici, Dionysii Cartusiani opera omnia,* favente pont. max. Leone XIII, II (Monstrolii: typis cartusiae, 1896–1935), 119–120.

54. Translation based on Cornelius van den Steen, called Cornelius à Lapide, *Commentaria in Scripturam Sacram,* editio nova (Paris: Vivés, 1868–1880), I, under *Ex. 34:29,* p. 746.

55. *Ibid.,* p. 747.

56. *Ibid.,* p. 746.

57. Quoted from, *The Holy Bible containing the Old and New Testaments, with Apocryphal Books, in the earliest English versions made from the Latin Vulgate by John Wycliffe and his Followers,* ed. Josiah Forshall and Frederic Madden (Oxford: Oxford University Press, 1850), p. 277, right column; for another phrasing see same page, left column.

58. As quoted in Strachan, *Early Bible Illustrations,* p. 14.

59. Thomas Godwyn, *Moses and Aaron, Civil and Ecclesiastical Rites Used by the Ancient Hebrews,* (1st ed. probably 1624; 12th ed., London, 1672), p. 158. The "p" in the above quote is Godwyn's reference to his marginal note where he directly alludes to Ra. Sa., who is Rashi.

60. On Adam see A. Wilmart, "Magister Adam Cartusiensis," *Mélanges Mandonnet,* II (Paris, 1930), 145–161; "Maitre Adam chanoine prémontré devenu chartreux à Witham," *Analecta Praemonstratensia,* IX (1933), 207–232; Smalley, *Study of the Bible,* pp. 180–181; Adam of Eynsham, *The Life of St. Hugh of Lincoln,* ed. Decima L. Douie and Hugh Farmer, 2 vols. (London, New York: Thomas Nelson, 1961), 2: 52–54; James Bulloch, *Adam of Dryburgh* (London: Church Historical Society, 1958).

61. For the Latin see *Pat. Lat.,* vol. 198, cols, 774–775.

62. Smalley, *Study of the Bible,* p. 181.

63. Cf. Comestor, see p. 85.

64. Smalley, *Study of the Bible,* p. 180.

65. Bulloch, *Adam of Dryburgh,* p. 1.

66. The difficulties that beset even the specialist are outlined by Smalley in her introduction, see pp. xi–xxii.

67. Smalley, *Study of the Bible,* p. xii. Furthermore, it is indeed possible that I have overlooked something of importance in print.

68. Adam of Eynsham, *The Life of St. Hugh of Lincoln,* 2:52–54.

69. The *double* grouping of rays as a rationalization for two horns contrasts with the Byzantine type as seen in the eleventh- and twelfth-century Octateuchs (fig. 7).

70. John A. Asher in his recent article in the *Encyclopaedia Britannica,* 1966 ed., says that there are over eighty extant manuscripts and manuscript fragments of this text; see under *Rudolf von Ems.*

71. See the introduction in Gustav Ehrismann, *Rudolfs von Ems Weltchronik* [Deutsche Texte des Mittelalter] (Berlin: Weidmann, 1915).

72. See Ehrismann for the German, *ibid.*, p. 170.

73. Compare Rudolf with Comestor; see Comestor's commentary, p. 85. For some recent thorough studies of Rudolf's poetry (with extensive bibliographies) see: Xenja von Ertzdorff, *Rudolf von Ems: Untersuchung zum höfischen Roman im 13. Jahrhundert* (Munich: Fink, 1967); and Helmut Brackert, *Rudolf von Ems: Dichtung und Geschichte* (Heidelberg: Carl Winter, 1968).

74. See Joseph Gantner, *Kunstgeschichte der Schweiz von den anfängen bis zum beginn des Jahrhunderts*, II (Frauenfeld, 1947), 241; see also Alfred Stange, *Deutsche Malerei der Gotik*, 8 vols. (Berlin: Deutscher kunstverlag, 1934–1938) 1:5; and see Erich Petzet, "Eine Prachthandschrift der Weltchronik des Rudolf von Ems," *Germanische-romanische Monatsschrift*, I (1909), 471, who dated it a little later. See also Joseph Gutmann's comments on the depiction of Moses in this manuscript in his review of Carl-Otto Nordström's book, *The Duke of Alba's Castillian Bible, Art Bulletin* LI (1969), 94.

75. See the extensive article on this MS by Konrad Escher, "Die Bilderhandschrift der Weltchronik des Rudolf von Ems in der Zentralbibliothek Zürich," *Mitteilungen der Antiquarischen Gesellschaft in Zürich*, vol. XXXI, pt. 4 (1935), pp. 5–43; and see Ganter, *Kunstgeschichte der Schweiz*, p. 240.

76. The upper half of this folio is quite interesting; it follows the text describing how Moses saw the back of God's head and neck; see Ehrismann, *Weltchronik*, p. 170. Radial horns were not always used in illustrations of the *Weltchronik*; occasionally Moses was simply given the usual two horns, see fig. D 152 in *Synagoga, Kultgeräte und Kunstwerke* [catalog], Städtische Kunsthalle Recklinghausen, Nov. 30, 1960–Jan. 15, 1961.

77. Émile Mâle, *The Gothic Image*, trans. Dora Nussey (1st ed., 1913; New York: Harper Torchbooks, 1958), pp. 392–396.

78. *Ibid.*, p. 393.

CHAPTER VIII

1. See Durandus's prayer, p. 98.

2. See Joseph Braun, *Die Liturgische Gewandung im Occident und Orient* (Freiburg im Breisgau: Herder, 1907), p. 437; and see Braun's article on the mitre in *The Catholic Encyclopedia*, 15 vols. (New York: Robert Appleton, 1907–1912), 10:405; see *Oxford Dictionary of the Christian Church*, ed. F. L. Cross (London: Oxford University Press, 1958), under *mitre*; and

see *Lexicon für Theologie und Kirche*, 10 vols. (Freiburg im Breisgau: Herder, 1957–1965), vol. 7 (1962), under *mitra*.

3. Braun, *Die Liturgische Gewandung*, p. 437.

4. See J. Deshusses' article on the mitre in the *Dictionnaire de droit canonique*, ed. R. Naz (Paris: Librairie Letouzey, 1957), vol. 6, under *mitre*, where he says, "Son origine historique est assez obscure. Telle que nous la connaissons, elle apparait vers le XI⁰ s."

5. Archdale A. King, *Liturgy of the Roman Church* (London, New York, and Toronto: Longmans, Green, 1957), p. 139.

6. Eduard Eichmann, *Weihe und Kronung des Papstes im Mittelalter* (Munich: Zink, 1951), p. 26.

7. *Ibid.*, p. 27.

8. *Ibid.*, pp. 29–31.

9. King, *Liturgy of the Roman Church*, p. 140; see also Braun, *Die Liturgische Gewandung*, p. 447; and see *Enciclopedia Cattolica*, 12 vols. (The Vatican, 1948–1954), vol. 8 (1952), under *mitra*. And for additional details on the later development and use of the mitre see P. Philipp Hofmeister, *Mitra und Stab der wirklichen Prälaten ohne bischöflichen Charakter* (1st ed., 1928; reprint; Amsterdam: Schippers, 1962), especially pp. 3–7; and see Pierre Salmon, *Mitra und Stab* (Mainz, 1960), a German translation of the *Étude sur les insignes du pontife dans le rit romain* (Rome, 1955), pp. 24–32; for a study dealing with the development of bishops' insignia during the early period of Christianity (though not related to our problem of the mitre), see Theodore Klauser, *Der Ursprung der bischöflichen Insignien und Ehrenrechte*, 1st pub. 1948 in *Bonner Akademische Reden* (Krefeld: Scherpe, 1953).

10. See Braun, *Catholic Encyclopedia*, p. 405; see *Enciclopedia Cattolica*, vol. 8, under *mitra* for a photographic reproduction of a conical shaped mitre taken of a folio from the Exultet roll of the cathedral at Bari, Italy.

11. Braun, *Die Liturgische Gewandung*, p. 459.

12. Perhaps it is of some significance that the general usage of the mitre on bishops' seals appears earlier in England and France than elsewhere, as noted by Braun, *Die Liturgische Gewandung*, p. 451.

13. See Braun, *Catholic Encyclopedia*, under *mitre*; and see King, *Liturgy of the Roman Church*, p. 143, who says "The depression and 'puff' on either side were caused by pressing the hand on the top, as it was put on." See King also for a brief history of the early use of the mitre, especially chap. 13: "Pontificalia," pp. 39 ff.

14. Braun, *Die Liturgische Gewandung*, p. 467.

15. *Ibid.*, p. 463.

16. *Ibid.*, p. 464.

17. See also the English seals illustrated in C. H. Hunter Blair, "Medieval Seals

of the Bishops of Durham," *Archaeologia*, LXXII (1922), 1–24, especially pl. I.

18. Braun, *Die Liturgische Gewandung*, p. 719.

19. Based on *Pat. Lat.*, vol. 177, col. 405.

20. *Ibid.*, vol. 205, col. 139.

21. *Ibid.*, vol. 217, col. 796.

22. See pp. 83–84.

23. See p. 83.

24. See *Oxford Dictionary of the Christian Church*, under *Durandus, William*; see also Lancelot C. Sheppard, *The Liturgical Books* (New York: Hawthorn, 1962), pp. 70 ff; and see also, V. Leroquais, *Les pontificaux manuscrits des bibliothèques publiques de France*, 3 vols. (Paris, 1937), LXXXII–XCIII.

25. This is the Latin as given to me in 1964 by Father Gelb, secretary to Cardinal McIntyre, Archbishop of Los Angeles. It is almost identical with the prayer of the Middle Ages. Compare the one in Michel Andrieu, *Le pontifical romain au moyen-âge*, 4 vols. *(Città del Vaticano: Biblioteca apostoliaca vaticana, 1938–1941), 3:389.*

26. Braun, *Die Liturgische Gewandung*, p. 486, suggests that the ceremony of giving over the mitre to the newly consecrated bishop must have been formed at the latest in the course of the twelfth century.

27. *Ibid.*

28. Leroquais, *Pontificaux manuscrits*, says, "Le premier qui en parle est le pontifical d'Avranches: 'Hic imponatur capiti eius mitra,' (Bibl. Nat. MS lat. 14832, fol. 62)," p. xci.

29. *Ibid.*

30. Sheppard, *Liturgical Books*, p. 70.

31. *Ibid.*

32. At least as of 1964.

33. This folio and its significance as testimony to an early ceremony for the imposition of the mitre have not, to my knowledge, been previously pointed out in the literature.

34. This translation by T. H. Passmore, *The Sacred Vestments* (an English rendering of the third book of the *Rationale Divinorum Officiorum* of Durandus, Bishop of Mende) (London: Sampson Low, Marston, 1899), pp. 94, 95. See also, the translation by A. Welby Pugin, *Glossary of Ecclesiastical Ornament and Costume* (London: Bohn, 1844), pp. 160, 161.

35. Based on [Denis le Chartreux, Doctoris ecstatici], *Dionysii cartusiani opera omnia*, favente pont. max. Leone XIII (Monstrolii: typis cartusiae, 1896–1935), 2:121.

36. I am indebted to Robert Brentano for this important reference. See Hugh the Chantor, *The History of the Church of York (1066–1127)*, trans.

Charles Johnson (London: Thomas Nelson, 1961). This is an excellent English translation with the Latin text printed on parallel pages.

37. Hugh the Chantor, *The History of the Church of York*, p. 49.

38. *Ibid.*, p. 50.

39. *Ibid.*

40. *Ibid.*

41. Habakkuk 3:4 (Vulgate). The horns are still part of the Authorized Version of the Bible of 1611. They were removed with the later Revised Version.

42. Apocalypse 12:3–4 (Vulgate).

43. Psalm 74:11 (Vulgate), and cf. Jerome, p. 78.

44. See chap. x of this study with reference to the ambiguous meaning of horns.

45. Nigel de Longchamps, *Speculum Stultorum*, ed. John H. Mozley and Robert R. Raymo (Berkeley and Los Angeles: University of California Press, 1960), p. 68.

46. Nigel Longchamp, *A Mirror for Fools*, trans. J. H. Mozley (Notre Dame, Ind.: University of Notre Dame Press, 1963), p. 56.

47. Nigel de Longchamps, *Speculum Stultorum*, p. 69.

48. Nigel Longchamp, *A Mirror for Fools*, p. 57.

49. See *The Pontifical of Egbert, Archbishop of York*, A.D. 732–736, ed. W. Greenwell (London: Surtees Society, 1853), pp. 2, 3, 4; see also Dorothy Bethurum, *The Homilies of Wulfstan* (Oxford: Clarendon Press, 1957), p. 353, nn. 21–25; and see her notes on Homily XVII, p. 351.

50. Bethurum, *Homilies of Wulfstan*, pp. 242–243.

51. Eadmer (writing some time in the last decade of the eleventh century) described the consecration of Anselm as Archbishop of Canterbury (1093), mentioning that a copy of the gospels was opened by the bishops over Anselm's head, but saying nothing about any of the episcopal vestments, Eadmer, *History of Recent Events in England*, trans. Geoffrey Bosanquet (London: Cresset Press, 1964), pp. 42–44.

52. Erwin R. Goodenough, *Jewish Symbols in the Greco-Roman Period*, 12 vols. (New York: Pantheon, 1953–1965), vol. 11, fig. 237.

53. Emile Mâle, *The Gothic Image*, trans. Dora Nussey (1st ed. 1913; New York: Harper Torchbooks, 1958), fig. 120, p. 241. The use of the side-horned bishop's mitre to depict the Jewish high priest's mitre is often found later too in Renaissance and post-Renaissance art, e.g., the high priest is so sculptured on the chancel screen (begun in 1514) inside Chartres, and the high priest is so represented in two frescoes by Guadenzio Ferrari, now in the Brera Gallery in Milan. And see Joseph Braun, *Tracht und Attribute der Heiligen in der Deutschen Kunst* (Stuttgart: Metzler, 1943), p. 762.

54. Passmore, *The Sacred Vestments*, p. 161.
55. *Ibid.*, p. 154; cf. the passage in Exod. 28:39.
56. Passmore, *The Sacred Vestments*, p. 177.
57. James Strachan, *Early Bible Illustrations* (Cambridge: Cambridge University Press, 1957), p. 18.
58. Bernardino Luini (1480–1532) so represents the Jewish high priest in "The Presentation of Mary to the Temple" (now in the Brera Gallery, Milan).
59. Strachan, *Early Bible Illustrations*, fig. 67.
60. See Theodor Ehrenstein, *Das alte Testament im Bilde* (Vienna: Kende, 1923), fig. 57, p. 465.
61. This has not to our knowledge been previously pointed out in the literature.
62. See p. 111.

CHAPTER IX

1. See chap. vii.
2. See p. 26.
3. See *The Story of Genesis and Exodus, an early English Song, about* A.D. *1250*, ed. Richard Morris (London: Early English Text Society, 1895), Line 3614, p. 103, and see note re line 3614 on p. 166.
4. See p. 85.
5. See J. J. Lamberts, "The Noah Story in the Cursor Mundi," *Medieval Studies*, XXIV (1962), 232, who stresses the popularity of this text by reason of the many times it was recopied; see also *The Cambridge History of English Literature*, ed. A. W. Ward and A. R. Waller, 15 vols. (Cambridge: Cambridge University Press 1963), 1:226.
6. *The Oxford Companion to English Literature*, ed. Paul Harvey, (3d ed.; Oxford: Clarendon Press, 1946), under *Cursor Mundi*.
7. *Cursor Mundi* (*The Cursur o the World*), ed. Richard Morris (London: Early English Text Society, 1874–1892), 1:21, 22, lines 233–240.
8. *Ibid.*, lines 240–264.
9. See the other three versions in the *Cursor Mundi*, 1:384, 385, lines 6655–6658.
10. *Cambridge History of English Literature*, 2:343.
11. *Ibid.*, and see *Oxford Companion to English Literature*, under *Cursor Mundi*.
12. *Cambridge History of English Literature*, 2:343.
13. See pp. 91–92.
14. See Erich Petzet, "Eine Prachthandschrift der Weltchronik des Rudolf von Ems," *Germanische-romanische Monatschrift*, I (1909), 465.
15. See p. 91.

16. A full-scale study of all the remarkable number of surviving manuscripts (beyond the scope of this book) would perhaps provide a more definitive answer.

17. Marion Lofthouse, " 'Le pèlerinage de vie humaine' by Guillaume de Deguileville," *Bulletin of the John Rylands Library*, XIX, no. 1 (Jan., 1935), 170.

18. John Lydgate, *The Pilgrimage of the Life of Man*, ed. F. J. Furnivall; introd. and notes by Katharine B. Locock (London: Early English Text Society, 1905), see p. xiii. Rosemond Tuve, in a recent study, *Allegorical Imagery* (Princeton, N. J.: Princeton University Press, 1966), pp. 145–218, has devoted an entire chapter to this single work of Guillaume. She states that it deserves this eminent place in her book since it has as its subject, "the basic allegorical theme, of which most others are variants or parts," p. 145.

19. Tuve, *Allegorical Imagery*, p. 145, argues that the first edition of the poem has merit even today; that it was the second redaction that was so verbose and faulty.

20. This has been most recently emphasized and documented by Tuve, *Allegorical Imagery*, pp. 145–151. A useful French edition was published (based on the first edition) which is helpful for comparison, see *Le pèlerinage de vie humaine*, ed. J. J. Stürzinger (London: Roxburghe Club, 1893).

21. Tuve, *Allegorical Imagery*, pp. 146–147.

22. Lofthouse, "Le pèlerinage," p. 176; and also Tuve, *Allegorical Imagery*, p. 148.

23. Tuve, *Allegorical Imagery*, pp. 149–150.

24. Lofthouse, "Le pèlerinage," p. 176.

25. Lydgate, *Pilgrimage*, p. xiii; and see Tuve, *Allegorical Imagery*, p. 149.

26. *Cambridge History of English Literature*, 2:170; and see Tuve, *Allegorical Imagery*, p. 149.

27. *The Ancient Poem of Guillaume de Guileville compared with The Pilgrim's Progress of John Bunyan*, ed. from notes by Nathaniel Hill (London: Basil Montagu Pickering, 1858). See also Lydgate, *Pilgrimage*, pp. liii; see also Lofthouse, "Le pèlerinage," p. 184; and see *Cambridge History of English Literature*, 2:200.

28. Lydgate, *Pilgrimage*, lines 1395–1399.

29. This is corroborated by Tuve, *Allegorical Imagery*, p. 158, who says: "The Lady Reason enters to give explanations and counsel, heard with profit by the Pilgrim but addressed to the interesting character who is consistently called Moses but is pictured either with the horns that traditionally identify that personage, or as a mitred Bishop. It is typical of allegory in the stricter sense, grounded as it was in a typological relationship between the Old and the New Law, that we should be expected to read this character constantly

as double, unobtrusively but insistently reminded that he is a 'vicaire of Moses or Aaron,' and that the horns of the mitre were foreshadowed in the older lawgiver's horns." See also Tuve, *Allegorical Imagery*, fig. 41, p. 159 showing another illustration of horned Moses delegating Sacraments of Extreme Unction, Oxf. Bodl. MS Douce 300 f. 5 (of the early fifteenth century).

30. Lydgate, *Pilgrimage*, lines 1429–1433. The bracketed portions are my interpolations in this quotation, and hereafter in other quotations from Lydgate's version of the poem.

31. Lydgate, *Pilgrimage*, lines 1580–1586.

32. Deguileville apparently was critical of some of the practices of certain of the Church officials and priests, see Lofthouse, "Le pèlerinage," p. 174.

33. Lydgate, *Pilgrimage*, lines 1625–1634.

34. *Ibid.*, lines 1644–1648.

35. *Ibid.*, lines 1663–1668.

36. *Ibid.*, lines 1696–1700.

37. *Ibid.*, lines 1749–1783.

38. *Ibid.*, lines 1797–1798.

39. *Ibid.*, lines 1831–1836.

40. *Ibid.*, lines 1871–1877.

41. *Ibid.*, lines 1891–1892.

42. *Ibid.*, lines 1994–2004.

43. *Ibid.*, lines 2184–2244.

44. *Ibid.*, lines 2283–2294.

45. *Ibid.*, lines 5209–5259.

46. *Ibid.*, lines 8860–8877.

47. See p. 71.

48. See pp. 71–73.

49. Melchizedek (Gen. 14:18) is a prefiguration of Christ as a king-priest. Christ is a priest after the order of Melchizedek, as king of righteousness and king of peace, and in the endlessness of his priesthood. On the other hand, the Aaronic priesthood typifies Christ's priestly work—see *The Scofield Reference Bible* (New York: Oxford University Press, 1917), Gen. 14:18.

50. Émile Mâle, *L'art religieux de la fin du moyen-âge* (Paris: Librairie Armand Colin, 1931), p. 279 where he states that fifteenth century Italy was the place of origin for the triumphal chariot of the faith (or Church) concept; see pp. 279–292 for his discussion of its use and development at the end of the Middle Ages.

51. Paul Durrieu, "Les manuscrits à peintures de la Bibliothèque de Sir Thomas Phillipps à Cheltenham," *Bibliothèque de l'école des Chartes*, 50 (1889), 400.

52. Paulin M. Paris, *Les manuscrits françois de la Bibliothèque du roi*, IV (Paris, 1841), 93–95.
53. T. H. Passmore, *The Sacred Vestments* (London: Sampson Low, Marston, 1899), p. 5.
54. *Ibid.*, p. 98.

CHAPTER X

1. John Brand, *Observations on the Popular Antiquities of Great Britain*, rev. Henry Ellis, 3 vols. (London: George Bell, 1900), under *cornutes*, pp. 181–202; see also *Oxford English Dictionary* (Oxford: Clarendon Press, 1961), under *horn*, n. 7.
2. See Maximilian Rudwin, *The Devil in Legend and Literature* (Chicago and London: Open Court, 1931), pp. 45 ff., for a description of the Devil as he developed during the Middle Ages.
3. See p. 78.
4. See p. 101.
5. John Lydgate, *The Pilgrimage of the Life of Man*, ed. F. J. Furnivall; introd. and notes by Katharine B. Locock (London: Early English Text Society, 1905), lines 1749–1783; see p. 114.
6. *Ibid.*, lines 14,336 to 14,337.
7. *Ibid.*, lines 14,191 to 14,193.
8. In the Palazzo Pubblico in Siena.
9. See Frederick Thomas Elworthy, *Horns of Honour* (London: John Murray, 1900), pp. 45–50.
10. An almost identical representation can be seen in another fourteenth-century copy of this text, see *Monumenta Judaica* [Katalog] (Köln, 1964), Abb. 16, cat. no. A–36.
11. See Henry Petersen, *Danske Adelige Sigiller* (Copenhagen, 1897), figs. 46, 69, 147, 202, 203, 223, 227, 271, 312, 411, 479, 655, 697, 888, 930.
12. See A. Thiset, *Danske Adelige Sigiller* (Copenhagen, 1905) where we find even more examples in the fifteenth and sixteenth centuries, than in the thirteenth and fourteenth centuries.
13. Wedding cupboards in the Danish National Museum in Copenhagen—as for example on a cupboard once belonging to the parents of Corfitz Ulfeldt, Chancellor Jacob Ulfeldt and Brigitte Brockenhuus who were married in 1599—include horn-crested helmets as part of the armorial bearings.
14. Beryl Smalley, *The Study of the Bible in the Middle Ages* (repr. of 2d ed., 1952; Notre Dame, Ind.: University of Notre Dame Press, 1964) p. xviii.
15. *Ibid.*, p. 25. Smalley points out that "according to the spiritual sense the

raising of Lazarus prefigures the sacrament of penance; Lazarus signifies a man in mortal sin, who repents, confesses and receives absolution"; and then tells that "an ignorant monk at St. Edmundsbury so confused the literal and spiritual senses as to teach in a sermon that *Lazarus died in mortal sin* and for that reason stank after three days."

16. Lynn White, jr., *Medieval Technology and Social Change* (Oxford: Clarendon Press, 1962), p. vii.

17. See *Monumenta Judaica* [Handbuch] (Köln, 1964), for a good brief review of the representations of Synagogue, pp. 750–755. See also Paul Weber, *Geistliches Schauspiel und Kirchliche Kunst* (Stuttgart: Neff, 1894).

18. Weber, *Geistliches Schauspiel*, p. 68; For a recent study of Synagogue see Wolfgang Seiferth, *Synagoge und Kirche im Mittelalter* (München: Kösel-Verlag, 1964).

19. The ass had both positive connotations (as the animal ridden by Jesus) and very negative ones (associated with the "stubborn" Jews) during the Middle Ages.

20. See p. 63.

21. See Louis Baillet, "Les miniatures du *Scivias* de Sainte Hildegard," *Monuments et Mémoires*, 19 (Paris, 1911), 49–149; see also Charles Singer, "Allegorical Representation of the Synagogue in a Twelfth Century Illuminated MS of Hildegard of Bingen," *The Jewish Quarterly Review*, V (1915), 267–288.

22. See Singer, "Representation of Synagogue," pp. 270–285 for the Latin and a translation.

23. London Society of Antiquaries, MS 59; see Margaret Rickert, *Painting in Britain: the Middle Ages* (Baltimore: Penguin, 1952), p. 112 for a description of this psalter.

24. George Warner, *Queen Mary's Psalter*, (London: Trustees of the British Museum, 1912), fol. 84ᵛ, pl. 147.

25. Discussed on p. 70.

26. Fol. 38ʳ of the Treasure of the Cathedral of Poitiers.

27. For a translation of canon 68 (with Latin on a parallel page), see Solomon Grayzel, *The Church and the Jews in the XIII Century*, (1st ed., 1933; New York: Hermon Press, 1966), pp. 308–309.

28. For some literature on this subject see Ulysse Robert, *Les signes d'infamie au moyen-âge* (Paris: Champion, 1891); Israel Abrahams, *Jewish Life in the Middle Ages* (London, Edward Goldston, 1932), pp. 320–323; Grayzel, *Church and Jews*, pp. 67–70; Joseph Reider, "Jews in Medieval Art," in *Essays in Antisemitism*, ed. Koppel S. Pinson (New York: Conference on Jewish Relations, 1942), pp. 51–52; Guido Kisch, *The Jews in Medieval Germany* (Chicago: University of Chicago Press, 1949), pp. 295–299, and

also Kisch, "The Yellow Badge in History," *Historia Judaica*, XIX (1957), 91–101.

29. Julius Aronius, *Regesten zur Geschichte der Juden* (Berlin: Simon, 1902), sect. no. 724, p. 302.

30. See Ioannes Dominicus Mansi, *Sacrorum Conciliorum Nova, et amplissima collectio* [facsimile copy of original ed. of 1758–1798] (Paris, 1903), vol. 23, col. 1174, that reads in part: "debent in habitu a Christianis, cornutum pileum, quem quidam . . ."

31. For abundant and varied examples of the Jewish medieval pointed hat see the many illustrations in Bernhard Blumenkranz, *Le juif médiéval au miroir de l'art chrétien* (Paris: Études Augustiniennes, 1966). See also a diagram of Jewish headdress from the thirteenth century in *The Jewish Encyclopedia* (New York-London: Funk and Wagnall, 1916), vol. 6, under *headdress*.

32. See p. 129 for one example of definite negative implications.

33. See Blumenkranz, *Le juif médiéval*, especially ch. iii, pp. 79–104; and see Hanns Swarzenski, *Die Lateinischen Illuminierten Handschriften des XIII. Jahrhunderts* (Berlin, 1936), for copious examples as in pls. 3, 26, 50; 27, 63, 68, 83, 90, 95, 115, 133, 135, 149, 169, and especially, pls. 81, 84, 98.

34. Joseph's position in medieval thought was not always a revered one; occasionally he is depicted in art and in liturgical dramas as a comic figure; see Blumenkranz, *Le juif médiéval*, pp. 117–122; and see V. A. Kolve, *The Play Called Corpus Christi* (Stanford, Calif.: Stanford University Press, 1966), pp. 248–253.

35. Discussed on p. 67.

36. See examples in Alexandre comte de Laborde, *La Bible moralisée, illustrée*, 5 vols. (Paris, 1911–1927), vol. I, pls. 34, 43, 57, 80, 95; vol. III, pls. 644, 646.

37. See Weber, *Geistliches Schauspiel*, p. 67 and fig. reproduced on p. 66; see also *Monumenta Judaica* [Handbuch], p. 752.

38. See Cecil Roth, *Essays and Portraits in Anglo-Jewish History* (Philadelphia: Jewish Publication Society of America, 1962), for a description of the members of the Norwich community, pp. 22–23.

39. *Exchequer of Receipt*, Jews' Roll, n. 87: Hilary Term, 17 Hen. III, in the Public Record Office, London.

40. See p. 127.

41. See Swarzenski, *Die Lateinischen*, fig. 516 on pl. 218.

42. *Ibid.*, fig. 520, pl. 220.

43. Stuttgart Landesbibliothek, Hist., fol. 418r.

44. Discussed on p. 129.

45. See pp. 91–92.

46. See pl. 1 in Erich Petzet, "Eine Prachthandschrift der Weltchronik des Ru-

dolf von Ems," *Germanische-romanische Monatsschrift*, vol. I (1909); and see Abb. 13 in Konrad Escher, "Die Bilderhandschrift der Weltchronik des Rudolf von Ems in der Zentralbibliothek Zürich," *Mitteilungen der Antiquarischen Gesellschaft in Zürich*, vol. XXXI, pt. 4 (1935).

47. See p. 129.

48. See Kisch, "The Yellow Badge," p. 107.

49. See *Monumenta Judaica* [Handbuch], figs. 63, 64, 67, 68, 70.

50. See Blumenkranz, *Le juif médiéval*, fig. 59 (Bibl. Nat. Fr. 166, fol. 40.^{v}).

51. Kisch, "The Yellow Badge," p. 104.

52. *Ibid.*

53. "And that each Jew after he shall be Seven Years old, shall wear a Badge on his outer Garment; that is to say, in the Form of the Two Tables joined, of yellow Felt, of the length of Six Inches, and of the Breadth of Three Inches," as Englished in that part of the Statutes of Edward I, called *The Statutes of Jewry*, 1 *Statutes of the Realm* 221 (Temp. Incert.). William Holdsworth, *A History of English Law* (Boston, 1922–1932), 1:46 gives the date as 3 Edw. I.

54. For a reproduction see Roth, *Essays and Portraits*, fig. 3, opposite p. 51; or the *Jewish Encyclopedia*, vol. 2, under *Badge*.

55. First published by Joseph Jacobs and Lucien Wolf, *Anglo-Jewish Historical Exhibition Catalogue* (London, 1887); see p. 9 for an account of the court proceedings where it is stated that Aaron son of Leo stood bail for one of the culprits, and is probably the man caricatured on this Roll.

56. See Roth, *Essays and Portraits*, fig. 9, and see his description on p. 25.

57. This translation was provided by Bengt Löfstedt and Ingrid Frank; for the Latin, see Weber, *Geistliches Schauspiel*, p. 68.

58. See p. 128.

59. See Grayzel, *Church and Jews*.

60. See Fritz Kynass, *Der Jude im Deutschen Volkslied* [a foreign dissertation] (Griefswald, 1934), pp. 18, 21; for example on p. 18.

> Aodam un Eavao
> Satten baie opt Sopha,
> Aodam laitn Pup gaon.
> Eva musste ruut goan.

61. *Ibid.*, p. 23.

62. *Ibid.*, pp. 28–30.

63. *Ibid.*, pp. 30–34.

64. *Ibid.*, p. 45.

65. *Ibid.*, pp. 45–46.

66. *Ibid.*, p. 47.

67. *Ibid.*, p. 50.

68. *Ibid.*, p. 49.
69. Grayzel, *Church and Jews*, p. 12.
70. *The Letters of St. Bernard*, trans. Bruno Scott James (London: Burns, Oates, 1953), letter No. 391: "To the English People."
71. See Joshua Trachtenberg, *The Devil and the Jews* (Cleveland and New York: Meridian, 1961).
72. *Ibid.*, pp. 44–53.
73. *Ibid.*, p. 227, n. 5. See also Norman Cohn, "The Horns of Moses," *Commentary Magazine*, XXVI, no. 3 (Sept., 1958), 220.
74. Here in Los Angeles, a woman reared in the South told me that during her childhood she often had heard "that the Jews cut the horns off their babies so no one would know!" A professor at the University of California at Los Angeles also stated that he was told, growing up in Germany, that Jews had horns.
75. See Georg Liebe, *Das Judentum in der Deutschen Vergangenheit* (Leipzig: Diederichs, 1903), p. 35.
76. Felix Singermann, *Die Kennzeichnung der Juden im Mittelalter* (Berlin, 1915), p. 20.
77. See p. 89.
78. That the ambiguous meanings of horns sometimes led to misunderstanding regarding the horns of the bishop's mitre is documented by William Durandus's scornful reprimand to heretics: "Yet do certain heretics condemn the Mitre with its horns, and the bishop wearing it; who allege unto the fostering of their error the words of John in the Apocalypse, *I beheld another beast coming up out of the earth, and he had two horns like a lamb, and he spake as a dragon.*" See T. H. Passmore, *The Sacred Vestments* (London: Sampson Low, Marston, 1899), p. 95.

Bibliography

Abrahams, Israel. *Jewish Life in the Middle Ages*. London: Edward Goldston, 1932. [1st pub. 1896.]

Adam of Eynsham. *The Life of St. Hugh of Lincoln*. Ed. Decima L. Douie and Hugh Farmer. 2 vols. London, New York: Thomas Nelson, 1961.

Aelfric [the Grammarian]. *Aelfric's Lives of the Saints*. Ed. Walter W. Skeat. 2 vols. London: Early English Text Society, 1881–1900.

————. *The Homilies of the Anglo-Saxon Church*. Ed. Benjamin Thorpe. 2 vols. London: Aelfric Society, 1844.

Alföldi, Andrew. "Cornuti: A Teutonic Contingent in the Service of Constantine the Great and its Decisive Role in the Battle at the Milvian Bridge," *Dumbarton Oaks Papers*, XIII (1959), 171–179.

Altaner, Berthold. *Patrology*. Trans. Hilda C. Graef. Freiburg: Herder; London: Thomas Nelson, 1960.

Anderson, M. D. *Drama and Imagery in British Churches*. Cambridge: Cambridge University Press, 1963.

————. *The Imagery of British Churches*. London: John Murray, 1955.

Andrieu, Michel. *Le pontifical romain au moyen-âge*. 4 vols. Città del Vaticano: Biblioteca apostolica vaticana, 1938–1941.

An Anglo-Saxon Dictionary. See Bosworth, Joseph.

An Anglo-Saxon Dictionary: Supplement. See Toller, T. Northcote.

Arbman, Holger. *Birka I. Die Gräber*. [Kungl. Vitterhets Historie och Antikvitets Akademien], Uppsala, 1943.

————. *The Vikings*. Vol. 21 in series, *Ancient Peoples and Places*. London: Thames and Hudson, 1961.

Aronius, Julius. *Regesten zur Geschichte der Juden*. Berlin: Simon, 1902.

Aubert, Marcel; Grodecki, Louis; Lafond, Jean; and Verrier, Jean. *Les vitraux de Notre-Dame et de la Sainte-Chapelle de Paris* [Corpus Vitrearum Medii Aevil]. Paris: Le comité international d'histoire de l'art, 1959.

Avery, Myrtilla. *The Exultet Rolls of South Italy*. Vol. II (plates), [no vol. I pub.], Princeton, N. J.: Princeton University Press, 1936.

Baillet, Louis. "Les miniatures du *Scivias* de Sainte Hildegarde," *Monuments et Mémoires*, 19 (Paris, 1911), 49–149.

Baum, Paull F. *Anglo-Saxon Riddles of the Exeter Book*. Durham, N. C.: Duke University Press, 1963.

Bede. [Ecclesiastical History], *A History of the English Church and People*. Trans. Leo Sherley-Price. Baltimore: Penguin, 1955.

————. *Lives of the First Five Abbots of Wearmouth and Jarrow*. Trans. Peter Wilcock. Sunderland: Hills, 1910.

Berg, Knut. "The Gosforth Cross," *Journal of the Warburg and Courtauld Institutes*. XXI (1958), 27–43.

Bernard of Clairvaux [St.]. *The Letters of St. Bernard*. Trans. Bruno Scott James. London: Burns, Oates, 1953.

Bethurum, Dorothy. *The Homilies of Wulfstan*. Oxford: Clarendon Press, 1957.

Biblia Latina. [Cum postillis Nicolai de Lyra et expositionibus Guillelmi Britonis in omnes prologos S. Hieronymi et additionibus Pauli Burgensis replicisque Matthiae Doering] Venice. [Bonetus Locatellus, for Octavianus Scotus, Aug. 8, 1489.]

Biblia Pauperum—Deutsche Ausgabe von 1471. Weimar: Gesellschaft der bibliophilen, 1906.

Biblia Pauperum, The Estergom Blockbook of Forty Leaves. Introd. and notes by Elizabeth Soltész. Budapest: Corvina Press, 1967.

Biblia Sacra iuxta Latinam Vulgatam Versionem ad codicum fidem, iussu Pii PP. XI, cura et studio monachorum Sancti Benedicti Commissionis pontificae a Pio PP. X institutae sodalium praeside Aidan Gasquet, S.R.E. Cardinale edita. Rome: Typis Polyglottis Vaticanis, 1926, et seq.

Biblia Sacra, Vulgatae editionis Sixti V Pontificis Maximi iussu recognita et Clementis VIII. Editiones Paulinae. Rome, 1957.

Blair, C. H. Hunter. "Medieval Seals of the Bishops of Durham," *Archaeologia*, LXXII (1922), 1–24.

Blair, Peter Hunter. *An Introduction to Anglo-Saxon England*. Cambridge: Cambridge University Press, 1962. [1st ed., 1956.]

Blumenkranz, Bernhard. *Le juif médiéval au miroir de l'art chrétien*. Paris: Études Augustiniennes, 1966.

Boase, T. S. R. *English Art, 1100–1216*. Oxford: Clarendon Press, 1953.

Boeckler, Albert. *Abendländische Miniaturen*. Berlin and Leipzig: de Gruyter, 1930.

Bond, Francis. *Fonts and Font Covers*. London, New York and Toronto: Henry Frowde, 1908.

Bosworth, Joseph. *An Anglo-Saxon Dictionary*. Ed. and enl. by T. Northcote Toller. London: Oxford University Press, 1898.

Boutemy, A. "De quelques enlumineurs de manuscrits de l'abbaye de Corbie dans la seconde moitié du XIIe siècle," *Scriptorium*, IV (1950), 246–252.

————. "Les manuscrits enluminés du nord de la France," *Scriptorium*, III (1949), 110–122.

Brackert, Helmut. *Rudolf von Ems: Dichtung und Geschichte*. Heidelberg: Carl Winter, 1968.

Brand, John. *Observations on the Popular Antiquities of Great Britain*. Rev. Henry Ellis [Sir]. 3 vols. London: George Bell, 1900.

Branston, Brian. *Gods of the North.* New York: Vanguard Press, n.d.

———. *The Lost Gods of England.* London: Thames and Hudson, 1957.

Braun, Joseph. *Die Liturgische Gewandung im Occident und Orient.* Freiburg im Breisgau: Herder, 1907.

———. *Tracht und Attribute der Heiligen in der Deutschen Kunst.* Stuttgart: Metzler, 1943.

Breitenbach, Edgar. *Speculum Humanae Salvationis,* eine typengeschichtliche untersuchung. [Studien zur Deutschen Kunstgeschichte, Heft 272]. Strasbourg, 1930.

Brøgger, A. W., and Shetelig, Haakon. *The Viking Ships.* Trans. Katharine John. Oslo: Dreyers, 1951.

Brøndsted, Johannes. *Danmarks Oltid.* 3 vols. København, 1957–1960.

———. "A Survey of Danish Prehistoric Culture," in catalog: *The Arts of Denmark,* for an exhibition organized by the Danish Society of Arts and Crafts and Industrial Design. United States, 1960–1961.

Brown, T. J.; Meredith-Owens, G. M.; and Turner, D. H. "Manuscripts from the Dyson Perrins Collection," *British Museum Quarterly,* XXIII (1961) 27–38.

Buchthal, Hugo. *The Miniatures of the Paris Psalter.* London: Warburg Institute, 1938.

Budge, E. A. Wallis. *The Life and Exploits of Alexander the Great.* 2 vols. London: Clay, 1896.

Bulloch, James. *Adam of Dryburgh.* London: Church Historical Society, 1958.

The Cambridge History of English Literature. Ed. A. W. Ward [Sir] and A. R. Waller. 15 vols. Cambridge: Cambridge University Press, 1963. [1932 ed.]

Campbell, A., ed. *The Chronicle of Aethelweard.* London, Edinburgh, Melbourne, Johannesburg, Toronto, Paris, New York: Thomas Nelson, 1962.

The Catholic Encyclopedia. 15 vols. New York: Robert Appleton, 1907–1912.

Chadwick, Nora K. "The Monsters and Beowulf," in *The Anglo-Saxons.* Ed. Peter Clemoes. London: Bowes and Bowes, 1959.

Chambers, Raymond Wilson. *Beowulf,* with a supplement by C. L. Wrenn. 3rd ed. Cambridge: Cambridge University Press, 1963. [1st ed., 1921.]

———. "The Continuity of English Prose from Alfred to More and his School," in *The Life and Death of Sir Thomas More.* London, New York, Toronto: Early English Text Society, 1932.

Chaney, William A. "Paganism to Christianity in Anglo-Saxon England," *Harvard Theological Review,* LIII (1960), 197–217.

Clark, Eleanor Grace. "The Right Side of the Franks Casket," *Publications of the Modern Language Association,* XLV (1930), 339–353.

Clemoes, Peter, ed. *The Anglo-Saxons.* (Studies in some Aspects of their History and Culture, presented to Bruce Dickins.) London: Bowes and Bowes, 1959.

Cohen, Gustave. *Anthologie du drame liturgique en France au moyen-âge.* Paris: Les éditions du Cerf, 1955.

――――. *La grande clarté du moyen-âge.* New York: Éditions de la maison française, 1943.

――――. "The Influence of the Mysteries on Art in the Middle Ages," *Gazette des Beaux-Arts* XXIV (July-Dec., 1943), 327–342.

――――. *Le théâtre en France au moyen-âge.* Paris: Presses Universitaires de France, 1948. [1st version appeared in 2 vols. in the *Bibliothèque Générale illustrée,* 1928.]

Cohn, Norman. "The Horns of Moses," *Commentary Magazine,* XXVI, no. 3 (Sept., 1958), 220–226.

A Concise Anglo-Saxon Dictionary. Ed. John R. Clark Hall and Herbert D. Meritt. 4th ed. Cambridge: Cambridge University Press, 1960.

Cook, Albert Stanburrough, ed. *The Old English Elene, Phoenix, and Physiologus.* New Haven: Yale University Press, 1919.

Cornelius van den Steen [Cornelius à Lapide]. *Commentaria in Scripturam Sacram.* Editio nova. Paris: Vivés, 1868–1880.

Cornell, Henrik. *Biblia Pauperum.* Stockholm: [Thule-tryck], 1925.

Craig, Hardin. *English Religious Drama of the Middle Ages.* Oxford: Clarendon Press, 1955.

Cramp, Rosemary J. "*Beowulf* and Archaeology," *Medieval Archaeology,* I (1957), 57–77.

Cursor Mundi (The Cursur o the World). A Northumbrian poem of the fourteenth century in four versions. Ed. Richard Morris. London: Early English Text Society, 1874–1892.

David, Henri. *Claus Sluter.* Paris: Éditions Pierre Tisné, 1951.

Davidson, Hilda R. Ellis. "Gods and Heroes in Stone," in *The Early Cultures of North-west Europe.* Ed. [Sir] Cyril Fox and Bruce Dickins. Cambridge: Cambridge University Press, 1950. Pp. 121–139.

――――.*Gods and Myths of Northern Europe.* Baltimore: Penguin, 1964.

[Davidson] Ellis, Hilda R. "Sigurd in the Art of the Viking Age," *Antiquity,* XVI (1942), 216–236.

Delaporte, Y. *Les vitraux de la cathédral de Chartres.* 4 vols. Chartres: Houvet, 1926.

Dickins, Bruce, ed. *Runic and Heroic Poems of the Old Teutonic Peoples.* Cambridge: Cambridge University Press, 1915.

Dictionary of National Biography. London: Oxford University Press, 1917, et. seq.

A Dictionary of the Bible. Ed. William Smith. 2 vols. 2d ed. Boston: Little, Brown, 1861.

Dictionnaire d'archéologie chrétienne et de liturgie. Ed. Fernand Cabrol and Henri Leclercq. 15 vols. in 30. Paris: Librairie Letouzey, 1907, et. seq.

Dictionnaire de droit canonique. Ed. R. Naz. Paris: Librairie Letouzey, 1935–1965.

Dictionnaire de la Bible. Ed. F. Vigouroux. 5 vols. Paris: Librairie Letouzey, 1926. [1st print. 1899.]

Dionysius the Carthusian [Denis le Chartreux, Doctoris ecstatici]. *Dionysii Cartusiani, opera omnia in unum corpus digesta ad fidem editionum coloniensium, cura et labore monachorum sacri ordiniis Cartusiensis.* 42 vols. in 44. Favente pont. max. Leone XIII. Monstrolii: Typis cartusiae, 1896–1935.

Dobbie, Elliott van Kirk, ed. *Beowulf and Judith.* New York: Columbia University Press, 1953.

Dodwell, C. R. *The Canterbury School of Illumination, 1066–1200.* Cambridge: Cambridge University Press, 1954.

————. *The Great Lambeth Bible.* London: Faber and Faber, 1959.

Du Chaillu, Paul B. *The Viking Age.* 2 vols. New York: Scribner's, 1889.

Dupont, Jacques. *Gothic Painting.* Geneva: Skira, 1954.

Durrieu, Paul. "Les manuscrits à peintures de la Bibliothèque de Sir Thomas Phillipps à Cheltenham," *Bibliothèque de l'école des Chartes,* 50 (1889), 400.

Eadmer. *History of Recent Events in England.* Trans. Geoffrey Bosanquet. London: Cresset Press, 1964.

Eerdmans, Bernardus Dirk. *The Covenant at Mount Sinai viewed in the Light of Antique Thought.* Leiden: Burgersdijk and Niermans, 1939.

Ehrenstein, Theodor. *Das alte Testament im Bilde.* Vienna: Kende, 1923.

Ehrismann, Gustav. *Rudolfs von Ems Weltchronik.* [Deutsche Texte des Mittelalter.] Berlin: Weidmann, 1915.

Eichmann, Eduard. *Weihe und Kronung des Papstes im Mittelalter.* Munich: Zink, 1951.

Elworthy, Frederick Thomas. *Horns of Honour.* London: John Murray, 1900.

Enciclopedia Cattolica. 12 vols. The Vatican, 1948–1954.

Encyclopaedia Biblica. Ed. T. K. Cheyne and J. Sutherland Black. 4 vols. London: Adam and Charles Black, 1901.

Encyclopaedia of Religion and Ethics. Ed. James Hastings. 4th imp. Edinburg: T. and T. Clark; New York: Scribner's, 1959. [1st imp., 1913.]

Ertzdorff, Xenja von. *Rudolf von Ems: Untersuchung zum höfischen Roman im 13. Jahrhundert.* Munich: Fink, 1967.

Escher, Konrad. "Die Bilderhandschrift der Weltchronik des Rudolf von Ems in der Zentralbibliothek Zürich," *Mitteilungen der Antiquarischen Gesellschaft in Zürich,"* XXXI, pt. 4 (1935) 5–43.

Farley, Mary Ann, and Wormald, Francis. "Three Related English Romanesque Manuscripts," *Art Bulletin,* XXII (1940), 157–161.

Focillon, Henri. *Peintures romanes des églises de France.* Paris: Hartmann, 1938.

Förster, Otto H. *Stefan Lochner ein Maler zu Köln. Köln:* Prestel, 1941.

Fox, Cyril [Sir]. *Pattern and Purpose: A Survey of Early Celtic Art in Britain.* Cardiff: National Museum of Wales, 1958.

Frankfort, Henri. *Art and Architecture of the Ancient Orient.* Baltimore: Penguin, 1954.

Friesen, Otto v. *Sparlösastenen* (Runstenen vid Salems Kyrka Sparlösa socken Vastergötland). [Kungl. Vitterhets Historie Och Antikvitets Akademiens Handlingar, Del 46:3]. Stockholm, 1940.

Gaillard, Georges. *The Frescoes of Saint-Savin.* New York and London: Studio Publications, 1944.

Gantner, Joseph. *Kunstgeschichte der Schweiz von den anfängen bis zum beginn des Jahrhunderts.* Vol. II. Frauenfeld, 1947.

Geijer, Agnes. *Birka III, Die Textilfunde aus den Gräbern.* [Kungl. Vitterhets Historie och Antikvitets Akademien]. Uppsala, 1938.

Gelling, Peter, and Davidson, Hilda Ellis. *The Chariot of the Sun.* London: J. M. Dent and Sons, 1969.

Gildas. *De Excidio et Conquestu Britanniae,* in *Monumenta Germaniae Historica,* Auctores Antiquissimi, XIII (1896), 25–85.

Giles, John A. *Old English Chronicles.* London: Bell, 1908.

Gillet, Louis. *Histoire artistique des ordres mendicants.* Paris: Laurens, 1912.

Godwyn, Thomas. *Moses and Aaron, Civil and Ecclesiastical Rites Used by the Ancient Hebrews.* 12th ed. London, 1672. [1st ed. probably 1624.]

Goldschmidt, Adolph. "English Influence on Medieval Art of the Continent," *Medieval Studies in Memory of A. Kingsley Porter.* 2 vols. Cambridge: Harvard University Press, 1939. 2: 709–728.

Gollancz, Israel [Sir]. *The Caedmon Manuscript of Anglo-Saxon Biblical Poetry, Junius XI in the Bodleian Library.* London: Oxford University Press, 1927.

Goodenough, Erwin R. *Jewish Symbols in the Greco-Roman Period.* 12 vols. New York: Pantheon, 1953–1965.

Grabar, André. *Byzantine Painting.* Lausanne and Geneva: Skira, 1953.

Grayzel, Solomon. *The Church and the Jews in the XIII Century.* New York: Hermon Press, 1966. [1st ed., 1933.]

A Greek-English Lexicon. Compiled by Henry George Liddell and Robert Scott. Oxford: Clarendon Press, 1867–1939.

Green, Charles. *Sutton Hoo.* London: Merlin Press, 1963.

Gressman, Hugo. *Moses und seine Zeit.* Göttingen: Vandenhoeck and Ruprecht, 1913.

Grodecki, Louis. *Chartres.* Paris: Draeger et Verve, 1963.

Guillaume de Deguileville. *Le pèlerinage de vie humaine.* Ed. J. J. Stürzinger. London: Roxburghe Club, 1893.

———. *The Ancient Poem of Guillaume de Guileville compared with the Pil-*

grims Progress of John Bunyan. Ed. from notes by Nathaniel Hill. London: Basil Montagu Pickering, 1858.

————. See Lydgate, John.

Gummere, Francis B., trans., *The Oldest English Epic.* New York: Macmillan, 1923. [1st ed., 1909.]

Gutmann, Joseph. A book review of Carl-Otto Nordström's *The Duke of Alba's Castillian Bible.* Art Bulletin, LI (1969), 91–96.

Hagen, Anders. *The Viking Ship Finds.* Oslo: Universitetets Oldsaksamling, 1960.

Hailperin, Herman. *Rashi and the Christian Scholars.* Pittsburgh: University of Pittsburgh Press, 1963.

Hardison, O. B., Jr. *Christian Rite and Christian Drama in the Middle Ages.* Baltimore: Johns Hopkins Press, 1965.

Harper's Bible Dictionary. Ed. Madeleine S. Miller and J. Lane Miller. 6th ed. New York: Harper, 1959.

Harrsen, Meta. *Central European Manuscripts in the Pierpont Morgan Library.* New York, 1958.

————. *Cursus Sanctae Mariae.* New York: Pierpont Morgan Library, 1937.

Haseloff, Arthur M. "Peintures, miniatures, et vitraux de l'époque romane," *Histoire de l'art.* Ed. A. A. Michel. Vol. I, pt. 2, chap. vii. Paris, 1905. Pp. 737 ff.

Hassall, W. O. *The Holkham Bible Picture Book.* London: Dropmore Press, 1954.

Hatto, A. T. "Snake-swords and Boar-helms in Beowulf," *English Studies,* XXXVIII, 4 (1957), 145–160.

Hawkes, Sonia Chadwick; Davidson, H. R. Ellis; and Hawkes, Christopher. "The Finglesham Man," *Antiquity,* XXXIX (1965), 17–31.

Henderson, George. "Cain's Jaw-Bone," *Journal of the Warburg and Courtauld Institutes,* XXIV (1961), 108–114.

Herbert, J. A. "A Psalter in the British Museum (Royal MS I.D.X.), Illuminated in England Early in the Thirteenth Century," *The Walpole Society,* III (1913–1914), 47–56.

Hesseling, D. C. *Miniatures de l'octateuque Grec de Symrna.* Leyden: Sijthoff, 1909.

Hodgkin, R. H. *A History of the Anglo-Saxons.* Appendix on Sutton Hoo by R. L. S. Bruce-Mitford. 2 vols. London: Oxford University Press, 1959. [1st ed., 1935.]

Hofmeister, P. Philipp. *Mitra und Stab der wirklichen Prälaten ohne bischöflichen Charakter.* Reprint. Amsterdam: Schippers, 1962. [1st ed., 1928.]

Holmqvist, Wilhelm. "The Dancing Gods," *Acta Archaeologica,* XXXI (1960), 101–127.

————. *Germanic Art during the First Millenium A. D.* [Kungl. Vitterhets Historie och Antikvitets Akademiens Handlingar, Del 90]. Stockholm, 1955.

————. "Viking Art in the Eleventh Century," *Acta Archaeologica*, XXII (1951), 1–56.

Hougen, Bjorn. "Osebergfunnets billedev," *Viking: tidsskrift for norrøn arkeologi*. Oslo, 1940. Pp. 85–124.

Hugh the Chantor. *The History of the Church of York, 1066–1127*. Trans. Charles Johnson. London: Thomas Nelson, 1961.

Jacobs, Joseph, and Wolf, Lucien. *Anglo-Jewish Historical Exhibition Catalogue*. London, 1887.

James, Montague Rhodes. "Illustrations of the Old Testament," in *A Book of Old Testament Illustrations of the Middle of the Thirteenth Century*. Ed. Sidney C. Cockerell, Cambridge: Roxburghe Club, 1927.

Jansson, Sven B. F. *The Runes of Sweden*. Trans. Peter G. Foote. London: Phoenix House, 1962.

————. *Runinskrifter i Sverige*. Uppsala: Almqvist and Wiksell, 1963.

Jerome [Saint]. S. Hieronymi Presbyteri Opera. *Commentariorum in Hiezechielem*, in *Corpus Christianorum*. Series Latina. LXXV. Turnholti: Typographi Brepols Editores Pontificii, 1964.

————. *The Homilies of Saint Jerome*. Trans. Sister Marie Liguori Ewald. Vol. 1 of *The Fathers of the Church*. Washington: Catholic University of America Press, 1964.

Kantorowicz, Ernest H. "The Carolingian King in the Bible of San Paola fuori le Mura," *Late Classical and Mediaeval Studies in honor of A. M. Friend*. Princeton, N. J.: Princeton University Press, 1955. Pp. 287–300.

Katzenellenbogen, Adolph. *Allegories of the Virtues and Vices in Medieval Art*. New York: Norton, 1964. [1st pub, 1939.]

Kauffmann, C. M. "The Bury Bible," *Journal of the Warburg and Courtauld Institutes*, XXIX (1966), 60–81.

Kemble, J. M., trans. *The Poetry of the Codex Vercellensis*. London: Aelfric Society, 1843.

Kendrick, T. D. *Late Anglo-Saxon and Viking Art*. London: Methuen, 1949.

————. "The Viking Taste in Pre-Conquest Art," *Antiquity*, XV (1941), 125–141.

Kennedy, Charles W. *An Anthology of Old English Poetry*. New York: Oxford University Press, 1960.

————. *Beowulf, the Oldest English Epic*. New York, London, Toronto: Oxford University Press, 1966. [1st ed., 1940.]

————. *Early English Christian Poetry*. New York: Oxford University Press, 1952.

Kenney, James F. *The Sources for the Early History of Ireland.* New York: Columbia University Press, 1929.

Kent, Charles W. *Elene an Old English Poem.* Boston and London: Ginn, 1889.

Kenyon, Frederic [Sir]. *Our Bible and the Ancient Manuscripts.* 4th ed., rev. London: Eyre and Spottiswoode, 1939. [1st ed., 1895.]

Ker, N. R. *Catalogue of Manuscripts Containing Anglo-Saxon.* Oxford: Clarendon Press, 1957.

King, Archdale A. *Liturgy of the Roman Church.* London, New York, and Toronto: Longmans, Green, 1957.

Kisch, Guido. *The Jews in Medieval Germany.* Chicago: University of Chicago Press, 1949.

————. "The Yellow Badge in History," *Historia Judaica,* XIX (1957), 91–145.

Klaeber, Fr., ed. *Beowulf and the Fight at Finnsburg.* 3rd. ed. Boston, New York, and Chicago: Heath, 1936.

Klauser, Theodore. *Der Ursprung der bischöflichen Insignien und Ehrenrechte.* Krefeld: Scherpe, 1953. [1st pub. in *Bonner Akademische Reden,* 1948.]

Klindt-Jensen, Ole. *Denmark before the Vikings.* Vol. 4 in the series, *Ancient Peoples and Places.* London: Thames and Hudson, 1957.

————. "Foreign Influences in Denmark's Early Iron Age," *Acta Archaeologica,* XX (1949), 1–229.

Koehler, Wilhelm. *Die Karolingischen Miniaturen.* Vol. I, pts. 1 and 2. Reprint. Berlin: Deutscher Verein für Kunstwissenschaft, 1963. [1st ed., 1930 and 1933.]

Künstle, Karl. *Ikonographie der Christlichen Kunst.* 2 vols. Freiburg im Breisgau: Herder, 1928.

Kynass, Fritz. *Der Jude im Deutschen Volkslied.* [A foreign dissertation]. Griefswald, 1934.

Laborde, Alexandre comte de. *La Bible moralisée illustrée.* 5 vols. Paris, 1911–1927.

Ladner, Gerhart. "Die Italienische malerei im 11. Jahrhundert," *Jahrbuch der Kunsthistorischen Sammlungen in Wien,* new series, V (1931), 33–160.

Lamberts, J. J. "The Noah Story in Cursor Mundi," *Medieval Studies,* XXIV (1962), 217–232.

Lauer, Philippe. *Les enluminures romanes des manuscrits de la Bibliothèque Nationale.* Paris: Éditions de la Gazette des Beaux-Arts, 1927.

Leroquais, V. *Les pontificaux manuscrits des bibliothèques publiques de France.* Text 3 vols., pls. 1 vol. Paris, 1937.

Lexicon für Theologie und Kirche. 10 vols. Freiburg im Breisgau: Herder, 1957–1965.

Liebe, Georg. *Das Judentum in der Deutschen Vergangenheit*. Leipzig: Diederichs, 1903.

Lofthouse, Marion. " 'Le pèlerinage de vie humaine' by Guillaume de Deguileville," *Bulletin of the John Rylands Library*, XIX, no. 1 (Jan., 1935), 170–215.

Loomis, Roger Sherman. "The Origin and Date of the Bayeux Embroidery," *Art Bulletin*, VI (1923), 3–7.

L'Orange, Hans Peter, and Gerkan, Armin von. *Der spätantike Bildschmuck des Konstantinsbogens*. [Studien zur spätantiken Kunstgeschichte]. 2 vols. Berlin: de Gruyter, 1939.

Lutz, J., and Perdrizet, P., eds. *Speculum Humanae Salvationis*. Texte critique, traduction inédite de Jean Mielot (1448). 4 vols. Mulhouse: Meininger, 1907–1909.

Lydgate, John. *The Pilgrimage of the Life of Man*. English trans. in 1426 from the French of Guillaume de Deguileville, 1330, 1355. Ed. F. J. Furnivall. Introd., notes, glossary, and indexes, Katharine B. Locock. London: Early English Text Society, 1905.

McCullock, Florence. *Medieval Latin and French Bestiaries*. Chapel Hill: University of North Carolina Press, 1960.

Magoun, Francis P. "On Some Survivals of Paganism in Anglo-Saxon England," *Harvard Theological Review*, XL (1947), 33–46.

Mâle, Émile. *L'art religieux de la fin du moyen-âge*. Paris: Librairie Armand Colin, 1931. [1st ed. 1908.]

———. *L'art religieux du XIIe siècle en France*. Paris: Librairie Armand Colin, 1928. [1st ed. 1922.]

———. *The Gothic Image*. Trans. Dora Nussey. New York: Harper Torchbooks, 1958. [1st ed. 1913.]

Malone, Kemp, trans. *Ten Old English Poems*. Baltimore: Johns Hopkins Press, 1941.

Mansi, Ioannes Dominicus. *Sacrorum Conciliorum Nova, et amplissima collectio* [facsimile copy of original ed. of 1758–1798]. Paris, 1903.

Martin, Henry. *La miniature française, XIIIe au XVe siècle*. Paris and Brussels: Van Oest, 1924.

Martin, Henry, and Lauer, Philippe. *Les principaux manuscrits à peintures de la Bibliothèque de l'Arsenal à Paris*. Paris, 1929.

Martin-Clarke, D. Elizabeth. *Culture in Early Anglo-Saxon England*. Baltimore: Johns Hopkins Press, 1947.

Maryon, Herbert. "The Sutton Hoo Helmet," *Antiquity*, XXI (Sept., 1947), 137–144.

Migne, Jacques Paul. *Patrologiae cursus competus*. Series Graeco-Latina. Paris, 1857–1902.

———. *Patrologiae cursus completus*. Series Latina. Paris, 1844–1864.

Millar, Eric G. *English Illuminated Manuscripts from the Xth to the XIIIth Century.* Paris and Brussels: Van Oest, 1926.

―――. *English Illuminated Manuscripts of the XIVth and XVth Centuries.* Paris and Brussels: Van Oest, 1928.

―――. *An Illuminated Manuscript of La Somme le Roy.* Oxford: Roxburghe Club, 1953.

Mitchell, H. P. "Flotsam of Later Anglo-Saxon Art," Parts I, II, III, IV, *Burlington Magazine,* XXXXII (1923), 63 ff., 162 ff., 303 ff.; XXXXIII (1923). 104 ff.

Monumenta Judaica [Handbuch]. Köln, 1964.

Monumenta Judaica [Katalog]. Köln, 1964.

Morey, C. R. "The Illustrations of Genesis" in C. W. Kennedy, *The Caedmon Poems.* London: Routledge; New York: Dutton, 1916.

Morgan, Edwin. *Beowulf.* Berkeley and Los Angeles: University of California Press, 1966.

Morgenstern, Julian. "Moses with the Shining Face," *Hebrew Union College Annual,* II (1925), 1–27.

Neher, André. *Moses and the Vocation of the Jewish People.* Trans. Irene Marinoff. New York: Harper Torchbooks; London: Longmans, 1959.

Neuss, Wilhelm. *Die katalanische Bibelillustration um die Wende des ersten Jahrtausends und die altspanische Buchmalerei.* Bonn and Leipzig: Kurt Schroeder, 1922.

Nigel (de Longchamps). *Speculum Stultorum.* Ed. John H. Mozley and Robert R. Raymo. Berkeley and Los Angeles: University of California Press, 1960.

Nigel (Longchamp). *A Mirror for Fools.* Trans. J. H. Mozley. Notre Dame, Ind.: University of Notre Dame Press, 1963.

Nordenfalk, Carl. *Early Medieval Painting.* [Lausanne]: Skira, 1957.

―――. *Romanesque Painting.* Lausanne and Paris: Skira, 1958.

Norling-Christensen, H. "The Viksø Helmets, a bronze-age votive find from Zealand," *Acta Archaeologica,* XVII (1946), 99–115.

Noth, Martin. *Exodus—a Commentary.* Trans. J. S. Bowden from German ed. of 1959. Philadelphia: Westminster Press, 1962.

The Old English Version of the Hepateuch, Aelfric's Treatise on the Old and New Testament and his Preface to Genesis, ed. from all the existing MSS and fragments with an introd. and three appendices together with a reprint of "A Saxon Treatise Concerning the Old and New Testament: Now First Published in Print with English of Our Time by William L'Isle of Wilburgham (1623)," and the Vulgate Text of the Heptateuch. Ed. S. J. Crawford. London: Early English Text Society, 1922.

O'Loughlin, J. L. N. "Sutton Hoo—The Evidence of the Documents," *Medieval Archaeology,* VIII (1964), 1–19.

Oppé, Adolf Paul. *Raphael*. London: Methuen, 1909.

Ottino della Chiesa, Angela, *Bernadino Luini*. Novara: Instituto geografico de Agostini, 1956.

The Oxford Companion to English Literature. Ed. Paul Harvey [Sir]. 3d ed. Oxford: Clarendon Press, 1946.

The Oxford Dictionary of the Christian Church. Ed. F. L. Cross. London: Oxford University Press, 1958.

Pächt, Otto. "The Pre-Carolingian Roots of Early Romanesque Art," *Studies in Western Art: Acts of the XX International Congress of the History of Art*. Ed. M. Meiss. 4 vols. Princeton, N. J.: Princeton University Press, 1963. 1:67–75.

———. *The Rise of Pictorial Narrative in Twelfth Century England*. Oxford: Clarendon Press, 1962.

———. *St. Albans Psalter (Albani Psalter)*. London: Warburg Institute, 1960.

Pächt, Otto, and Alexander, J. J. G. *Illuminated Manuscripts in the Bodleian Library Oxford, I*. Oxford: Clarendon Press, 1966.

Panofsky, Erwin. *Early Netherlandish Painting*. 2 vols. Cambridge: Harvard University Press, 1953.

Paris, Paulin M. *Les manuscrits françois de la Bibliothèque du roi*. IV. Paris, 1841.

Passmore, T. H. *The Sacred Vestments*. [An English rendering of the third book of the *Rationale Divinorum Officiorum* of Durandus, Bishop of Mende]. London: Sampson Low, Marston, 1899.

Paulys Real-Encyclopädie der Classischen Altertumswissenschaft. Stuttgart: Metzler, 1894, et seq.

The Pentateuch and Haftorahs. Ed. late Chief Rabbi Dr. J. H. Hertz, C. H. London: Soncino Press, 1952.

The Pentateuch and Rashi's Commentary, a Linear Translation into English. Trans. Abraham Ben Isaiah [Rabbi] and Benjamin Sharfman [Rabbi]. Brooklyn, N. Y.: Jewish Publication Society of Philadelphia, 1949.

Pentateuch with Targum Onkelos, Haphtaroth and Rashi's Commentary. Trans. M. Rosenbaum and A. M. Silbermann in collaboration with A. Blashki and L. Joseph. New York: Hebrew Publishing, [1935].

Petersen, Henry. *Danske Adelige Sigiller*. Copenhagen, 1897.

Petzet, Erich. "Eine Prachthandschrift der Weltchronik des Rudolf von Ems," *Germanische-romanische Monatsschrift*, I (1909), 465–490.

Pfeilstücker, Suse. *Spätantikes und Germanisches Kunstgut in der Frühangelsächsischen Kunst*. Berlin: Deutscher kunstverlag, 1936.

Plancher, Urbain [Dom]. *Histoire générale et particulière de Bourgogne*. 4 vols. Dijon, 1739–1781.

Plummer, John. *Liturgical Manuscripts*. New York: Pierpont Morgan Library, 1964.

The Pontifical of Egbert, Archbishop of York, A. D. 732–766. Ed. W. Greenwell. London: Surtees Society, 1853.

Pope-Hennessy, John. *Fra Angelico*. London: Phaidon Press, 1952.

Porcher, Jean. *French Miniatures from Illuminated Manuscripts*. London: Collins, 1960.

Pugin, A. Welby. *Glossary of Ecclesiastical Ornament and Costume*. London: Bohn, 1844.

Rawlinson, George. *Moses: His Life and Times*. London: James Nisbet, 1887.

Réau, Louis. *Iconographie de l'art chrétien*. 6 vols. Paris: Presses Universitaires de France, 1955–1959.

Regularis Concordia. Trans. Thomas Symons. London: Thomas Nelson, 1953.

Reider, Joseph. "Jews in Medieval Art," *Essays on Antisemitism*. Ed. Koppel S. Pinson. New York: Conference on Jewish Relations, 1942. Pp. 45–56.

Rice, David Talbot. *English Art, 871–1100*. Oxford: Clarendon Press, 1952.

Rickert, Margaret. *Painting in Britain: the Middle Ages*. Baltimore: Penguin, 1954.

Robert, Ulysse. *Les signes d'infamie au moyen-âge*. Paris: Champion, 1891.

Robinson, H. Wheeler, ed. *The Bible in its Ancient and English Versions*. Oxford: Clarendon Press, 1940.

Rosenthal, Erwin I. J. "Rashi and the English Bible," *Bulletin of the John Rylands Library*, XXIV (1940), 138–167.

Roth, Cecil. *Essays and Portraits in Anglo-Jewish History*. Philadelphia: Jewish Publication Society of America, 1962.

Rudwin, Maximilian. *The Devil in Legend and Literature*. Chicago and London: Open Court, 1931.

Ryan, J. S. "Othin in England," *Folklore*, 74 (1963), 460–480.

Salmon, Pierre. *Mitra und Stab* [German trans. of *Étude sur les insignes du pontife dans le rit romain* of 1955]. Mainz, 1960.

Saunders, O. Elfrida. *English Illumination, I*. 2 vols. Firenze: Pantheon, 1928.

———. *A History of English Art in the Middle Ages*. Oxford: Clarendon Press, 1932.

Saxl, Fritz. *English Sculptures of the Twelfth Century*. Ed. Hanns Swarzenski. Boston: Boston Book and Art Shop, [1952].

Schapiro, Meyer. A book review of J. C. Webster, *The Labors of the Months in Antique and Medieval Art to the End of the Twelfth Century*. *Speculum*, XVI no. 1 (Jan., 1941), 131–137.

———. "The Image of the Disappearing Christ—the Ascension in English Art

Around the Year 1000," *Gazette des Beaux-Arts*, XXIII (March, 1943), 135–152.

——. Preface to *Illustrations for the Bible by Marc Chagall*. New York: Harcourt, Brace, 1956.

Scheftelowitz, I. "Das Hörnermotiv in den Religionen," *Archiv für Religionswissenschaft*, XV (1912), 451–487.

Schmidt, Gerhard. *Die Armenbibeln des XIV. Jahrhunderts*. Graz-Köln: Böhlaus Nachf., 1959.

Seiferth, Wolfgang. *Synagoge und Kirche im Mittelalter*. München: Kösel-Verlag, 1964.

Sepet, Marius. "Les prophètes du Christ," *Bibliothèque de l'École des Chartes*, XXVIII (1866–1867), 1–27, 211–264; XXIX (1867–1868), 105–139, 261–293; XXXVIII (1877), 397–443.

Septuaginta. Ed. Alfred Rahlfs. 2 vols. Stuttgart: Privilegierte württembergische Bibelanstalt, 1952.

Sheppard, Lancelot C. *The Liturgical Books*. New York: Hawthorn, 1962.

Shereshevsky, Esra. "Hebrew Traditions in Peter Comestor's Historia Scholastica," *The Jewish Quarterly Review*," LIX (April, 1969), 268–289.

Shetelig, Haakon, and Falk, Hjalmar. *Scandinavian Archaeology*. Trans. E. V. Gordon. Oxford: Clarendon Press, 1937.

Singer, Charles. "Allegorical Representation of the Synagogue in a Twelfth Century Illuminated MS of Hildegard of Bingen," *Jewish Quarterly Review*, V (1915), 267–288.

Singermann, Felix. *Die Kennzeichnung der Juden im Mittelalter*. Berlin, 1915.

Smalley, Beryl. *The Study of the Bible in the Middle Ages*. Repr., 2d. ed., 1952. Notre Dame, Ind.: University of Notre Dame Press, 1964.

Smetana, Cyril L. "Aelfric and the Early Medieval Homiliary," *Traditio*, XV (1959), 163–204.

Souers, Philip Webster. "The Franks Casket: Left Side," *Harvard Studies and Notes in Philology and Literature*, XVIII (1935), 199–209.

——. "The Magi on the Franks Casket," *Harvard Studies and Notes in Philology and Literature*, XIX (1937), 249–254.

——. "The Top of the Franks Casket," *Harvard Studies and Notes in Philology and Literature*, XVII (1935), 163–179.

Speculum Humanae Salvationis. A fifteenth-century English translation, *The Miroure of Mans Saluacionne*. Printed from a manuscript in the possession of Alfred Henry Huth. London: [Privately printed], 1888.

Stange, Alfred. *Deutsche Malerei der Gotik*. 8 vols. Berlin: Deutscher kunstverlag, 1934–1938.

Stenberger, Mårten. *Det forntida Sverige*. Uppsala: Almqvist and Wiksells, 1964.

————. *Sweden.* Trans. Alan Binns. Vol. 30 of series, *Ancient Peoples and Places.* London: Thames and Hudson, 1962.

Stenton, F. M. *Anglo-Saxon England.* Oxford: Clarendon Press, 1947. [1st ed., 1943.]

————, gen. ed. *The Bayeux Tapestry.* London: Phaidon, 1965. [1st ed., 1957.]

Stettiner, Richard. *Die Illustrierten Prudentius–Handschriften im Mittelalter.* 2 vols. Berlin: Grote, 1895 and 1905.

Stevens, C. E. "Gildas Sapiens," *English Historical Review,* LVI (1941), 353–373.

Stjerna, Knut. "Helmets and Swords in *Beowulf,*" *Essays on Questions Connected with the Old English Poem of Beowulf.* Trans. and ed. John R. Clark Hall. London: Viking Club Society for Northern Research, 1912.

Stolpe, Hjalmar, and Arne, T. J. *La nécropole de Vendel.* [Kungl. Vitterhets Historie och Antikvitetsakademien, mono. no. 17]. Stockholm, 1927.

Stone, Lawrence. *Sculpture in Britain: the Middle Ages.* Baltimore: Penguin Books, 1955.

The Story of Genesis and Exodus, an early English Song, about A. D. *1250.* Ed. Richard Morris [Rev.]. London: Early English Text Society, 1895.

Strachan, James. *Early Bible Illustrations.* Cambridge: Cambridge University Press, 1957.

Studer, Paul. *Le mystère d'Adam.* Manchester: Manchester University Press, 1949. [1st ed., 1918.]

Suhr, E. G. "The Horned Moses," *Folklore,* 74 (1963), 387–395.

The Sutton Hoo Ship-Burial, a provisional guide. 8th imp. London: Trustees of the British Museum, 1961. [1st ed., 1947.]

Swarzenski, Georg. *Die Salzburger Malerei.* 2 vols. Leipzig: Hiersmann, 1913.

Swarzenski, Hanns. *Die Lateinischen Illuminierten Handschriften des XIII. Jahrhunderts.* Berlin, 1936.

————. *Monuments of Romanesque Art.* Chicago: University of Chicago Press, 1967. [1st ed., 1954.]

Synagoga, Kultgeräte und Kunstwerke [catalog]. Städtische Kunsthalle Recklinghausen, Nov. 30, 1960–Jan. 15, 1961.

Tacitus. *The Complete Works of Tacitus.* Trans. Alfred John Church and William Jackson Brodribb. New York: Random House, 1942.

Thiset, A. *Danske Adelige Sigiller.* Copenhagen, 1905.

Thompson, Edward Maunde [Sir]. "English Illuminated Manuscripts—A.D. 700–1066," *Bibliographica,* I (1895–1896), 129–155.

Thompson, R. Lowe. *The History of the Devil . . . the Horned God of the West.* London: Kegan Paul, Trench, Trubner, 1929.

Toller, T. Northcote. *An Anglo-Saxon Dictionary: Supplement.* Oxford: Clarendon Press, 1921.

Trachtenberg, Joshua. *The Devil and the Jews*. Cleveland and New York: Meridian, 1961. [1st ed., 1943.]

Tselos, Dimitri. "English Manuscript Illustration and the Utrecht Psalter," *Art Bulletin*, XLI, no. 2 (June, 1959), 137–149.

Turnure, James H. "Etruscan Ritual Armor: Two Examples in Bronze," *American Journal of Archaeology*, LXIX, no. 1 (Jan., 1965), 39–48.

Turville-Petre, E.O.G. *Myth and Religion of the North, the Religion of Ancient Scandinavia*. New York: Holt, Rinehart and Winston, 1964.

Tuve, Rosemond. *Allegorical Imagery*. Princeton, N. J.: Princeton University Press, 1966.

Unterkircher, Franz, and Schmidt, Gerhard. *Die Wiener Biblia Pauperum Codex Vindobonensis 1198*. 3 vols. Graz, Wien, Köln: Verlag Styria, [1962].

Van Buren, E. Douglas. "Concerning the Horned Cap of the Mesopotamian Gods," *Orientalia*, XII (1943), 318–327.

Warner, George [Sir]. *Descriptive Catalogue of Illuminated Manuscripts in the Library of C. W. Dyson Perrins*. 2 vols. Oxford: Oxford University Press, 1920.

————. *Queen Mary's Psalter*. London: Trustees of the British Museum, 1912.

Watson, Arthur. *The Early Iconography of the Tree of Jesse*. London: Oxford University Press, 1934.

Weber, Paul. *Geistliches Schauspiel und Kirchliche Kunst*. Stuttgart: Neff, 1894.

Weigelt, Curt H. *Giotto des Meisters Gemälde*. Stuttgart: Deutsche verlagsanstalt, 1925.

Weitzmann, Kurt. *Illustrations in Roll and Codex*. Princeton, N. J.: Princeton University Press, 1947.

————. *The Joshua Roll*. Princeton, N. J.: Princeton University Press, 1948.

Werner, Joachim. "Eberzier von Monceau-Le-Neuf (Dép. Aisne)—ein beitrag zur Entstehung der völkerwanderungszeitlichen Eberhelme," *Acta Archaeologica*, XX (1949), 248–257.

The Westminster Dictionary of the Bible. Ed. John D. Davis. 5th ed. rev. Henry S. Gehman. Philadelphia: Westminster Press, 1944.

Westwood, J. O. *Palaeographia Sacra Pictoria*. London: Bohn, n.d.

White, Caroline Louisa. *Aelfric, a New Study of his Life and Writings*. Yale Studies in English. Boston, New York, and London: Lamson, Wolffe, 1898.

White, Lynn, jr. "Eilmer of Malmesbury, an Eleventh Century Aviator," *Technology and Culture*, II (1961), 97–111.

————. *Medieval Technology and Social Change*. Oxford: Clarendon Press, 1962.

Williams, A. Lukyn. *Adversus Judaeos*. Cambridge: Cambridge University Press, 1935.

Wilmart, A. "Magister Adam Cartusiensis," *Mélanges Mandonnet*, II (Paris, 1930), 145–161.

————. "Maitre Adam chanoine prémontré devenu chartreux à Witham," *Analecta Praemonstratensia*, IX (1933), 207–232.

Wilson, David M. *The Anglo-Saxons*. London: Thames and Hudson, 1960.

Wilson, David M., and Klindt-Jensen, Ole. *Viking Art*. London: George Allen and Unwin, 1966.

Withrow, W. J. "Sorel Etrog," *Canadian Art*, no. 97 (May/June, 1965), pp. 20–22.

Woodruff, Helen. "The Illustrated Manuscripts of Prudentius," *Art Studies*. Vol. 7. Cambridge: Harvard University Press, 1929. Pp. 33–79.

Wormald, Francis. *The Benedictional of St. Ethelwold*. London: Faber and Faber, 1959.

————. "Decorated Initials in English MSS from A.D. 900 to 1100," *Archaeologia*, XCI (1945), 107–135.

————. "The Development of English Illumination in the Twelfth Century," *The Journal of the British Archaeological Association*, 3d series, VIII (1943), 31–49.

————. *English Drawings of the Tenth and Eleventh Centuries*. London: Faber and Faber, 1952.

————. "Late Anglo-Saxon Art: Some Questions and Suggestions," *Studies in Western Art: Acts of the XX International Congress of the History of Art*. Ed. M. Meiss. 4 vols. Princeton, N. J.: Princeton University Press, 1963. Vol. I.

————. "The Survival of Anglo-Saxon Illumination after the Norman Conquest," *Proceedings of the British Academy*, XXX (1944), 127–145.

Wrenn, C. L. *Anglo-Saxon Poetry and the Amateur Archaeologist*. London: Lewis, 1962.

Wright, David. *Beowulf, a prose translation*. Baltimore: Penguin, 1964. [1st ed., 1957.]

Wycliffe, John. *The Holy Bible, containing the Old and New Testaments, with the Apocryphal Books, in the earliest English versions made from the Latin Vulgate by John Wycliffe and his Followers*. Ed. [Rev.] Josiah Forshall and [Sir] Frederic Madden. Oxford: Oxford University Press, 1850.

Young, Karl. *The Drama of the Medieval Church*. 2 vols. Oxford: Clarendon Press, 1933.

Index

Aaron, 64, 98, 99, 103, 105, 106, 111, 117.
See also Jewish high priest; Moses

Abbot's mitre, horns of: Nigel de Longchamp's interpretation, 101–103; Petrus Cantor's interpretation, 97. *See
also* Bishop's mitre, horns of

Abel, 129, 131

Abraham, 62, 117, 134

Adam, 134

Adamus Scotus: background of, 89, 90;
horned Moses concept, 88–90, 93, 121,
136; possible influence of, 90; sources
for, 89; treatise on threefold sense of
tabernacle, 88–90

Aelfric: background of, 23–25; educational zeal, 24, 25, 55, 56; on heathen
gods and practices, 54, 55; Latin writings, 24; literal emphasis of, 25, 26;
literary merit, 23, 25, 26; patriotic zeal,
57; patrons, 24, 25; popularity, 25;
vernacular writings, 24–26

Aelfric Paraphrase, illuminations: artists,
15; dating, 15; earlier models for, 14–
15; iconographic innovations in, 16, 18,
20; literalism of, 16, 19; Moses, horned
in, 13, 14, 15–17, 26, 27, 51, 57, 61, 62,
92, 94, 107, 146n.22, 147n.29, 147n.30;
possible influence from liturgical drama, 33–35; reflecting ancient traditions, 48, 49; Scandinavian influence
in, 50, 51; style and quality, 15, 16

Aelfric Paraphrase, text: date of, 25; extant copies of, 25; as a vernacular
translation, 24–26, 87. *See also* Aelfric

Aestii, 40

Aethelweard, 24, 25

Aethelwold, St., 24, 29, 30

Alexander, 3

Alfred the Great, 23

Ammon, 3

Andrew of St. Victor, 85

Aquila (Bible version), 77, 78, 168n.5

Arch of Constantine, 40, 41

Augustine, mission of, 52

Avranches, Bibliothèque de la Ville MS
210, 96

Bayeux tapestry, 51

Bede, St.: on Exod. 34:29, 83; on heathenism, 52, 53; on horns of the two Testaments, 97, 99

Benedict Biscop, 15

Benedictional of St. Aethelwold, 16

Benty-Grange helmet, 42

Beowulf: date of, 23, 48; helmets in, 44,
46, 47, 48, 51, 52; Scandinavian elements in, 50; and Sutton Hoo, 43, 44;
symbolism, 48. *See also* Helmets (or
headdress) with animal motifs; Sutton
Hoo

Bible moralisée: influences from stained
glass, 68, 69; mixed iconographic traditions in, 68, 69, 72; Moses, horned in,
69, 70; Moses with double grouping of
rays, 69, 72, 73, 90; Moses without
horns, 69

Biblia Pauperum: mixed iconographic
traditions in, 71, 72; Moses, horned in,
72, 73, 75, 117; Moses with double
grouping of rays, 73, 91; Moses without horns, 72; typological method of,
71, 117, 119

Birka figurine, 45, 46

Bishop: consecration of, 97–99, 176n.51;
as descendant of Moses, 103–106, 110–
116; ordination of, 103; seals of, 95,
96. *See also* Bishop's mitre; Bishop's
mitre, horns of

Bishop's mitre: anachronistically depicted, 96; in Eastern Church, 106; his-

Illustrations

1. "Alexander the Great with Ammon horns,"
on coins issued by Lysimachus, ca. 300 B.C.
Burton Y. Berry Collection,
American Numismatic Society, New York.

2. Stele of Naramsin.
Mesopotamia,
ca. 2340–2180 B.C.
Louvre.

3. Akkadian seal impression, ca. 2340–2180 B.C.
Bibliothèque Nationale, Paris.

5. Gem engraved head wearing
the basket of Serapis,
the horn of Ammon, and
the rays of Phoebus.
Late Hellenistic period.

4. Stele inscribed with the code of Hammurabi
(detail). Mesopotamia, ca. 1792–1750 B.C. Louvre.

6. "Moses receiving the Law." Mosaic in San Vitale, Ravenna, sixth century A.D.

7. "Moses' shining face." Byzantine Octateuch, twelfth century A.D.
   Vat. Gr. 746, folio 254ᵛ.

8. "Moses receiving the Law." Bible of Moutier-Grandval, A.D. 834–843.
British Museum Add. 10546, folio 25ᵛ.

9. "Moses receiving the Law." Vivian Bible
(First Bible of Charles the Bald), A.D. 844–851.
Bibliothèque Nationale Lat. 1, folio 27ᵛ.

10. "Moses receiving the Law." Bible of San Paolo
fuori le mura, ca. A.D. 870., folio 30ᵛ.

11. "Moses receiving the Law" (detail). Farfa Bible,
ca. A.D. 1000. Vat. Lat. 5729, folio 6ᵛ.

12. "Moses receiving the Law." Schematic drawing of
a fresco from Saint-Savin-sur-Gartempe, France,
late eleventh or early twelfth century.

HFROHGYHD SEODRID
DE BOC DEIS GENEMHED
OH EBRFIS UNE CRA · 7 LE
UITICUS OH GRECISC ·
¬ MIHISTERIALIS OH
LEDEH · DÆTIS ÐEHUNG
BOC · OH EHGLIS · FOR
ÐAH DE ÐARA SACER
DA ÐEHUHGA SYHD ÐAR

DOH · ÅPRITEI ———— —

Ðrihten clypode to moyre onþære halgan puþþung þrop
þduþ cpæð · Sege iþna hela beaþnum · gyf hpile toþer pille
gode offrunga bringan · of nytenum · þæt is of hryþerú
7 of sceapum · 7 to offrung beþam fullan beon rezole · þe
bringe he of hryþerum an unpemme ozan cealf toþære
halgan rope durja · ðrihten myð · toge gladienne · 7 þrece

14. (*Above, l.*) "Moses vesting" (detail). Aelfric Paraphrase, ca. A.D. 1025–1050. British Museum Cotton Claudius B. IV, folio 107ᵛ.

15. (*Above, r.*) "Moses communicating with God" (detail). Aelfric Paraphrase, ca. A.D. 1025–1050. British Museum Cotton Claudius B. IV, folio 111ʳ.

16. (*Below, l.*) "Moses communicating with God" (detail). Aelfric Paraphrase, ca. A.D. 1025–1050. British Museum Cotton Claudius B. IV, folio 113ᵛ.

17. (*Below, r.*) "Aaron and Miriam rebuked by God" (detail). Aelfric Paraphrase, ca. A.D. 1025–1050. British Museum Cotton Claudius B. IV, folio 116ᵛ.

18. "Moses murmured against" (detail). Aelfric Paraphrase,
ca. A.D. 1025–1050. British Museum Cotton Claudius B. IV, folio 121ʳ.

19. "Moses communicating with God" (detail). Aelfric Paraphrase,
ca. A.D. 1025–1050. British Museum Cotton Claudius B. IV, folio 121ᵛ.

20. (*Above, l.*) "Moses numbering the Israelites" (detail). Aelfric Paraphrase, ca. A.D. 1025–1050. British Museum Cotton Claudius B. IV, folio 128ʳ.

21. (*Above, r.*) "Moses encouraging Joshua" (detail). Aelfric Paraphrase, ca. A.D. 1025–1050. British Museum Cotton Claudius B. IV, folio 136ᵛ.

22. (*Below, l.*) "Moses and Joshua in the tabernacle" (detail). Aelfric Paraphrase, ca. A.D. 1025–1050. British Museum Cotton Claudius B. IV, folio 137ʳ.

23. (*Below, r.*) "Moses giving the Law" (detail). Aelfric Paraphrase, ca. A.D. 1025–1050. British Museum Cotton Claudius B. IV, folio 138ᵛ.

24. "Moses blessing the tribes and the death of Moses."
Aelfric Paraphrase, ca A.D. 1025–1050.
British Museum Cotton Claudius B. IV, folio 139ᵛ.

25. "Moses blessing the tribes and the death of Moses." Bible of San Paolo fuori le mura, ca. A.D. 870., folio 49ᵛ.

26. "The division of the 'elect' from the 'damned.'" Register of
Newminster, ca. A.D. 1016–1020. British Museum Stowe MS 944, folio 7^r.

27. Rock carving (detail). Tanum parish,
    Bohuslän, Sweden, ca. 1000–800 B.C.

28. Viksø helmets, ca. 800–400 B.C.
    National Museum of Denmark.

29. Bronze statuette.
Grevensvaenge,
ca. 800–500 B.C.
National Museum
of Denmark.

30. Gundestrup cauldron (detail), Celtic iron age. National Museum of Denmark.

31. Gundestrup cauldron (detail), Celtic iron age. National Museum of Denmark.

32. Celtic bronze helmet,
ca. 25 B.C. British Museum.

33. The "cornuti" (detail). Arch of
Constantine, Rome, fourth century A.D.

NORDIC WARE

MINNEAPOLIS 16, MINNESOTA
TESTED RECIPES ON REVERSE SIDE

34. Trademark on a baking pan,
    twentieth century.

35. Danish fisherman dressed as a Viking
    for a twentieth century Copenhagen
    pageant.

36. Bronze plate from Sweden, seventh century A.D.
    Stockholm Historical Museum.

37. Bronze plate from Sweden,
seventh century A.D. Stockholm Historical Museum.

38. Benty Grange helmet from Derbyshire,
sixth or seventh century A.D. Sheffield City Museum, England.

39. Sutton Hoo helmet from East Anglia, England, sixth or seventh century A.D. British Museum.

40. Horned figure on Sutton Hoo helmet (detail), sixth or seventh century A.D. British Museum.

41. Finglesham buckle from Kent, England, grave 95, ca. seventh century A.D.

42. Sparlösa stone (detail). Sweden,
ca. A.D. 800.

44. Metal figurine from Birka, Sweden,
first half of the tenth century A.D.
Stockholm Historical Museum.

43. Tapestry reconstructed from fragments found in the Oseburg grave,
ca. A.D. 850. University Museum of Oslo.

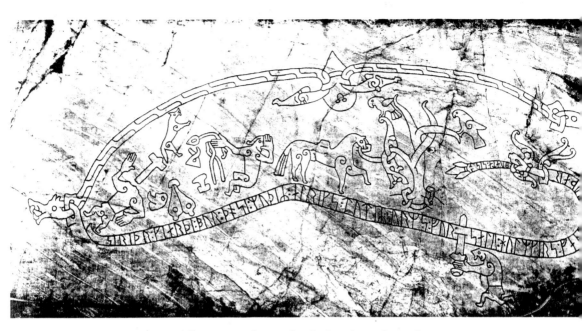

45. Rune stone from Ramsundberget, Södermanland, Sweden, eleventh century A.D.

46. Swedish Vendel helmet from grave 14 (detail),
seventh century A.D. Stockholm Historical Museum.

47. "Moses addressing the Israelites." Bible of Bury St. Edmunds,
ca. A.D. 1135. Corpus Christi College MS 2, folio 94ʳ.

48. "Tree of Jesse." Shaftesbury Psalter, second quarter of
the twelfth century A.D. British Museum Lansdowne MS 383, folio 15ʳ.

49. "Moses receiving the Law."
Gebhardt Bible from Admont,
ca. A.D. 1130. Vienna Nationalbibliothek
Ser. nov. 2701–02, folio 68ᵛ.

50. "Moses after the reception of the Law."
Gebhardt Bible from Admont,
ca. A.D. 1130. Vienna Nationalbibliot[h]
Ser. nov. 2701–02, folio 69ʳ.

51. "Moses receiving the Law."
Great Lambeth Bible, ca. A.D. 1150.
Lambeth Palace Library
MS 3, folio 52ʳ (detail).

52. "Tree of Jesse." Great Lambeth Bible, ca. A.D. 1150.
Lambeth Palace Library MS 3, folio 198ʳ.

53. "Moses receiving the Law." Psalter of Henry of Blois, ca.
A.D. 1150–1160. British Museum Cotton Nero C. IV, folio 4ʳ (detail).

54. "Exposition of Leviticus." Folio of a manuscript coming from Corbie, France, end of twelfth century A.D. Bibliothèque Nationale Lat. 11564, folio 2ʳ.

55. "Moses communicating with God." Manerius Bible, late twelfth century A.D. Bibliothèque Sainte-Geneviève MSS 8–10, folio 69ᵛ.

56. "Moses with the ark," and "Moses with the grapes of the Promised Land."
English Psalter, A.D. 1200. Bibliothèque Nationale Lat. 8846, folio 2ᵛ (detail).

57. "Moses teaching." English
Bible, early thirteenth century
A.D. British Museum Add.
MS 15452, folio 54ʳ (detail).

58. Statue of Moses. St. Mary's Abbey,
York, England, ca. A.D. 1200.
Yorkshire Museum, York.

59. "Miracle of the water," and "Moses and the Brazen Serpent."
English Psalter, first quarter of the thirteenth century A.D.
Bayerische Staatsbibliothek Codex Monacensis Lat. 835, folio 20ʳ.

60. "Moses and the Burning Bush," and "Moses and Aaron before Pharaoh."
English Psalter, first quarter of the thirteenth century A.D.
Bayerische Staatsbibliothek Codex Monacensis Lat. 835, folio 18ʳ.

61. "Moses receiving the Law." *Cursus Sanctae Mariae*, A.D. 1215.
Pierpont Morgan Library MS 739, folio 16ʳ.

62. "Moses before the Burning Bush."
Part of a stained glass window, Cathedral of Chartres,
first quarter of the thirteenth century A.D.

63. "Moses holding the tablets of the Law."
Part of the north rose window,
Notre-Dame of Paris, ca. A.D. 1250.

64. (Right) "Moses and the Brazen Serpent."
Part of a stained glass window, Cathedral
of Bourges, thirteenth century A.D.

65. "Moses receiving the Law." Psalter of Blanche of Castille,
ca. A.D. 1230. Bibliothèque de l'Arsenal MS 1186, folio 14ʳ.

67. "Moses with the tablets of the Law."
Bible moralisée, ca. A.D. 1250. Oxford
Bodleian 270b, folio 57ᵛ (detail).

66. "Moses with the tablets of the Law."
Bible moralisée, ca. A.D. 1250. Oxford
Bodleian 270b, folio 52ʳ (detail).

68. "Moses with 'rays.'" *Bible moralisée*,
ca. A.D. 1250. Oxford Bodleian 270b,
folio 56ʳ (detail).

69. "Moses." *Bible moralisée*,
ca. A.D. 1250. Oxford Bodleian 270b,
folio 184ʳ (detail).

70. "Moses." *Bible moralisée*,
ca. A.D. 1250. Oxford Bodleian 270b,
folio 216ʳ (detail).

71. *(Right)* "Transfiguration."
English Psalter,
early thirteenth century A.D.
British Museum Royal
MS I. D. X., folio 4ʳ.

72. "Moses receiving the Law," and
"The Worship of the Golden Calf."
Psalter of St. Louis,
ca. A.D. 1253–1270.
Bibliothèque Nationale
Lat. 10525, folio 35ᵛ (detail).

73. "Moses receiving the Law."
Latin Bible from France,
ca. A.D. 1260.
Pierpont Morgan Library
MS 109, folio 86ᵛ (detail).

74. "Crucifixion." Psalter of Yolande de Soissons,
ca. A.D. 1275. Pierpont Morgan Library MS 729, folio 345ᵛ.

75. "Moses receiving and shattering the tablets of the Law."
La Somme le Roy, ca. A.D. 1295. British Museum Add. MS 54180, folio 5ᵛ.

76. "Moses." Detail of an initial in a Latin Bible from Abbey of St. Martin, Tournai, second half of the thirteenth century A.D.

77. "Moses reading the Law." Spanish Bible, ca. A.D. 1293. British Museum Add. MS 50003, folio 61ᵛ (detail).

78. "Moses before the Burning Bush." *Biblia Pauperum*,
ca. A.D. 1414. Bayerische Staatsbibliothek
Cod. Lat. 8201, folio 81ʳ (detail).

79. "Moses receiving the Law." *Biblia Pauperum*,
ca. A.D. 1414. Bayerische Staatsbibliothek
Cod. Lat. 8201, folio 89ʳ (detail).

80. "The rain of manna." *Speculum Humanae Salvationis,*
fourteenth century A.D. Stiftsbibliothek, Kremsmünster,
Codex Cremifanensis 243, folio 21ᵛ.

81. "The Last Supper." *Biblia Pauperum*, Nördlingen, A.D. 1471.

82. Moses sculpture (detail), by Claus Sluter.
Chartreuse de Champmol, Dijon, A.D. 1404.

a quinte hyſtour
et œruenie q̃ moyſe
eſcripſt en grœ eſt
apelee œutœrono
mes. Ceſt a dire la
ſeconœ loy. Car œu
terõ uaut autãt
cõme ſecõns et noma cõme loys. $u
a dire œutœronome ſeconœ loy. pour
œque alz luurs eſt apeleʒ ſeconœ loys
ont aucuns ēœ qui dient q̃l fuirẽ
·y·loys au temps aus hebrueus. dont
lune fu donnee œ dieu œ la q̃le nous
auons parle es luurs œuant diʒ et
lautœ moyſes œ̃na. qui eſt contenue

83. "Moses speaking to the Israelites." Bible historiale de Guyart des Moulins,
ca. A.D. 1403. Bibliothèque de l'Arsenal MS 5212, folio 128ᵛ.

84. Moses sculpture by Michelangelo,
ca. A.D. 1513–1515. San Pietro in Vincoli, Rome.

85. "Moses on Mt. Sinai." Detail of a fresco by
     Bernadino Luini, ca. A.D. 1520. Pinacoteca de Brera, Milan.

86. "Moses striking the rock."
     French Bible, sixteenth century A.D.
     Bibliothèque Nationale Lat. 1429, folio 45ʳ (detail).

87. "Moses receiving the Law"
and "shattering the tablets."
German sculptured relief
by Veit Stoss, sixteenth century A.D.
Bayerisches Nationalmuseum.

88. "Moses." Dutch tile, late eighteenth
or early nineteenth century.

89. Moses sculpture by Sorel Etrog, 1960s.
Los Angeles County Museum of Art.

90. "Moses giving the Law." *Weltchronik*, ca. A.D. 1255–1270.
Bayerische Staatsbibliothek Codex Monacensis Germ. 6406, folio 68ʳ.

91. "Moses giving the Law." *Weltchronik*, ca. A.D. 1340–1350.
Zürich Zentralbibliothek MS Rh. 15, folio 87ʳ (lower portion).

92–96. English bishops' seals, twelfth century A.D.

97. "The Donation of Richard II
of Normandy to Bishop Manger of Avranches."
Mont-Saint-Michel, ca. A.D. 1160. Bibliothèque
de la ville d'Avranches MS 210, folio 19ᵛ.

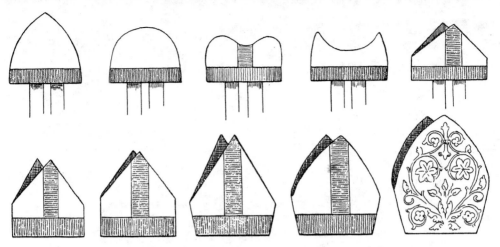

98. Development of the mitre from the eleventh century until the present time.

99. "Gregory the Great."
S. *Gregorius Magnus Dialogi*, abbey of Saint-Laurent,
Liège, second half of the twelfth century A.D.
Bibliothèque Royale de Belgique MS 9916, folio 2ᵛA.

100. "St. Augustine and the bishop Aurelius." *S. Augustinus Epistolae*, ca. A.D. 1200. Bibliothèque Royale de Belgique MS II 2526, folio 1ᵛe (detail).

101. Consecration of a bishop. *Pseudo-Isidorus Decretales*, abbey of Bonne-Espérance, second half of the twelfth century A.D. Bibliothèque Royale de Belgique MS II 2532, folio 6A (detail).

102. Nicolas of Lyra's diagram for
the High Priest of Exodus in a
fifteenth century Bible.
Biblia Latina cum postillis
Nicolai de Lyra et . . . , Venice
[Bonetus Locatellus,
for Octavianus Scotus, 1489.]

103. Diagram from Christian III's
Bible (Danish), A.D. 1550.
Norsk Folkemuseum.

104. Diagram from Frederic II's Bible (Danish), A.D. 1589. Norsk Folkemuseum.

בגדי קדש לאהרן אחיך

105. Frontispiece to a
Zohar (detail).
Amsterdam, 1706.

106. Ritual cover for festivals.
Austria, eighteenth century.
Jewish Museum, New York.

107. "Moses confirming the Pilgrim." French manuscript,
early fifteenth century A.D. John Rylands Library French MS 2, folio 5ʳ–1.

108. "Moses gives three kinds of ointment to a bishop."
French manuscript, early fifteenth century A.D.
John Rylands Library French MS 2, folio 5ʳ–2.

109. "Moses gives Grace of God to the monks."
French manuscript, early fifteenth century A.D.
John Rylands Library French MS 2, folio 8ᵛ–1.

110. "Memory carries the armour; the Pilgrim asks Moses for bread."
French manuscript, early fifteenth century A.D.
John Rylands Library French MS 2, folio 43ʳ–2.

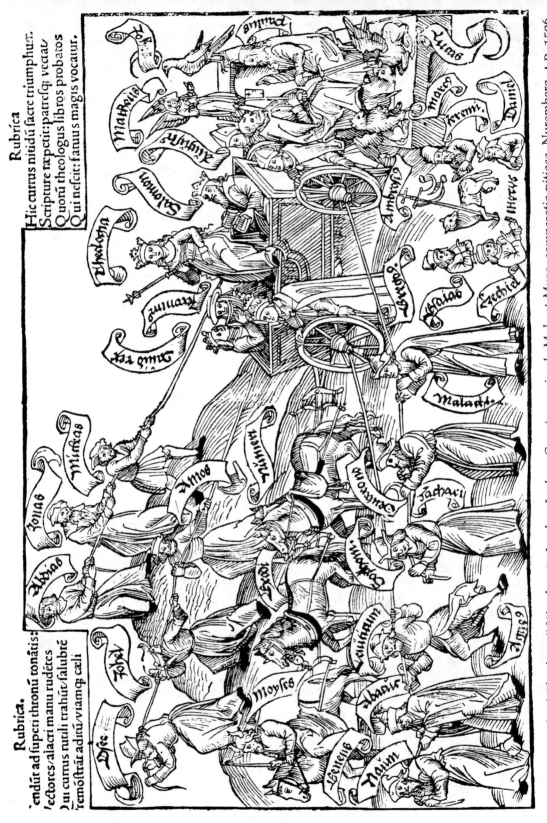

111. "Triumph of Theology." Woodcut in Jacobus Locher, *Carmina varia, de Mula et Musa, comparatio vitiosa,* Nuremberg, A.D. 1506.

112. Jean Germain, *Le chemin de paradis*. French manuscript, ca. A.D. 1460. Philadelphia Free Library MS E 210.

113. Jean Germain, *Le chemin de paradis*. French manuscript, ca. A.D. 1460. Philadelphia Free Library MS E 210.

114. "David and the three valiants."
Speculum Humanae Salvationis,
mid-fourteenth century A.D.
Bayerische Staatsbibliothek
Codex Monacensis Lat. 146,
folio 12ʳ (detail).

115. "Synagogue." *Scivias*
of Hildegard of Bingen,
ca. A.D. 1170. Wiesbaden
Scivias MS, folio 35ʳ.

116. "Crucifixion." Psalter of Robert de Lindesey,
ca. A.D. 1214–1222. Society of Antiquaries MS 59, folio 35ᵛ.

117. "Moses receiving the Law" and "Synagogue." *La Somme le Roy*, ca. A.D. 1295. Bibliothèque de l'Arsenal MS 6329, folio 7ᵛ.

118. "Christ in Majesty." Missal of Poitiers,
end of the fifteenth century A.D., folio 38ʳ
(detail). Treasure of the Cathedral, Poitiers.

119. "The kiss of Judas." Choir screen of
Naumburg Cathedral, thirteenth century A.D.

120. "Cain and Abel." *Cursus Sanctae Mariae*, ca. A.D. 1215.
Pierpont Morgan Library MS 739, folio 9ᵛ.

121. "Humility and sinner," and "Pride and hypocrite."
La Somme le Roy, ca. A.D. 1295. British Museum
Add. MS 54180, folio 97ᵛ.

122. "Hypocrite worshipping the Beast."
La Somme le Roy, ca. A.D. 1295. British Museum
Add. MS 54180, folio 14ᵛ.

123. Caricature of English Jews.
Head of a roll of the Issues
of the Exchequer, A.D. 1233.
Public Record Office, London.

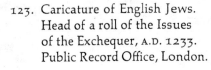

124. Title page to
Antiquitates Judaicae
(detail), ca. A.D. 1170–1190.
Württembergische Landesbibliothek Hist.,
folio 418ʳ.

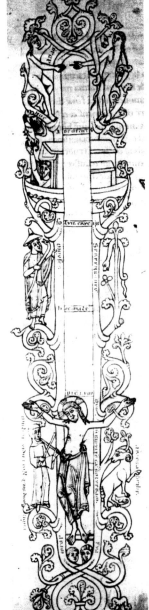

125. Caricature of an
English Jew in the
margin of Essex Forest Roll,
A.D. 1277. Public Record
Office, London.

126. Title page by Lucas Cranach for Luther's
Von den Juden und ihren Lügen, A.D. 1543.

Der Jůden Er= barkeit.

Alhie siehstu der Jůden Tantz/
Jr Gottes Lestrung vnd Finantz/
Wie sie den Son Gotts verspeyen/
All Christen vermaledeyen.
Darzu all Christlich Oberkeit/
Weils nicht gerhet so ists jn leid.
Auch jr grewliche Wucherey/
Noch sind sie bey alln Herren frey.
Betracht doch solchs du fromer Christ/
Du seyst gleich hoch/ odr wer du bist.
Las dir dis Buch zu hertzen gan/
Gott wird eim jeden gebn sein lohn.

ANNO. M. D. LXXI.

127. "Der Juden Ehrbarkeit" (caricature). Print of A.D. 1571.

128. Caricature of Jews. Early eighteenth century print.

MOSES
AND MONOTHEISM

by
Sigmund
Freud

a VINTAGE BOOK, originally published by Alfred A. Knopf, Inc. 95¢

129. Paperback cover for
Moses and Monotheism.

130. Cover of advertising brochure
of Mount Sinai Memorial Park and Mortuary,
1960s, Los Angeles, California.

In Sacred Jewish Tradition

Mount Sinai Memorial-Park
AND MORTUARY